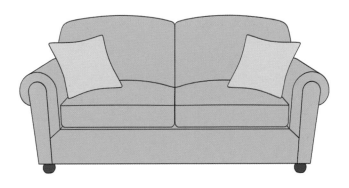

STEP-BY-STEP
home
DESIGN&DECORATING

STEP-BY-STEP
home
DESIGN&DECORATING

CLARE STEEL

London, New York, Munich,
Melbourne, Delhi

Illustrator Tim Loughhead
Step-by-step photography Kate Davis
Location photography Carolyn Barber
Editor Susannah Steel
Designer Anne Fisher

DK UK
Project Editor Robert Sharman
Senior Art Editor Glenda Fisher
Editorial Assistant David Fentiman
Design Assistants Danaya Bunnag, Jade Wheaton
Managing Editor Dawn Henderson
Managing Art Editor Christine Keilty
Senior Presentations Creative Caroline de Souza
Senior Jacket Creative Nicola Powling
Senior Production Editor Jennifer Murray
Senior Production Controller Claire Pearson
Creative Technical Support Sonia Charbonnier
Publisher Mary-Clare Jerram

DK INDIA
Senior Editors Alicia Ingty, Dorothy Kikon
Senior Art Editor Neha Ahuja
Project Designer Era Chawla
Designer Anjan Dey
Managing Editor Glenda Fernandes
Managing Art Editor Navidita Thapa
DTP Designer Sourabh Challariya
Senior DTP Designer Tarun Sharma
DTP Manager Sunil Sharma

First published in Great Britain in 2012
by Dorling Kindersley Limited, 80 Strand, London WC2R 0RL

Penguin Group (UK)

2 4 6 8 10 9 7 5 3 1

001 – 179007 – Mar/2012

Copyright © 2012 Dorling Kindersley Limited

This edition created for The Book People Limited
Hall Wood Avenue, Haydock, St Helens, WA11 9UL

A CIP catalogue record for this book is available from the British Library.

ISBN 978-1-4093-8718-3

Printed and bound in China by Hung Hing

Discover more at www.dk.com

CONTENTS

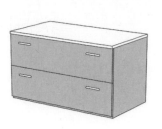

LAUNDRY ROOM 328

OUTSIDE SPACE 346

APPENDICES

PROJECT TEMPLATES 386

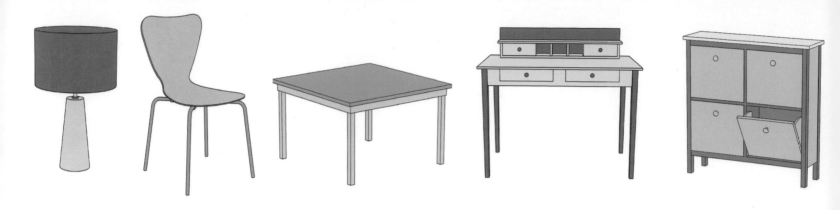

FOREWORD

Over the past 15 years, I have worked for a broad selection of interiors magazines as a stylist and writer, creating room sets to inspire readers, and nuts-and-bolts features on just about everything homes and property related to inform them.

During this period I moved house three times. Each house I bought was in a different state of repair, and each time I became more ambitious. The first required a minor makeover; the second needed some character adding, and the latest, a 1920s semi-detached property, needed to be completely gutted – new electrics, plumbing, windows, the lot!

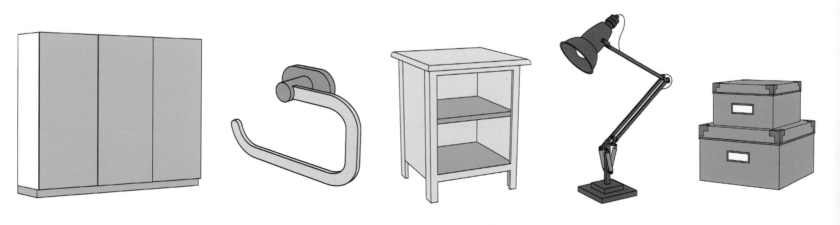

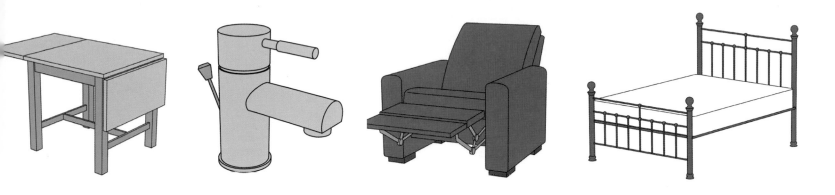

I approached each project relying on the knowledge I'd begun to build up and the experience I'd gained through work, but life would have been much easier if I had had a book like this one from the very beginning.

We all know that designing and decorating a home can be expensive, time-consuming, and, at times, stressful, which is why I have worked with Dorling Kindersley to create this step-by-step approach that will hopefully save you time, money, and a lot of stress.

We aim to take you right through the practical side of the process, so that you can do the work on your home in the right order and so that you can make an informed choice about materials and finishes before you

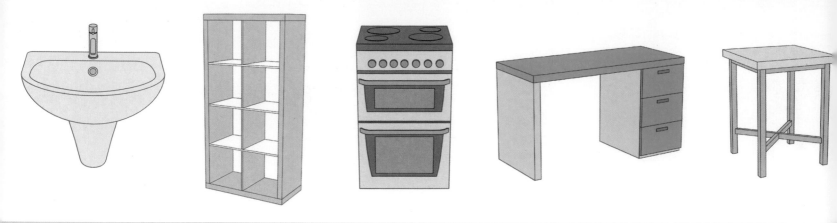

buy. We have covered every material you might need – from taps to carpets – to suit every home's style and every homemaker's approach and tastes. In these guides, we have aimed to provide lots of information to help you stick to your budget, too. There are also practical projects – presented step by step, naturally – to help you tackle DIY tasks and create unique features for your home.

Aside from the practical details, we've also approached the decorative side of transforming a home with gusto. In doing so, we have broken down the processes you need to go through to create a defined style for your home in a way that's achievable, affordable, and appealing to you and your family. There are mood board tutorials whereby we

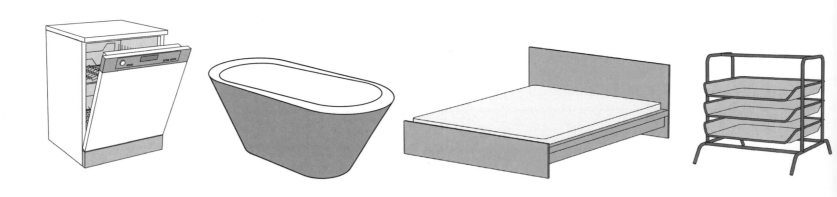

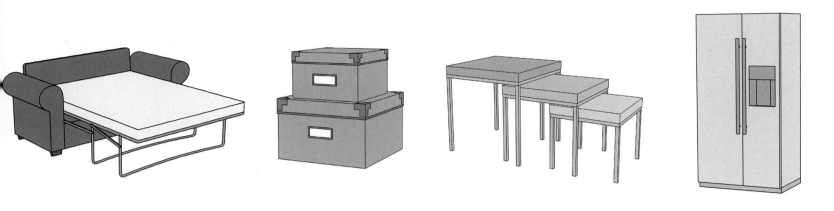

advise you how to pull your room's colour scheme and layout together so that it works practically and decoratively. There are also "5 ways with…" features to inspire ideas and help you find design suggestions that will work for your home.

In short, whether you're a beginner to transforming a home or a seasoned revamper like me, I think you'll find this book an indispensible guide and an inspiration to be more ambitious with your home's makeover than you might otherwise have been.

Clare

Clare Steel

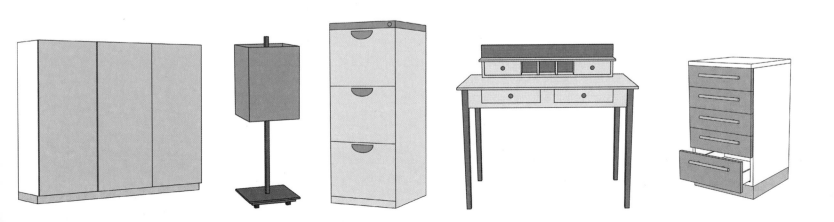

HOW TO USE
THIS BOOK

This book is designed to plot a logical course through the designing and decorating of your home. Everything in the book is presented step by step, making it the perfect reference for any would-be designer who doesn't know where to start, or for any budding renovator keen to make sure that their comprehensive overhaul is planned and executed to perfection.

If you are opening this book for the first time, begin with "Where do I start?" on pages 14–17. The principles discussed here are relevant to any, and every, room and reading this will provide a useful introduction to the most fundamental things you should consider when approaching any redecorating job.

Thereafter, there is a chapter for every room in the house, including outside space. The sequence in which each chapter is structured represents a suggestion for how to approach the work. You may find that, in places, it suits you to approach tasks in a different order and often this will be entirely possible. We do, however, recommend that you at least read the features that open each chapter – "What to do when…", "Create a mood board", and "Layout considerations" – before you undertake any work. Doing so will, we hope, help you to identify any likely problems or complications from the outset.

There follows a brief introduction to the various types of feature that appear in this book.

WHAT TO DO WHEN...

There is a logical order in which any redecorating job should be approached. Failing to observe this can cause problems and could result in you having to redo work. These features guide you through the correct process for each room. The text assumes a fairly comprehensive revamp, involving replastering, replacing windows, and so on; if you are undertaking a more minor refurbishment, you need only focus on the parts that concern you.

CREATE A MOOD BOARD

Next, we look at the process by which you will decide on the room's new appearance, focusing on colour, texture, pattern, and style. You may already have strong ideas about how you want the room to look. Or, on the other hand, you may not know where to start. If you are in the former camp, these features will allow you to check that your ideas work as a coherent scheme and find out sooner rather than later if anything doesn't work; if the latter, they will guide you through the whole process to help you come up with the perfect scheme for your room.

LAYOUT CONSIDERATIONS

Your ideal room should not only look amazing; it should also offer perfect functionality. These features will get you thinking about how you will use the room and ensure that you arrange the component parts in such a way that everything works smoothly and nothing is awkward. Not everyone notices a well-thought-out room, but they certainly notice an ill-thought-out one; these features will help ensure yours is the former.

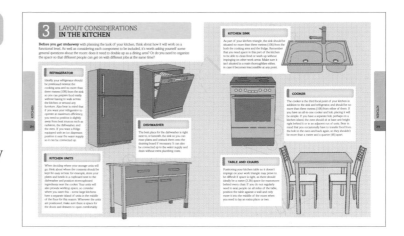

CHOOSE A...

There is a lot of choosing involved in redecorating a room: flooring, lighting, furniture, fixtures, and fittings all need to be selected. Much of this book is devoted to helping you make these decisions and choose the options that are best for you and your home. This book is not a catalogue and cannot hope to be comprehensive in showing every variation of tap, light fitting, armchair, or refrigerator. Instead, we have endeavoured to present every generic option, without going into the sort of subtle variations that can only be explored by comparing specific brands and models.

When comparing materials, we found that certain qualities were invariably important, and we have therefore included icons that will show at a glance how each material rates in those fields. "Durability" is represented by a hammer icon , "maintenance" by a brush. A low, medium, or high rating is denoted by the icon appearing singly, as a pair, or in triplicate. We have also endeavoured to always state, within the accompanying text, whether a material is low-, medium-, or highly priced. We believe that this approach provides

a useful at-a-glance guide, although please bear in mind that most materials vary in quality and that a material identified as typically "highly durable" or "low maintenance" may not always live up to this billing depending on the type you opt for and the supplier you use.

🔨🔨🔨 Highly durable	🖌🖌🖌 High maintenance
🔨🔨 Medium durability	🖌🖌 Medium maintenance
🔨 Low durability	🖌 Low maintenance

OTHER FEATURES

The other features that appear in this book are less fundamental to the process of designing and decorating a room but we hope they provide plenty of inspiration.

"Plan the perfect..." features look at a handful of small spaces in the home and show you how to approach them. Many of the subjects – outdoor kitchens; walk-in wardrobes – will not be applicable to every home; others, however, such as the kitchen work triangle, are much more universal.

"5 ways with..." features (and also "6 ways with…", "7 ways with…" etc.) demonstrate several approaches to a particular design idea, such as displaying art, creating a feature wall, or using the space under the stairs.

Projects also appear throughout the book, with step-by-step instructions and photography showing you how to undertake many DIY-style and craft-based projects.

WHERE DO I START?

Whether you've moved into a new home or are redesigning and decorating a room in your existing home, planning your scheme step by step gives you the best chance of making it a success. Whichever room you're thinking about, there are some key points you need to consider before you get going.

1 THINK ABOUT DIRECTION

The direction a room faces has an important effect on the amount and type of light it gets and the mood this creates. Bear this in mind when considering your colour scheme.

NORTH-FACING ROOM
A north-facing room is light-starved and the light it gets is cool. You can enliven a dark, north-facing room by using light, warm shades of colour.

SOUTH-FACING ROOM
Rooms facing south may be flooded with light and the quality of light is warm. You can temper a very bright, sunny room by using cool colours.

EAST-FACING ROOM
This is flooded with sunlight in the morning, but tonally cooler in the afternoon. Your colours need to work in both environments, so compare the effect of the changing light.

WEST-FACING ROOM
This is tonally cooler in the morning than in the afternoon. Again, your chosen colours need to suit both kinds of light.

Flooded with light A south-facing room is bathed in warm light throughout the day. Using cool colours as your basis offsets this to create a clean, sleek, fresh feel. You could go super-cool with white walls and floors and cream furniture and accessories.

2 CONSIDER TIME OF DAY

What time of day do you usually use the room and, therefore, how do you want it to "feel"? Consider this when planning your colours – walls, floors, furniture, and accessories.

MORNING
If it's a room you principally use in the morning, you may wish to decorate it so that it feels bright and invigorating.

EVENING
If it's a room you use to relax in the evening, you might want it to feel soothing and calming. It may not see much natural light, so consider the effect of electric lights on your colours.

DAY AND NIGHT
If the room is used in the day and evening, choose colours that will ensure the room feels comfortable at all times.

Morning colours Experiment with swatches of colour that feel invigorating – colours that encourage you to wake up and welcome the day.

Evening colours You may wish to consider calming, restful colours that will help to create an environment in which you can unwind.

Day and night colours Compare versatile colours that will enable you to achieve the feel you want at all times of the day, and compare how the colours react to the changing light.

This will help you to decide not only how to decorate your room, but also what you can do to influence how large or small the room feels. Good proportions needn't just include high ceilings or generous width and length – large, sparsely dressed windows in a smaller room can also contribute to how spacious the room feels.

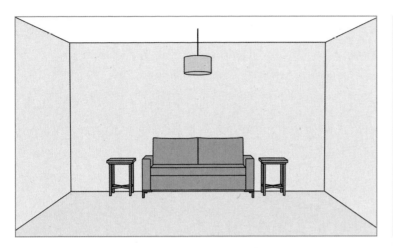

Deepen and widen Make a narrow, low-ceilinged room feel wide and bright by keeping both your flooring and walls a light colour.

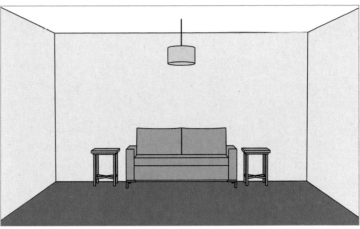

Widen Make a small, low-ceilinged room seem wider by matching a dark floor with a light-coloured ceiling and surrounding walls.

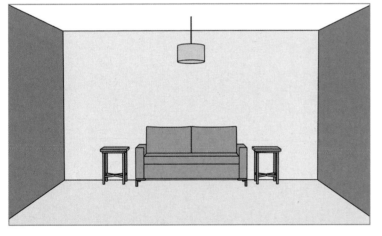

Narrow and make taller A low-ceilinged, wide space that lacks unity can be made to feel narrower, taller, and more cohesive with dark opposing walls and a light floor and ceiling.

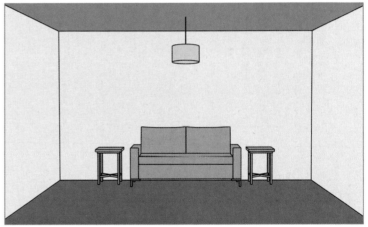

Widen and lower A large, lofty room can be made to feel cosier and more intimate with a dark floor and ceiling and light-coloured walls.

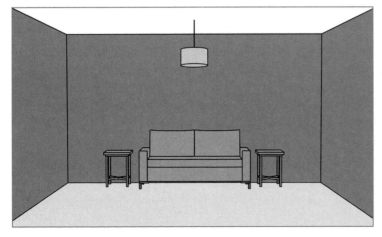

Narrow and deepen You can make a bright, large impersonal space feel warmer and more contained with a light floor and ceiling and dark-coloured walls.

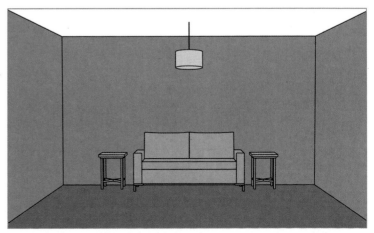

Narrow, deepen, and lower Make a large, low-ceilinged room feel cosy, intimate, and basement-like by matching a dark floor and walls with a light-coloured ceiling.

4 COMBINE COLOURS

Your colour choice will be based on the direction, use, and proportions of your room, but it's your combination of colours that will enable you to achieve the balance you desire.

LIGHT TO BOLD

Light, cool colours make a room feel more spacious, but can make it seem less inviting. So for a small, north-facing room with cream walls and light-coloured neutral furnishings, add an injection of extra interest with a bold-coloured rug.

BOLD TO LIGHT

Warm, deep colours make a room feel welcoming, but can also make it feel smaller. So take a large, south-facing room and treat it to bold, dark walls, but temper this with white or neutral flooring and cool, stylish furniture, perhaps with some textural interest.

Light-coloured walls can make a space feel larger.

Neutral floors complement the light-coloured walls.

Bold accessories add interest and warmth.

Bold walls make a room feel cosy and welcoming.

Understated floors offset the darker walls.

Cool accessories keep the room feeling fresh.

5 CREATE A FOCAL POINT

Nominating a feature within a room to be the focal point will help you to bring your scheme together. The focus may be an obvious feature that's part of the existing architecture of the room, or something that you create yourself to draw the eye and anchor the room. You can create or enhance a focal point in a number of ways, some of which are shown below.

Embellish The existing fire surround is further highlighted by dramatic art and impressive artefacts.

Construct The dark-coloured panel and large ornate mirror bring the focal point of the room to the stylish bath, creating a unified and relaxing mood.

Dress The French windows in this simple room are dressed with showy monochrome curtains, which draw the eye to the light.

Create contrast The recessed wall behind this shelving is painted in a vibrant contrasting colour, which draws the eye. The objects on the shelves are also carefully chosen and artfully placed to enhance the effect.

6 SELECT FURNITURE

Use what you've learnt about style and colour to choose your furniture and consider your room's proportions to get the size and shape of your items right. Don't forget comfort!

THINK ABOUT HEIGHT

A room with a low ceiling suits low items of furniture best, so if your ceiling's low, choose a low-backed sofa or a bed that's low to the floor, such as a futon. High-ceilinged rooms can house a tall, ornately framed bed, or even a four-poster bed, and still feel balanced.

ADD INTEREST

If your room's general scheme is fairly plain in terms of colour and pattern, or if its architecture is uninteresting, you can use furniture to introduce curvaceous shapes and finishes and to add texture in its upholstery and materials. Choose sofas, chairs, tables, and beds with this in mind.

Low or high? The height of your furniture is dictated by the height of your room.

Be adventurous Voluptuous shapes and unusual textures add interest to a plain room.

7 LAYER IT UP

The style of your room should not be conjured up artificially so that your whole house becomes a slave to a single overworked theme or so that each room has a contrived individual look. Ideally, your rooms should evolve slowly, so you might come up with a basic scheme and build from there over a period of weeks or months – layer by layer.

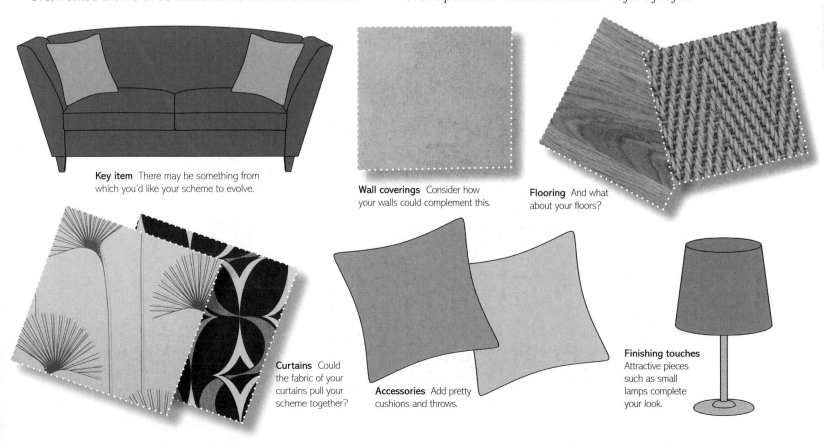

Key item There may be something from which you'd like your scheme to evolve.

Wall coverings Consider how your walls could complement this.

Flooring And what about your floors?

Curtains Could the fabric of your curtains pull your scheme together?

Accessories Add pretty cushions and throws.

Finishing touches Attractive pieces such as small lamps complete your look.

KITCHEN

1 WHAT TO DO WHEN
REVAMPING YOUR KITCHEN

The sheer number of components involved in redesigning a kitchen means that it requires particularly careful scheduling. The majority of your time will probably be spent preparing for the kitchen to be fitted, but if you do this job properly the rest of the refit should run smoothly. Get your redesign right first time with this step-by-step approach.

1 PLAN YOUR LAYOUT

Use graph paper to draw a plan to scale of your kitchen. Include windows and doors and all measurements. Then plan the position of units, appliances, and electric points. Moving the plumbing, gas supply, or electric points for appliances will increase costs, as will having the washing machine, dishwasher, and sink in different locations.

2 CONSIDER THE LIGHTING

The right lighting is vital, especially bright task lighting in food preparation areas. Put dimmable lighting in the dining area and also include inviting ambient lighting if possible.

3 VISIT A KITCHEN DESIGNER

When you have a firm idea of the layout and budget, get the input of a kitchen designer, whether high street or upmarket. If you have time, visit two other designers to compare prices and pick out any clever design ideas.

4 ORDER YOUR KITCHEN

You'll be given the choice of booking your own fitter or having the kitchen company's fitter install your kitchen when you order it. The latter is a wise choice – though sometimes not the cheapest option – as someone familiar with the design will fit it more quickly, and can easily resolve any problems with a delivery, such as the odd missing piece. If you want to book your own electrician, builder, and plumber instead, do so now. Also order your appliances now.

5 REMOVE YOUR OLD KITCHEN

Once the delivery date is confirmed (and not before), get your old kitchen removed. The fitter you've booked could do this for you at an extra cost, but ensure that this price also includes the disposal of the old kitchen, and bear in mind that gas pipes need capping by a qualified registered engineer (Gas Safe Register in the UK).

6 BEGIN THE FIRST FIX

The new electric cables and pipes need to be installed now. Double-check the position of all the electric sockets, both behind appliances and at work surface level. The electrician – if not the kitchen company's installer – will need a set of the finalized plans to get this right.

7 LAY THE KITCHEN FLOOR

If your floor is uneven, the appliances and units won't sit neatly, so have it levelled once any underfloor work has been completed. If you're having underfloor heating, it can be installed at this point. Then lay the new floor and keep it well protected while the rest of the work is completed.

8 PLASTER AND PAINT

Wiring and plumbing make a mess of walls, so they may have to be plastered. Once the plaster is dry, give the ceiling, walls, and woodwork a coat of primer and a couple of coats of paint. This will save you having to worry about splattering your new kitchen with paint later.

9 TAKE DELIVERY OF THE KITCHEN

Even if the kitchen company's fitter is installing your kitchen, it's well worth checking off all the boxes yourself when your units arrive. Open up every box to ensure that all the hinges and screws are included. Check the units for damage, too, and have them replaced as soon as possible if there are any problems.

10 INSTALL THE UNITS AND WORKTOP

If your kitchen arrives flat-packed, assemble it carefully to prevent warping later on. Begin with base units in one corner, ensuring each is perfectly fitted and level before moving on. Either the kitchen fitter or you can then install the worktop.

11 FIT THE SINK AND APPLIANCES

The kitchen fitter will fit the sink once the worktop is in place, unless you have chosen a composite or Corian® worktop, perhaps with an integral sink, which must be measured before being factory-cut. Allow a gap of a couple of days for this process to take place. With the sink in place, the taps can then be connected. Wooden or stone worktops may need treating with oil or sealing once in place. Then have a professional connect and check all your appliances.

12 FIT THE SPLASHBACKS

Fit and finish the splashbacks, ensuring that they are templated (measured) before being fixed in place to allow for the electrical sockets. The walls may need some touching up after this.

13 ORGANIZE THE SECOND FIX

Any wiring or plumbing that hasn't been taken care of can be completed now, including any light fittings.

14 TAKE CARE OF FINAL DETAILS

Finishing touches like plinths (or kickboards) can be fitted now, as can cornicing, doors, drawers, door handles, and so on. Check that everything works properly, from appliances to soft-closing drawers.

2 CREATE A MOOD BOARD FOR YOUR KITCHEN

Working on a mood board for your kitchen is, in many ways, simpler than for other rooms because much of the room will be dominated by unit doors, drawer fronts, and worktops. Spend time now carefully considering whether you want a homely, studiedly contemporary, or traditional-style kitchen, using the mood board to help you build up your theme and achieve the look you want.

1 **FIND PICTURES OF ROOMS**, including open-plan kitchen diners and dining rooms, that you like, or which have elements that attract you. Cut pictures from magazines, copy them from books, or print them off websites and spread them on the floor or a table. As you begin to narrow the choice of pictures down to a manageable few, you should see a theme begin to emerge, whether it's a preference for textures, a particular colour palette, or a retro feel.

Stick your favourite picture, or two or three pictures if you have several preferences, to the mood board as a starting point for your design.

2 **DO YOU HAVE A KEY ITEM** that has emerged from the pictures you've chosen, or is something you already own, such as a set of dining chairs, a retro-style food mixer, or a picture? Use this item to inspire your scheme, whether as a colour, unusual texture, or theme for the room.

Incorporate images of key items you want to include in your design, or you already own – such as a table and chairs – into your mood board.

3 **PICK A BACKGROUND WALL COLOUR** that will enhance the look of the units you like, or that zones the room into dining and cooking areas. Some walls will be partly covered with a splashback, so consider the colour of these, too. They needn't match, but there should be a cohesion between them and the units. Attach a tile, paint colours, and any other samples to the mood board for reference.

If your units will be bright or glossy, pick an understated or neutral colour as a background shade for the walls.

Think about including at least two accent colours in your scheme.

An accent colour can be a subtle variation of, or a dramatic contrast to, your background wall colour.

4 **INTRODUCE TWO ACCENT COLOURS** that link visually to your background colour, and consider adding a third accent colour in small splashes. Play around with the proportions of the colour combinations using fabric and paint swatches and floor samples to see if they work successfully.

Pick a strong contrasting accent colour if you want touches of bright, bold detail.

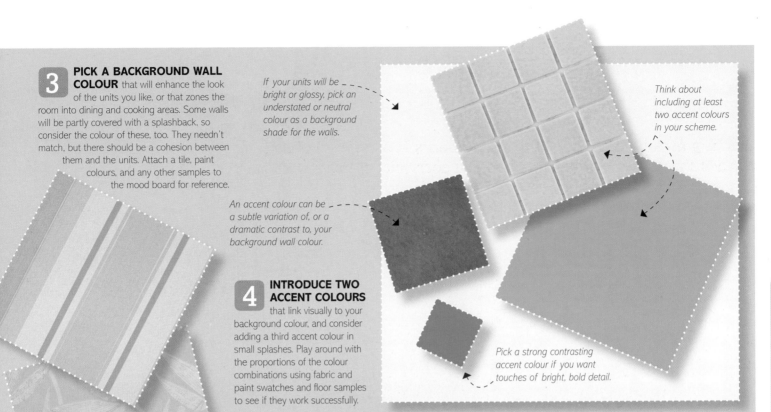

5 **ADD PATTERN & TEXTURE** with a grainy wood worktop or unit doors, for example, or with patterned tiles, wallpaper, a fabric blind, a natural stone for tiles and walls, or a composite worktop. Include roughly woven storage baskets, grained wood cutting boards, or ribbed china bowls for added texture. Stick wallpaper and fabric swatches and pictures of tiles and floor and worktop surfaces to the mood board to find the look you're aiming for.

If your kitchen is large, add pattern with wallpaper, for example, but don't add more than two patterns to the room.

Select a range of materials and different textures as options for the floor, walls, worktops, and storage.

6 **CHOOSE NEW FURNITURE** such as a dining table, chairs, a sideboard, or extra storage. Shape and size are just as important as looks, so check carefully before you buy to see if the pieces will sit comfortably in the room. Also use the colour and textural elements of your mood board to check which material your furniture should be made from.

7 **ADD THE FINISHING TOUCHES** such as light fittings, pictures, and china; stick pictures of your choices to your mood board. If you like to revamp rooms regularly, pick plain and textured accessories and add splashes of an accent colour with the odd item here and there to unite the whole scheme.

Accessories in an accent colour or contemporary material add to a fun, creative look.

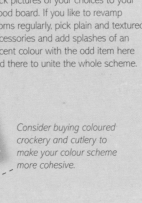

Consider buying coloured crockery and cutlery to make your colour scheme more cohesive.

3 LAYOUT CONSIDERATIONS
IN THE KITCHEN

Before you get under way with planning the look of your kitchen, think about how it will work on a functional level. As well as considering each component to be included, it's worth asking yourself some general questions about the room: does it need to double up as a dining area? Or do you need to organize the space so that different people can get on with different jobs at the same time?

REFRIGERATOR

Make the placement of the refrigerator, or fridge-freezer, one of your earliest considerations as it comprises part of the "work triangle" – see pages 26–27 for more information on this. Also bear in mind that if you want your refrigerator to operate at maximum efficiency, you need to position it slightly away from heat sources such as radiators and dishwashers, as well as the oven. If you want a refrigerator equipped with an ice dispenser, position it near the water supply so it can be connected up.

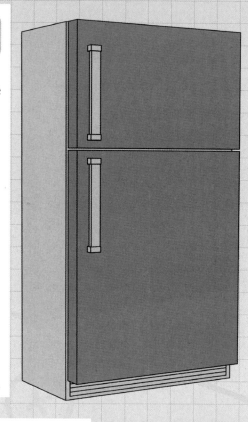

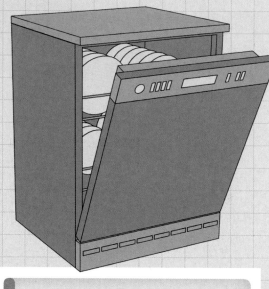

DISHWASHER

The best place for the dishwasher is right next to, or beneath, the sink so you can rinse plates and unstack them onto the draining board if necessary. It can also be connected up to the water supply and drain without extra plumbing costs.

KITCHEN UNITS

When deciding where your storage units will go, think about where the contents should be kept for easy access: for example, store your plates and bowls in a cupboard next to the dishwasher and position storecupboard ingredients near the cooker. Your units will also provide worktop space, so consider where you want this – some large kitchens have a separate island of units in the middle of the floor for this reason. Wherever the units are positioned, make sure there is space for the doors and drawers to open comfortably.

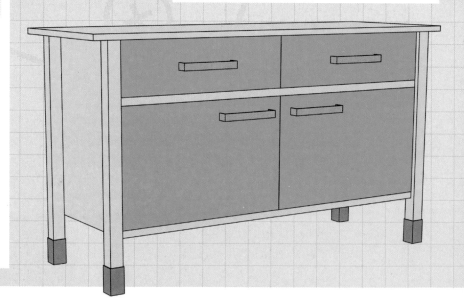

KITCHEN SINK

The sink is the second point of the work triangle (see pages 26–27), so think about its positioning early on, at the same time you decide where the cooker and refrigerator will go. Remember that you need space in this part of the kitchen to be able to clean food or wash up without impinging on other work areas. Make sure it isn't situated in a main thoroughfare either.

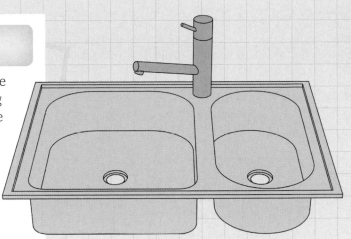

COOKER

As the cooker is the third point of the work triangle, its ideal location will be partly determined by the relative positioning of the sink and refrigerator. Placing your cooker is made simpler if you have an all-in-one unit combining oven and hob. If the hob is separate from the oven, on a kitchen island, say, the oven should be within easy reach – immediately behind, perhaps, or in an adjacent run of units. As you may have to transfer food from the hob to the oven and back again, the two components shouldn't be more than 120cm (4ft) apart.

TABLE AND CHAIRS

Positioning your kitchen table so it doesn't impinge on your work triangle may prove to be difficult if space is tight, as there should ideally be a metre (3ft) space for manoeuvre behind every chair. If you do not regularly need to seat people on all sides of the table, position the table against a wall and only move it into the middle of the room when you need to lay an extra place or two.

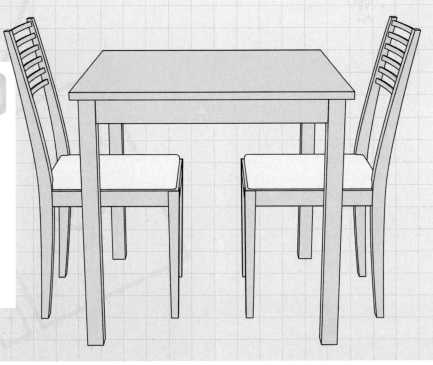

PLAN THE PERFECT
KITCHEN WORK TRIANGLE

To create a smoothly functioning kitchen, it is helpful to understand the concept of the work triangle. This states that there are three key points in any kitchen: a cooking area (the cooker), a food storage area (the refrigerator), and a cleaning area (the sink). Here's how to plan your space around these three points.

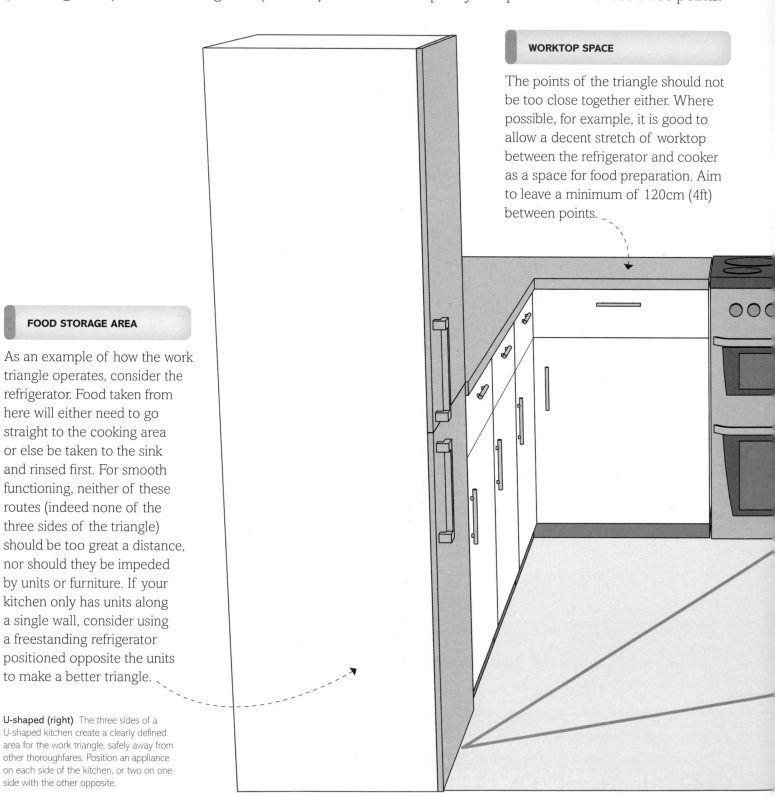

WORKTOP SPACE

The points of the triangle should not be too close together either. Where possible, for example, it is good to allow a decent stretch of worktop between the refrigerator and cooker as a space for food preparation. Aim to leave a minimum of 120cm (4ft) between points.

FOOD STORAGE AREA

As an example of how the work triangle operates, consider the refrigerator. Food taken from here will either need to go straight to the cooking area or else be taken to the sink and rinsed first. For smooth functioning, neither of these routes (indeed none of the three sides of the triangle) should be too great a distance, nor should they be impeded by units or furniture. If your kitchen only has units along a single wall, consider using a freestanding refrigerator positioned opposite the units to make a better triangle.

U-shaped (right) The three sides of a U-shaped kitchen create a clearly defined area for the work triangle, safely away from other thoroughfares. Position an appliance on each side of the kitchen, or two on one side with the other opposite.

COOKING AREA

When cooking, you need to quickly and easily be able to obtain ingredients from the refrigerator and also to transfer used pots and pans to the sink or surrounding worktop. To this end, the maximum recommended distance between points of the work triangle is 3m (10ft), in a straight line.

CLEANING AREA

Moving from the refrigerator to the sink to rinse your food, on to the cooking area, then back to the sink with your used pots – all of this is made much simpler if you can avoid any thoroughfares intruding on the work triangle. Another thing that will aid economy of movement is locating your dishwasher as close as possible to the sink, so that any pans left to soak have to travel the shortest possible distance afterwards.

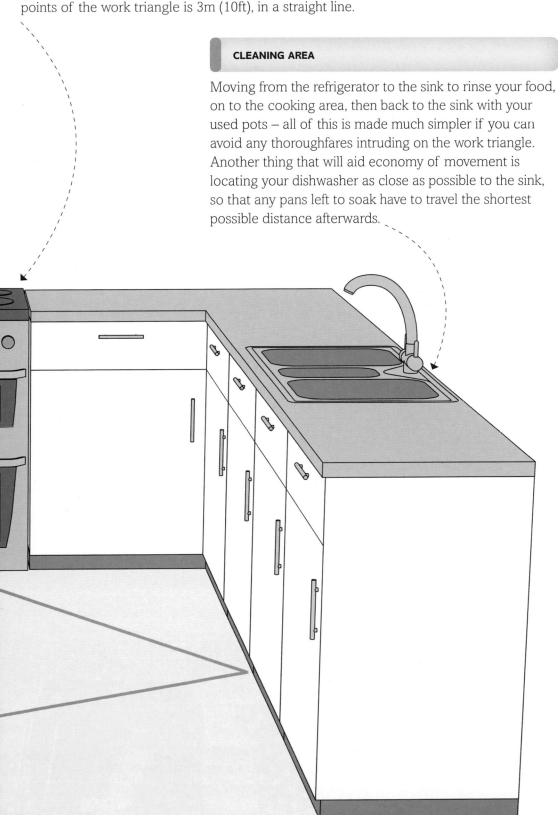

OTHER KITCHEN SHAPES

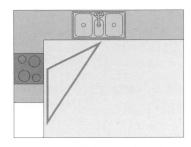

L-shaped In an L-shaped kitchen where the units run along two adjacent walls, two points of the triangle should be sited along one wall and the other point along the second wall. Think carefully about which appliances should go together.

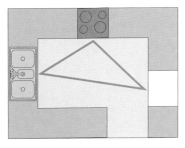

G-shaped A G-shaped kitchen can be laid out much like a U-shaped kitchen, with an appliance on each of the three sides, or alternatively you can site one of the points of the triangle within the peninsula.

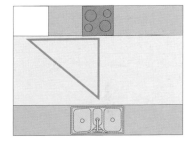

Galley Galley kitchens tend to be a thoroughfare, making the work triangle imperfect, but in all other respects you can create a smoothly functioning workspace by positioning two appliances along one wall and the other opposite.

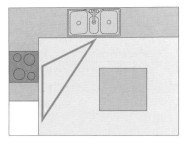

Island feature If you add an island feature to an L- or U-shaped kitchen, you can either use the island as the site for the sink or cooker, or else put the appliances against the walls and simply position the island so it does not encroach on the work triangle.

4 CHOOSE KITCHEN UNITS

Choosing your kitchen units needs careful planning so that you get the right configuration to perfectly suit your needs. Start by asking yourself whether you prefer fitted or freestanding units, and then consider individual elements – what storage do you need, and what finish do you want for the doors?

1 FITTED OR FREESTANDING

Two factors will influence your choice: the look, and your budget. Fitted kitchens look smarter and utilize space effectively, but informal freestanding kitchens can be a cheaper option with no fitting costs, so you may be able to afford a better-quality kitchen.

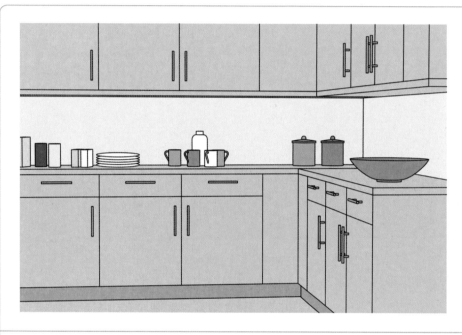

FITTED

Fitted kitchens – where runs of units are fixed to the wall – maximize storage and use space efficiently, so they are practical for all room sizes. Buy the units separately and hire a trusted tradesperson to install them, or opt for a specialist company that will take care of everything from design through to installation.

FREESTANDING

Freestanding kitchens can comprise separate stand-alone cabinets, drawers, islands, and other units. They are flexible, as you can add to them or rearrange the layout – and even take them with you if you move. Freestanding units work best in larger kitchens as they don't use space as efficiently as fitted versions.

2 CHOOSE YOUR BASIC UNITS

Fitted kitchens can include base and wall units, and possibly tall cabinets, which should cater for all storage requirements. Consider exactly what you want to store and how often you'll want to access it before you buy.

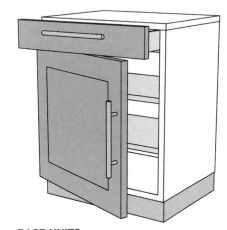

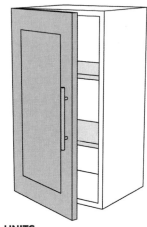

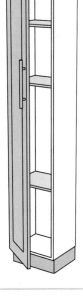

BASE UNITS

Cabinets between the floor and worktop range in size from 30cm (12in) to 100cm (39in) wide. High-line units have single or double doors, usually with shelves inside; drawer-line cabinets feature one or more drawers.

WALL UNITS

Wall-mounted cabinets are also 30cm (12in) to 100cm (39in) wide and vary in height (pick according to the height of your ceiling). Leave a gap of at least 45cm (18in) between the worktop and the underside of the cupboard.

HIGH UNITS

These floor-to-ceiling units include narrow pull-out cabinets, which provide easy access to stored items, and larder units with shelves that can store practically anything from food to china. Both types of unit finish level with the tops of wall units, and provide valuable extra storage space while taking up minimal floor space.

3 CHOOSE STORAGE OPTIONS

A wide selection of internal fittings and storage accessories for cupboards and drawers will help to keep your contents secure and surfaces clutter-free. Note down what needs storing and how often it is used to determine which type of storage you need.

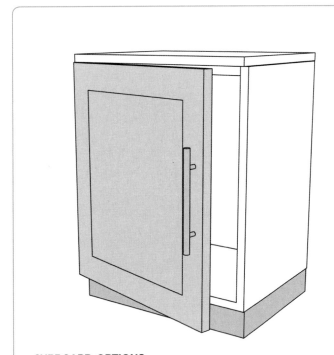

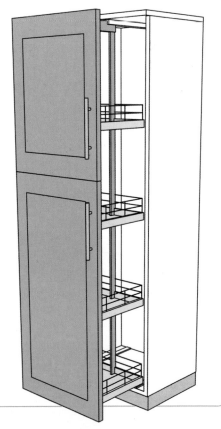

CUPBOARD OPTIONS

Standard cupboards may well suit all your storage needs, but if not, you could add least one wide cupboard of 60cm (24in) or more. If you want, you can also include half-depth cupboards for small items like tins and herbs.

PULL-OUT LARDER

Tall pull-out larder storage units incorporate wire baskets on runners, making spices, cans, and groceries easy to spot and reach for. They are available in various widths and look best positioned by a fridge. Ideally they should also be near a counter or a table so the contents are easier to load and unload.

KITCHEN

29

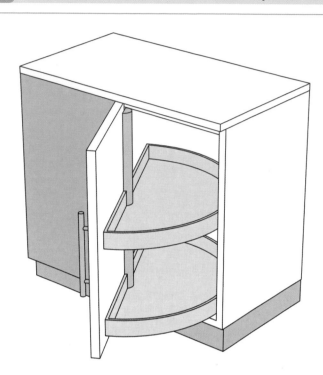

CAROUSEL

A carousel helps you utilize corner space that would otherwise be difficult to access. They are available as rectangular units with semicircular shelves (shown above) or L-shaped units with three-quarter-circular shelves that spin all the way around.

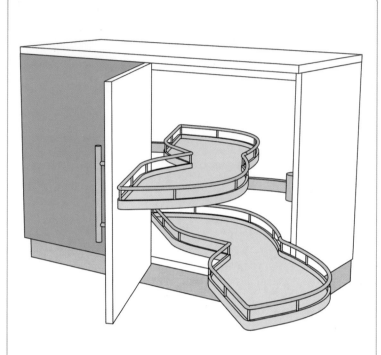

PULL-OUT CORNER UNIT

Another great way of making use of otherwise restricted corner space, these units have shelves mounted on a hinged arm. With the door open, the shelves will swing out, giving you easy access to the entire contents.

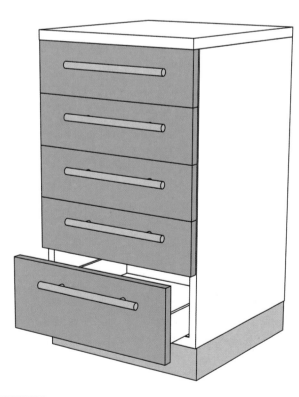

DRAWERS

The traditional method of kitchen storage, drawers can be used for anything from cutlery and tea towels to fine china. Drawer units are best located low enough so that you can see into the drawers when they are opened.

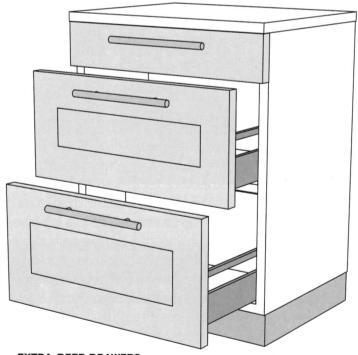

EXTRA-DEEP DRAWERS

Fashionable in contemporary kitchens, these oversized drawers are deep enough to hold stacked-up dinnerware, saucepans, and electrical appliances. Opt for a soft-close mechanism, which ensures that the drawers close gently and quietly to minimize any accidents or noise.

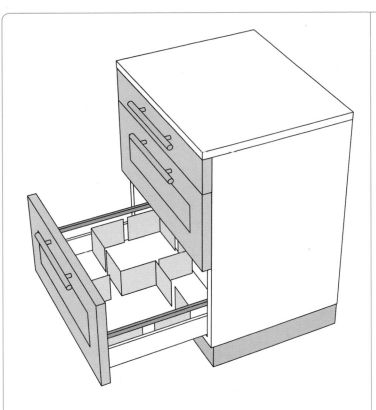

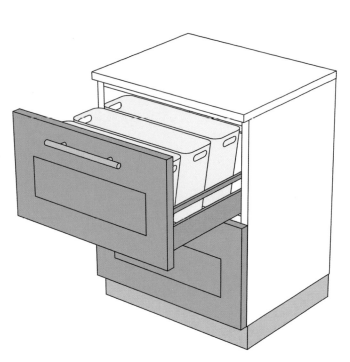

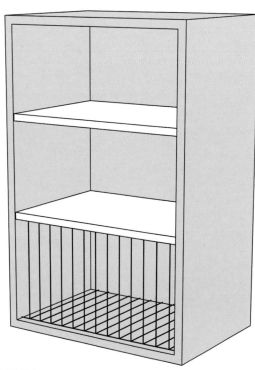

DRAWER DIVIDERS

Wooden or plastic inserts, which separate and secure various items in drawers, include cutlery and utensil trays, knife blocks, and plate holders – vertical pegs that prevent stacks of plates from being disturbed when the drawer is moved.

PULL-OUT WASTE BINS

Keep your household waste organized and out of sight with bins that slide out on runners, concealed behind doors or drawer fronts. Make sure the number of bin compartments is appropriate for the refuse/recycling system in your area.

PLATE RACK

The benefit of a plate rack is that it keeps plates separated and upright so they are less likely to gather dust. It is a practical buy if you have expensive dinnerware that you want on show and that you would rather not stack. Often built into a wall unit, a plate rack can be an insert for deep drawers.

WINE RACK

A wine rack allows bottles of wine to rest lying down. Available in varying sizes, this feature can be installed inside wall or base units, as a pull-out from a cupboard door, or fitted as a separate unit, often as an infill between two wider cabinets.

4 CHOOSE DOORS

The appearance and style of a kitchen depends very much on the style of the cabinet doors. Manufacturers offer a choice of solid doors, which can be panelled or flush, or glass-panelled doors with various types of surround.

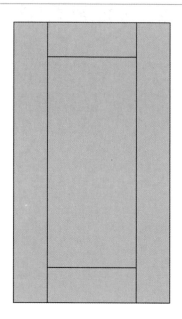

SOLID

Flat, flush doors are sleek, contemporary, and easy to keep clean. Panelled doors consist of a sunken panel surrounded by a frame. Shaker-style doors suit all types of kitchen, and tongue and groove and arched panels are ideal for traditional schemes.

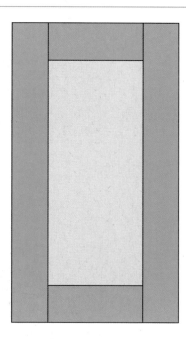

GLASS PANEL

Glass-panelled doors are often used alongside solid doors in wall units to provide contrast. Frosted glass is popular, but go for clear glass if you want to display the items inside. The cupboards may also be lit from within, providing a gentle glow that illuminates the contents.

5 CHOOSE THE FINISH

The material and colour you choose for the cabinet doors are the crucial factors in creating your look. In a large room you could try two coordinating shades or finishes, such as gloss and wood – but avoid using any more than two.

WOOD EFFECT

Cost-effective laminated wood-effect doors are made by heat-bonding patterned paper onto MDF; veneered doors consist of MDF covered with a thin layer of real wood.

SOLID WOOD

Warm wood is environmentally friendly, and the doors are available in finishes from pale ash through to deep mahogany. The high quality is reflected in the price.

PAINTED

Made from solid wood or coated MDF, painted doors are often found in country-style kitchens. The doors can be finished in any paint colour you like.

GLOSS

Made from MDF onto which a high-gloss thermofoil layer has been glued at high pressure, these shiny flush doors are available in many colours.

STAINLESS STEEL

This tough material creates an industrial, contemporary look. The doors are made from MDF wrapped in brushed steel. The overall effect is very striking, if expensive.

GLASS

Choose from frosted or clear glass with a wooden or MDF frame. These doors are available as single-framed panels or paned windows, which suit traditional rooms.

6 CHOOSE HANDLES

Smart handles can make all the difference, transforming an ordinary kitchen into something special, or helping to create a particular effect. Use identical handles throughout the room to give a streamlined effect and prevent the scheme looking messy.

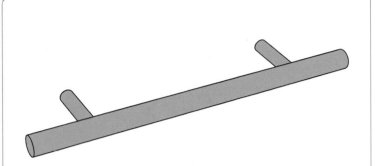

T-BAR

T-bar handles are angular in shape and are available in various lengths and finishes. Opt for a sleek, minimalist finish if you have a contemporary kitchen, or pick more intricate designs if you have chosen a classic scheme.

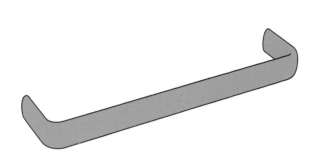

D AND BOW

D handles are simple and smart in style, with a softer look than T-bar handles due to their curved corners. Bow handles are similar, but consist of a single, sweeping curve. Both these styles are available in various lengths, thicknesses, and profiles.

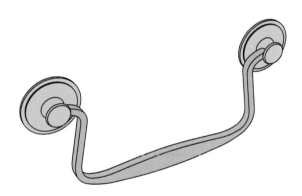

DROP HANDLES

Drop-pendant, drop-bar, and drop-ring handles are used almost exclusively in traditional kitchens and are hinged, unlike other types of handles. Simply lift them up and pull to open drawers and cupboards.

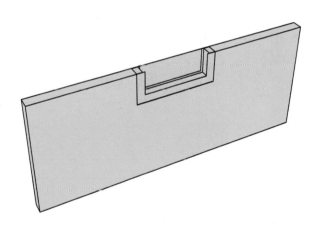

RECESSED HANDLES

Also known as integrated pulls, recessed handles create a flush, streamlined effect and are a trademark of an ultra-modern kitchen. They are usually positioned at the tops of drawers and cabinets, and include moulded grooves and metal-inset handles.

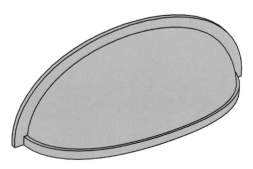

CUP HANDLES

These traditional metal handles are typically found on drawers rather than cupboards. Available in brushed nickel, chrome, or antique brass, they often feature in Shaker-style kitchens, where they add a stylish finishing touch.

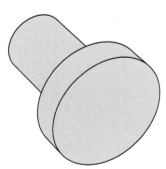

KNOBS

If you want to choose from the widest selection of sizes, materials, and shapes, opt for a traditional knob design. Pick wooden or porcelain finishes for a classic kitchen, or brushed or polished metal to give your cabinets a contemporary twist.

5 CHOOSE WORKTOPS

A good-quality worktop can really lift the look of a kitchen – even if you have bought plain units on a budget – so it's worth spending as much as you can afford on it. Bear in mind that you get what you pay for in terms of quality, and that you should follow the manufacturer's care instructions carefully so it lasts well.

CHOOSE THE MATERIAL

There is a vast range of worktop materials to choose from, and there can be a huge variation in the quality of each type. Check the durability of the material you prefer and whether it is suitable for use around the hob and sink before you buy.

GRANITE
Expensive and extremely hardwearing, granite is available in a polished high-gloss finish or a honed matt finish. It won't need resealing for 10 years or so.

COMPOSITE STONE
Made of resin, minerals, and acrylic, medium-priced hardwearing composite stone comes in a range of colours. Choose a smooth or slightly grainy textured surface.

LAVA STONE
Lava stone is a natural volcanic stone that can be glazed in any colour or finish. It is very expensive, but it is claimed that nothing can damage its surface.

WOOD
Medium to high in price, hardwood gives a warm look. Choices vary from pale beech to dark wenge. Reseal the wood annually, or sooner if it starts to lose its sheen.

GLASS
Mid- to high-priced toughened glass is scratch-, heat-, and acid-resistant, and may crack only if heavy objects are dropped onto it. Choose tinted or coloured glass.

STAINLESS STEEL
Popular in professional kitchens, medium-priced stainless steel is durable, hygienic, and can be made in almost any shape and size. Any scratches will add to its appeal.

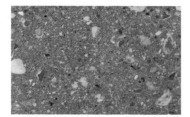

CONCRETE
High-priced concrete worktops are set on site or cast using a template made to your specification. Different finishes are available. Treat the surface with sealant before use.

CORIAN®
This high-priced surface has a semi-matt, non-porous finish that is extremely hardwearing. It is easy to care for and any scratches can be removed professionally.

LAMINATE
Laminate worktops come in many different guises including wood, stone, and granite effect. They are not as hardwearing as the real thing, but are a much cheaper option.

CARING FOR YOUR WORKTOP

Follow these tips to keep your worktops in good condition.

Clean wooden worktops with a soft cloth and warm soapy water. Mop up spills immediately.

For granite worktops, use a non-abrasive neutral detergent and dry it with a chamois to maintain the shine. Use wire wool to clean drainer grooves, a water-based stain remover to remove wine and tea stains, and an alkaline degreaser to remove grease and oil.

Clean Corian® using a kitchen spray and a cloth. Remove hard water marks with a limescale remover and grease and red wine with detergent. You may need to use bleach to remove tea and coffee stains.

Use a soft cloth and warm soapy water to clean laminate surfaces. Remove stubborn marks with a cream cleaner or a mild bleach solution. Use a bleach solution on stronger stains like red wine.

To treat glass, concrete, or stainless steel, wipe with a soft cloth and soapy water to remove marks. Polish with a microfibre cloth to give shine. Use baby oil on stainless steel to keep it looking new.

For composite and stone, use a soft, damp cloth and a mild detergent.

6 CHOOSE
SPLASHBACKS

You should choose your splashback at the same time as your work surface. You needn't use the same material, but you should pick something that complements it. Whether you choose to have a small upstand or a whole wall of your chosen material is a matter of personal taste.

CHOOSE THE MATERIAL

Your splashback material, above all else, needs to be practical and easy to clean. However, it's also a good opportunity to add interest to your walls, so consider adding colour with glass, pattern with tiles, or warmth with wood.

TILED

Probably the most popular choice, tiles are easy to clean and stain resistant, although you should steer clear of unglazed finishes as they are porous and will stain if splashed. If you have a large kitchen, consider using bigger tiles for your splashback.

GLASS

A good choice for modern kitchens, toughened glass splashbacks are usually custom-made, although you can buy pre-cut panels that normally come in 70cm (28in) widths. They come in a huge range of colours; look for those that are UV stable so they won't fade.

WOOD

A solid wood splashback will need to be treated regularly – either every three months, or when you notice that it has lost its sheen – so that it continues to repel water and oil splashes. It is not suitable for use behind a hob, as it may become scorched.

STAINLESS STEEL

Stainless steel is extremely hardwearing, hygienic, and easy to clean. Its surface may scratch over time, but that is part of its appeal and complements its tough, industrial look. Stainless steel splashbacks are available in various sizes.

12 CHOOSE FLOORING

The floor in your kitchen is likely to suffer from more wear and tear than any other room in your home, so choose something that can deal with all your requirements. As well as choosing something that looks good, you also need to consider how much maintenance it will require.

1 CHOOSE THE LOOK

Flooring that's suitable for a kitchen broadly falls into three types: tiles, wood, and seamless. Tiles and poured floors create a contemporary look and can withstand the most wear; wood and tiles are good choices if you want an informal, rustic look.

TILED

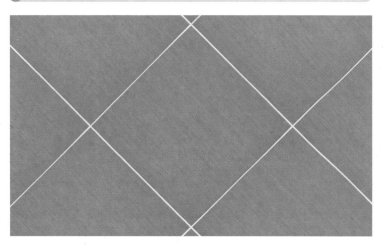

A tiled floor is the classic choice for a kitchen. When choosing tiles, consider the size and finish: large tiles make a space look contemporary, while smaller tiles give a room a more traditional feel. The more grouting there is, the more cleaning the floor will need.

WOODEN

Wooden floors should be well sealed, and must be able to withstand both the foot traffic of a busy space and the raised moisture levels of a cooking area. Planks can appear visually longer and wider, so are a good choice for small and narrow kitchens.

SEAMLESS

Seamless designs, which include sheet vinyl, rubber, and linoleum, and poured floors like concrete and resin are essentially one piece of flooring without any joins. The latest sheet flooring designs are quite upmarket and a good choice for small areas.

CHECKLIST

- **When calculating the amount** of tiles, hardwood or laminate flooring you need for your project, add at least 10% extra to the total amount as a contingency.

- **If you are laying tiles,** particularly large tiles, your sub-floor must be perfectly level. If you have floorboards, you will need to cover them first with marine plyboard.

- **If you have a sound, flat concrete floor** or an existing flat tiled floor, you can lay new tiles straight on top, but check first that the raised level of the new floor will not obstruct any doors or other moveable items in the room.

2

CHOOSE THE MATERIAL

The material you choose will largely depend on your budget and whether you prefer the look and solidity of tiles or a warmer, softer feel like vinyl or rubber. If you are having underfloor heating, check which materials are suitable to use with it first.

TILES

PORCELAIN

Hardwearing porcelain is a versatile choice available in a variety of prices, designs, and glazed and unglazed finishes. Seal unglazed tiles before and after grouting.

CERAMIC

Ceramic tiles are good for large areas. Available in a variety of colours, shapes, and textures, they are cheap, hardwearing, stain-resistant, and don't need sealing.

QUARTZ COMPOSITE

If you want a co-ordinated look for your worktops and floor, this may be a good choice. It doesn't stain, hides dirt, and rarely chips or cracks, but it is expensive.

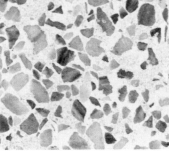

TERRAZZO

This expensive flooring is made of marble chippings set into cement with a colour pigment added. Endless combinations of colours and finishes can be achieved.

CONCRETE

Extremely hardwearing but costly, concrete tiles are available in various sizes with a polished or matt finish. The polished effect is easier to clean, so suits a kitchen.

TERRACOTTA

Medium-priced terracotta is very porous so the tiles must be sealed to avoid staining. Choose from a range of shapes such as classic square or brick-shaped tiles.

TRAVERTINE

Though expensive, this natural stone floor is available in either a sleek, polished finish or a rustic, tumbled look with soft edges and a sponge-like appearance.

LIMESTONE

These expensive tiles range from chalky white to honey in colour, and often reveal details of fossils within. Choose polished gloss tiles or rougher, matt finishes.

SLATE

The uneven "chipped" surface of black or grey slate sometimes has flecks of gold or orange, and always creates a dramatic look. It is medium to high in price.

LAMINATE

These laminated decorative fibreboard tiles are available in a range of colours and designs, including slate and travertine, and are a cheaper or medium-cost alternative.

VINYL

Vinyl gives an authentic look of the material it mimics. Prices depend on the brand. Cheaper versions have self-adhesive backing, so are easy to stick to the floor.

RUBBER

Medium-priced rubber comes in a range of colours and textures. Smoother surfaces are easy to clean; low-profile textures, like studs, provide extra grip underfoot.

WOODEN

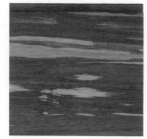

HARDWOOD

Good medium- to high-cost choices that will not react to heat and moisture include mahogany, walnut, and teak. Buy pre-sealed or seal with lacquer or linseed oil.

ENGINEERED WOOD

The construction of this medium-priced wood (layers of hard- and softwood boards topped with hardwood timber) means that it's less likely to warp than hardwood.

BAMBOO

Bamboo is medium- to high-cost and eco-friendly. While moisture-tolerant, it still needs to be sealed. It can either be left in its natural colour or stained.

LAMINATE

Low- to medium-cost laminate planks have realistic textured finishes and detailing to give the appearance of real boards like oak, maple, and teak.

VINYL

Wood-effect vinyl looks authentic and is easier to care for than the real thing. It is available in a range of prices. Expensive vinyls should be professionally fitted.

SEAMLESS

CONCRETE

A poured concrete floor is installed whole, then polished into a perfectly smooth surface. It is an expensive option, but comes in a range of colours and is durable.

RESIN

An expensive poured resin flooring offers a seamless finish. Highly contemporary, it's available in both matt and gloss finishes and a range of colours.

RUBBER

Practical, hardwearing, and warm underfoot, medium-cost rubber comes in a huge range of colours and textures – the smoother surfaces are easier to keep clean.

VINYL

Modern sheet vinyl is cheap or mid priced and is available in a huge range of designs that reproduce the look and texture of many different floor surfaces.

LINOLEUM

Medium-priced linoleum is made of natural, sustainable ingredients. It is easy to clean and scratches or dents only if heavy objects are dropped on or dragged across it.

ZONING YOUR KITCHEN FLOOR

If you have a large open-plan kitchen dining space, dividing the dining and cooking floor areas into separate zones will make your scheme look more successful.

- **Choose a rug in colours** that match the palette of your kitchen and place it beneath the dining table and chairs. Ensure that you buy a rug large enough so all the chair legs can stand on it comfortably, even when they are pulled out.

- **Avoid picking light-coloured flooring** or a rug with a deep pile or weave that will retain dropped food, and choose a material that's easy to clean.

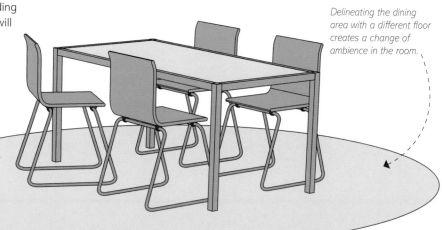

Delineating the dining area with a different floor creates a change of ambience in the room.

13 CHOOSE WALL COVERINGS

If you want to make your kitchen look visually stimulating, think about using more than one material on the walls: a mixture of decorated walls could look more interesting and may help your budget. Just remember, though, that your walls should complement rather than eclipse your kitchen units.

1 CHOOSE THE MATERIAL

When considering different materials for your kitchen, you should always bear in mind how much cleaning and maintenance each surface will require and whether it might be splashed by water or food.

TILES

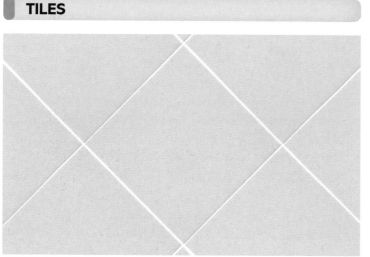

Tiles are a practical choice for a kitchen, especially behind the sink and hob where they can be easily cleaned if splashed. There are a wide range of designs, colours, and finishes available to suit both traditional and contemporary kitchens.

PAINT

Paint can be used on all walls in a kitchen, but if you're planning to use it near the sink or hob, choose one – such as kitchen & bathroom paint – that resists moisture and wipes clean easily, and avoid textured paints, which won't be so easy to wipe down.

WALLPAPER

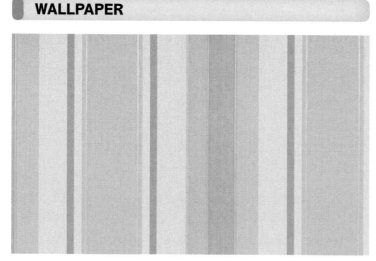

As with paint, it's worth choosing wallpaper that can withstand moisture if you're having it in the kitchen. It's best not to use these papers near a cooking or wet area; if you do, a clear glass splashback over the top gives you the best chance of keeping it protected.

CLADDING

If you want a rustic look, wood cladding is a good choice and a less expensive alternative to tiles. It needs to be well protected with a varnish, oil, or paint to resist moisture. Although it will withstand use around a wet area, it should not be used behind a hob.

2 CHOOSE THE TYPE

The type of material you pick will be very much dictated by the style of your house and the kitchen units themselves. If you are going to choose a combination of materials, ensure that they complement each other.

TILES

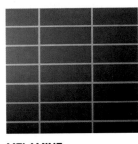

CLASSIC
Plain, square, or rectangular tiles are a low- to medium-cost choice. For a contemporary look, use grey grout – it looks good and doesn't show dirt.

BRICK
Give your kitchen a retro look with medium-priced brick-shaped tiles. Typically made of ceramic with a gloss or matt surface, they have a straight or bevelled edge.

MOSAIC
Good for contemporary spaces, medium- to high-cost mosaic tiles come in a range of materials and finishes such as silver, mirror glass, and glitter glass.

MELAMINE
Low-cost melamine panels are available in a selection of plain colours and patterned designs. They can be used on all walls except those behind a gas hob.

LARGE FORMAT
You may only need one row of large tiles (80 x 80cm/31 x 31in) to create a splashback, but your walls do need to be perfectly flat. They come in a range of prices.

PAINT

KITCHEN & BATHROOM
These medium- to high-priced paints withstand moisture and often offer mould protection, too. They are only available in a limited range of colour choices.

MATT
Unless your kitchen is badly ventilated, use matt emulsion on all walls except those behind a sink and hob. This paint is available in a range of prices.

SILK OR SHEEN
With a surface that can easily be wiped, medium-priced silk and soft sheen paints are a good choice. Their subtle sheen helps to reflect light around the room.

EGGSHELL
Tough and washable, mid-priced eggshell paint can be used on all surfaces in a bathroom, including skirting boards and any wood panelling, as well as walls.

BLACKBOARD PAINT
If you have a contemporary kitchen and enough light and space to paint a wall black, create a noticeboard using low- to medium-cost blackboard paint.

WALLPAPER

VINYL
Medium-priced vinyl wallpapers are designed for rooms with a higher moisture content, although don't use them behind a sink.

PLAIN OR PATTERNED
Standard wallpapers come in a range of prices. If you want to use it behind the sink or oven, protect it with a clear glass panel.

CLADDING

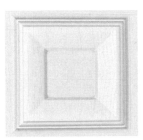

WAINSCOT
Medium-priced wainscot panels need to be painted, so pick a paint with a soft sheen to match that of your skirting boards.

TONGUE & GROOVE
Cover this low- to medium-priced panelling in a paint suitable for a kitchen, such as eggshell. Don't install it behind a hob, however.

14 CHOOSE KITCHEN LIGHTING

Kitchen lighting needs to be chosen with precision because it's the one area of the home – other than a workshop or home office, perhaps – where you need spaces to be lit well enough for you to work. Include ambient lighting, too, and accent lighting to show off any design elements.

1 CHOOSE YOUR LIGHTING

How you light your kitchen depends to some degree on how big it is. If it's a tiny room, you will probably want to focus on ambient and task lighting. If the room is large, or part of an open-plan living space, you can be more creative.

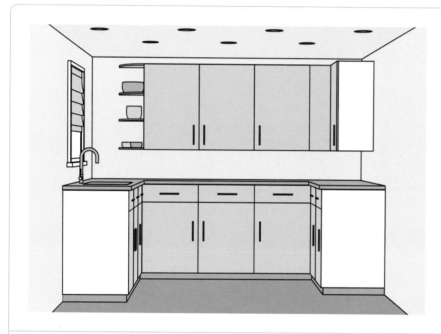

AMBIENT
Most kitchens have overhead lighting in addition to task lighting. If you have a large open-plan kitchen diner and living space, fitting a dimmer switch will allow you to lower the brightness of the overhead lighting once the cooking is over and the eating begins.

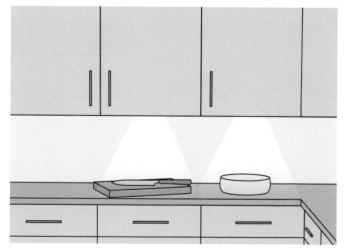

TASK
Task lighting is a must for a kitchen, whatever its size. Position it directly over the worktop so that no shadows are cast as you bend forward to chop vegetables, for example. If your kitchen is small and lighting options are limited by your budget, designate a task area – ideally near the hob – and ensure that it is lit well.

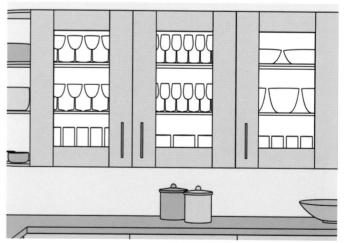

ACCENT
Accent lighting can make a room seem larger. Place lights on the underside, on top of and inside glazed wall cabinets, and at skirting board level to stretch your space and highlight your kitchen's design. Or use accent lighting as you would in a living room, focusing spotlights on pictures or an impressive range cooker, for example.

It is important to create a space that you and your family will enjoy spending time in, as well as one that is practical to work in. The aim should be to choose a combination of fittings that will cover all your lighting needs.

CEILING LIGHTS

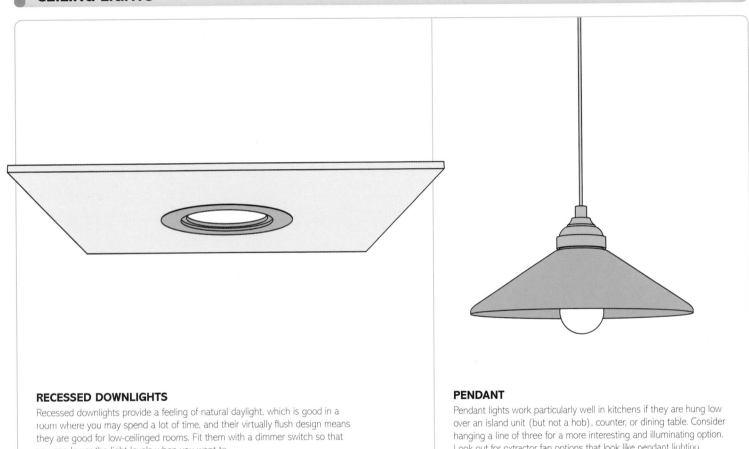

RECESSED DOWNLIGHTS

Recessed downlights provide a feeling of natural daylight, which is good in a room where you may spend a lot of time, and their virtually flush design means they are good for low-ceilinged rooms. Fit them with a dimmer switch so that you can lower the light levels when you want to.

PENDANT

Pendant lights work particularly well in kitchens if they are hung low over an island unit (but not a hob), counter, or dining table. Consider hanging a line of three for a more interesting and illuminating option. Look out for extractor fan options that look like pendant lighting.

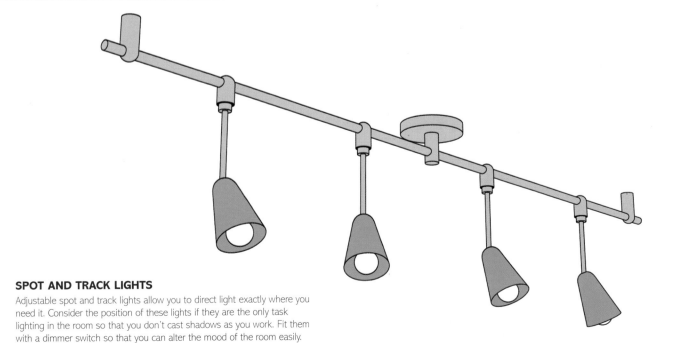

SPOT AND TRACK LIGHTS

Adjustable spot and track lights allow you to direct light exactly where you need it. Consider the position of these lights if they are the only task lighting in the room so that you don't cast shadows as you work. Fit them with a dimmer switch so that you can alter the mood of the room easily.

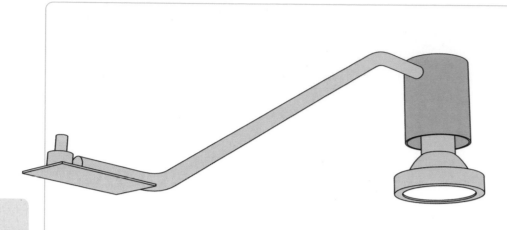

OVER CABINET

Swan neck fittings are fitted at the front of the top of wall cabinets to cast light down onto the doors and illuminate preparation areas. Or, you can have lights concealed on top of the cupboard – they simply light the space above the unit. Both types create decorative accent lighting in the evening.

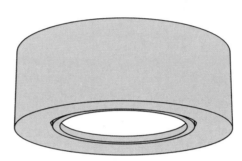

UNDER CUPBOARD

Under-cupboard lighting provides task lighting for when you are preparing food and also creates decorative additional lighting if you are dining in the kitchen. The lights should be mounted towards the middle of the underside of a wall cabinet so that the light is evenly distributed and doesn't cast shadows.

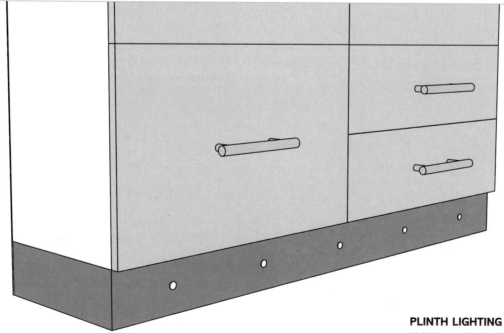

PLINTH LIGHTING

Highlight your kitchen floor using plinth lights. These lights are available in either LEDs or halogen lamps, and come in a range of designs that are fixed into the plinth panel around the bottom of your kitchen units.

15 CHOOSE WINDOW TREATMENTS

Before you choose what to dress your kitchen window with, decide if you want the window dressing to hide or show off the view outside? Secondly, does the window sit near a sink and require something that can withstand splashing? And, finally, how much impact should the window dressing make decoratively?

1 CHOOSE THE TYPE

Kitchen window dressings must be practical because they are subjected to more humidity than most other rooms. You also need to consider how easy your choice will be to keep clean, since over time it will become greasy and dust-covered.

BLINDS

Blinds are a popular choice in a kitchen, as they can sit neatly within the recess of a window and are less likely to get splashed. Choose a fabric that's mould-resistant and easy to wipe, and add decorative detail with pattern or a sculpted lower edge.

CURTAINS

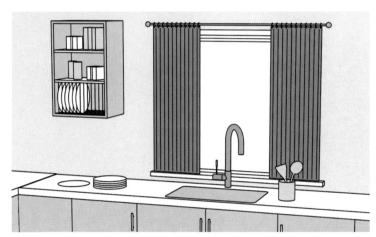

If you want curtains in your kitchen, choose ones that are machine-washable, as they're likely to pick up kitchen odours, grime, and dust. If you have two windows in your kitchen, choose a blind for the cooking area and curtains for the dining area.

SHUTTERS

A practical choice in a kitchen, shutters can be wiped clean easily. Choose from full-height, tier-on-tier, or café-style shutters, which only cover the bottom half of your window. Opt for a white or pale wood finish if you want to reflect light.

FILM

Window film offers complete privacy without blocking out all natural light. It can be bought by the metre or made to measure, and is easily fixed to your interior windowpanes. It is a good choice for a small space when you don't want a fancy window dressing.

2 CHOOSE THE STYLE

Kitchens are busy, often small rooms and typically need window dressings in a simple style. However, that doesn't mean they have to be plain – you can add pattern or texture with both fabric and wood finishes.

BLINDS

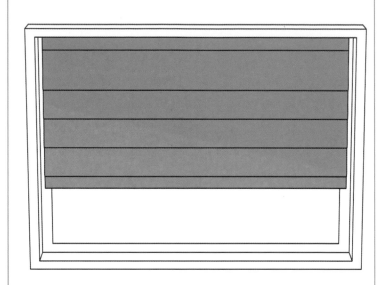

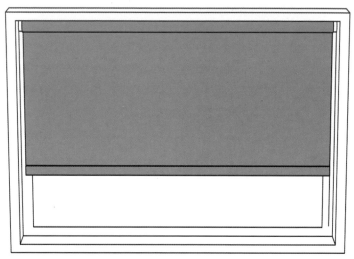

ROMAN

If you want your kitchen to feel homely rather than functional, consider a Roman blind. These blinds are available in a wide choice of fabrics, although you may want to consider using a patterned rather than plain design so it doesn't show marks easily.

ROLLER

Roller blinds are a fairly inexpensive option, so are a good choice in kitchens with wider windows. You can have roller blinds made to measure, although most ready-made blinds can be cut to size and, providing you're a competent DIYer, they are easy to fit. Choose blinds made from moisture-resistant fabrics.

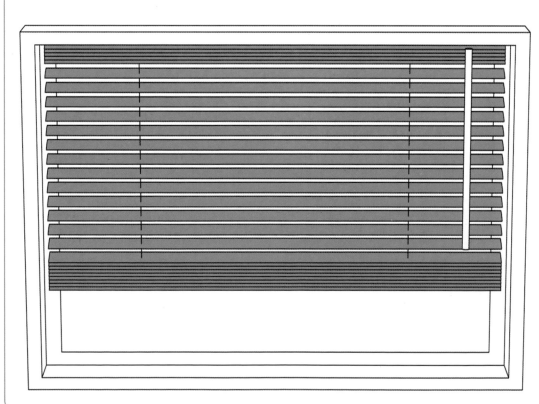

VENETIAN

Made from metal or wood, Venetian blinds are an easy-to-clean, functional choice for your kitchen. They will give your windows a streamlined look, which is ideal if you have a contemporary kitchen. They're available in a choice of materials, colours, and slat widths.

CURTAINS

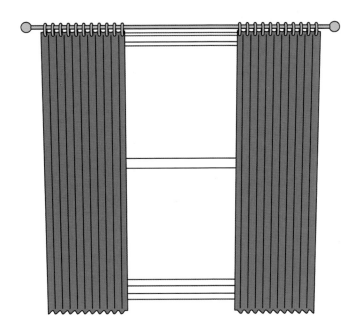

SILL LENGTH

Sill-length, or just below sill-length, curtains in a washable cotton are a good choice for small, recessed windows in a kitchen. Choose light fabrics that can be washed or find patterns that will hide grime or splashes – but be aware that this curtain length can look old-fashioned, so pick your fabric design with care.

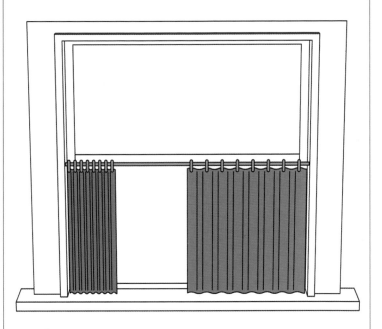

CAFÉ CURTAINS

Café curtains are hung from a rod or curtain wire that is fixed inside the window recess either halfway down a window, or aligned with the central horizontal frame between two panes of glass. They are designed to screen the lower half of the window to offer privacy, but still allow light in and enable you to see out.

SHUTTERS

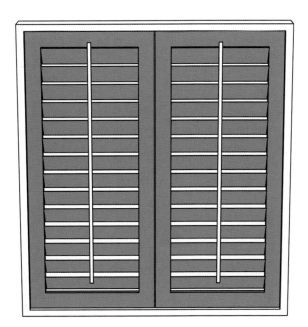

LOUVRE

Depending on the wood or paint finish you choose, louvred shutters suit most kitchen styles, whether traditional or contemporary. If your window is behind your sink, make sure that you will be able to open the shutters without hitting the tap.

FILM

PLAIN OR PATTERNED

If you are opting for window film, give some thought to whether you want to add interest with a pattern or motif, or whether you are happy to keep it plain. If you are teaming the film with another window dressing, such as curtains, for which you are using a patterned fabric, take care to avoid a clash of patterns.

MAKE
A ROMAN BLIND

Like roller blinds, Roman blinds allow more natural light into a room than thick curtains or drapes, but they dress a window more extravagantly than a simple roller blind. The cords and rods attached to the reverse of the blind enable it to be pulled into neat folded pleats when not covering the window.

WHAT YOU NEED

- Fabric with a straight weave
- Lining material
- Tape measure and ruler
- Scissors
- Pins
- Iron
- Velcro
- Sewing machine
- Roman blind kit
- Pencil or pen
- Glue
- Spirit level and screwdriver

1 CUT THE FABRIC AND LINING

1 MEASURE YOUR WINDOW to determine what size the finished blind needs to be. You will need to decide whether the blind will hang inside or outside the window recess.

2 CUT OUT THE FABRIC, adding 15cm (6in) to the length and 8cm (3in) to the width. Then cut out the lining material: this needs to be the same length as the main fabric (15cm/6in longer than the final length of the blind) but the width should only be that of the final blind – no extra allowance is needed.

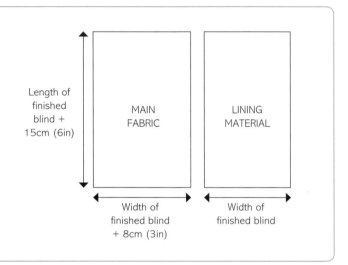

Length of finished blind + 15cm (6in)

MAIN FABRIC

LINING MATERIAL

Width of finished blind + 8cm (3in)

Width of finished blind

2 STITCH ON THE LINING

1 PLACE THE FABRIC face down on a flat surface and lay the lining over the top. Align the edges of the two fabrics on both sides and pin them together (there will be slightly more fabric than lining).

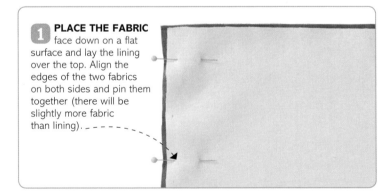

2 SEW THE SIDES together with a seam allowance of 2cm (¾in).

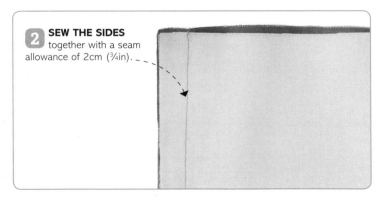

3 TURN THE JOINED FABRICS inside out so the fabric is the right way round. Lay the blind on a flat surface and make sure that the extra strip of fabric at either side of the lining is 2cm (¾in) on each side. Use a hot iron to press the fabric edges flat.

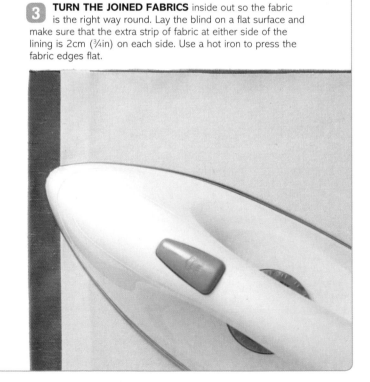

3 | ATTACH THE VELCRO

1 FOLD THE TOP of the blind over: the fold should be 3–4cm (1¼–1½in), depending on how wide your Velcro is.

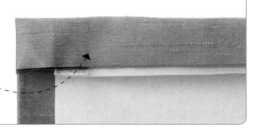

2 TRIM THE EDGE of the fabric, if necessary, to neaten it, then press the fold flat with the iron.

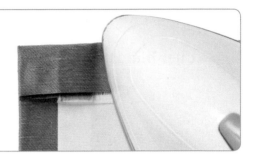

3 FOLD THE TOP CORNERS into triangles, tuck them under the pressed fold, and pin one half of the Velcro onto the fabric fold.

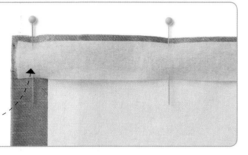

4 SEW THE VELCRO in place.

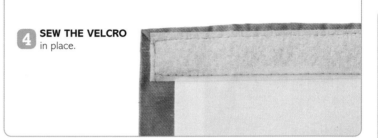

4 | SEW ON THE TAPES

1 TO DETERMINE WHERE to attach the tapes (which comprise the pockets for the rods), you need to divide the blind into sections. A blind with three rods needs to be divided into three equal sections plus a further section that is half the size. You should also make allowance for the headrail at the top of the blind.

To calculate the positions of the tapes, begin with the intended final length of your blind, as determined at step 1. Take away 5cm (2in) for the headrail. Then divide the resulting figure by 3.5 (relating to the three equal sections plus one half-size section; if your blind is to have four rods, divide the figure by 4.5 instead).

The example (right) shows how this would work for a blind 110cm (44in) long. Subtracting 5cm (2in) for the headrail gives you a figure of 105cm (42in). Dividing this by 3.5 gives you a figure of 30cm (12in). This will be the size of your three full-size panels.

Again you need to make allowance for the headrail, so measure 5cm (2in) from the top of the blind, then measure and mark (using a pencil or pen) a line 30cm (12in) below. Mark two further lines at 30cm (12in) intervals. The bottom of the blind once hemmed will be 15cm (6in) below the lowest tape; you can mark this line now if you want but you should still check it is correct by holding the blind up to the window (see step 5) before hemming.

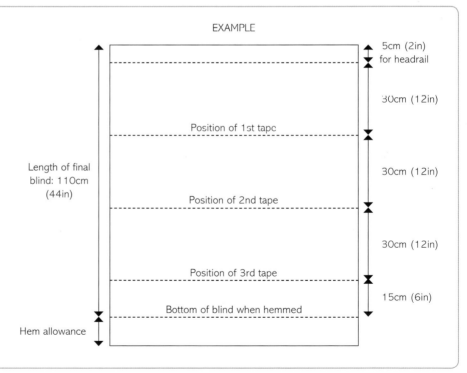

EXAMPLE

- 5cm (2in) for headrail
- 30cm (12in)
- Position of 1st tape
- 30cm (12in)
- Position of 2nd tape
- 30cm (12in)
- Position of 3rd tape
- 15cm (6in)
- Bottom of blind when hemmed

Length of final blind: 110cm (44in)

Hem allowance

2 PIN THE THREE LENGTHS of tape onto the lining at the marked points.

3 SEW THE TAPES onto the blind.

5 FOLD OVER THE BASE

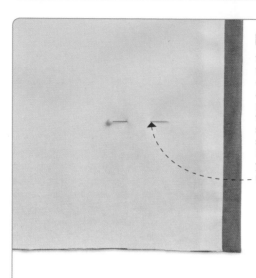

1 HOLD THE BLIND up to the window to check where the bottom edge needs to be and mark a line with pins. (If you marked the bottom edge at step 4 and you are satisfied that your line is in the correct place, you will not need to mark it again.)

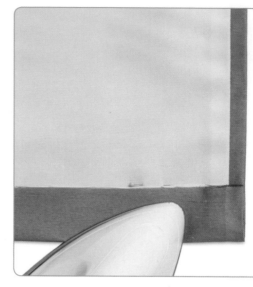

2 FOLD OVER THE BOTTOM of the fabric so it sits just below the line of pins and press it flat with the iron.

3 FOLD THE FABRIC over again (this second fold will make a channel, or pocket, in which the weight bar will sit). Secure the fold in place with pins.

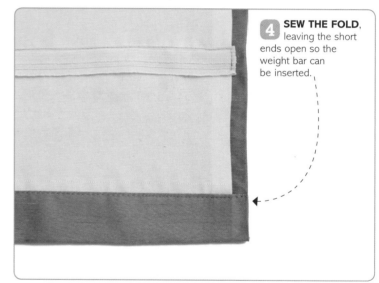

4 SEW THE FOLD, leaving the short ends open so the weight bar can be inserted.

6 INSERT THE WEIGHT BAR AND RODS

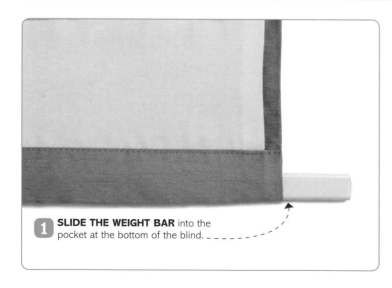

1 SLIDE THE WEIGHT BAR into the pocket at the bottom of the blind.

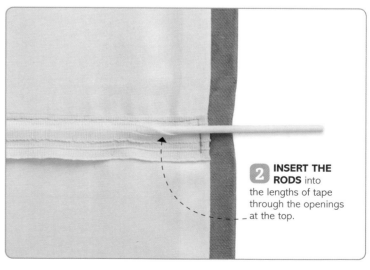

2 INSERT THE RODS into the lengths of tape through the openings at the top.

1 **GLUE THE OTHER LENGTH** of Velcro to the blind mechanism, then attach the mechanism to the blind by firmly pressing the two lengths of Velcro together.

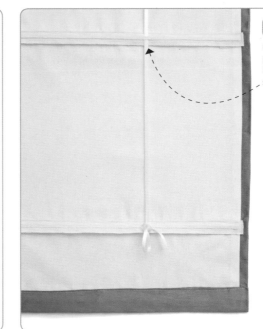

2 **THREAD UP THE BLIND,** making sure the cords pass through each length of tape at the same point.

8 FIX THE BRACKETS

1 **TO GAUGE THE RIGHT HEIGHT** of the brackets on the window, measure the position of the brackets on the blind and transfer these measurements to the window frame or recess. Draw a straight line between the two points using a spirit level.

2 **SCREW THE BRACKETS** to the window frame or wall. Attach the blind. Fix a cleat to the wall, if needed, at the side the pulley will hang to secure the blind in place when it is raised.

17 CHOOSE KITCHEN TABLE AND CHAIRS

A table and chairs is a key piece of furniture – whether it will be going in your kitchen, a dining room, or an open-plan living area. Think about whether you would rather prioritise a convivial atmosphere or spacious dining, and whether you prefer a sophisticated, integrated look or a more relaxed setting.

1 DECIDE ON TABLE SIZE

As a minimum, your table needs to be large enough to accommodate your usual number of diners, and if you regularly have guests you should also think about the logistics of fitting extra people in. The space available is the other major consideration and, particularly in a kitchen, you need to ensure there will be plenty of room to manoeuvre around it once it is in place.

2 CHOOSE SHAPE OF TABLE

Most tables are either round (circular or oval), square, or rectangular. You will usually find that one shape suits the dimensions of your room better than the others, but think too about the number of diners and which shape will best accommodate them.

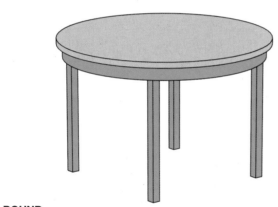

ROUND
Good for sociable dining, a round table allows everyone sitting around it to see and talk to each other easily. You can fit different numbers of chairs around a round table without leaving anyone stuck on a corner or at one end of the table.

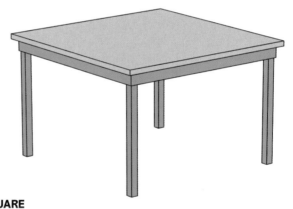

SQUARE
Square tables are suited to square rooms, as they make the most of the available space. If the table is only ever used to seat four or fewer people, the equal length of its sides means that each person has plenty of elbow space while eating.

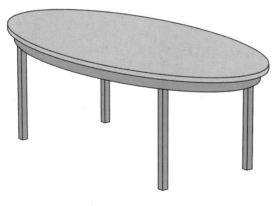

OVAL
Oval tables are often a good choice for rectangular rooms. If you entertain large groups, or if the number of people at your table often varies, the curved ends of an oval table make it easy to accommodate everyone without anyone having to sit on a corner.

RECTANGULAR
As most rooms are rectangular, this shaped table may well make the best use of space. These designs are available in a wide selection of lengths and widths to suit your room's dimensions, and even the smallest design can seat more than four people comfortably.

3

CHOOSE TYPE OF CHAIRS

If you like a streamlined, coordinated look, choose chairs that match your table. If you prefer your dining area to have a less formal atmosphere, go for chairs that aren't a perfect match, or choose a selection of different styles for a fun, individual look.

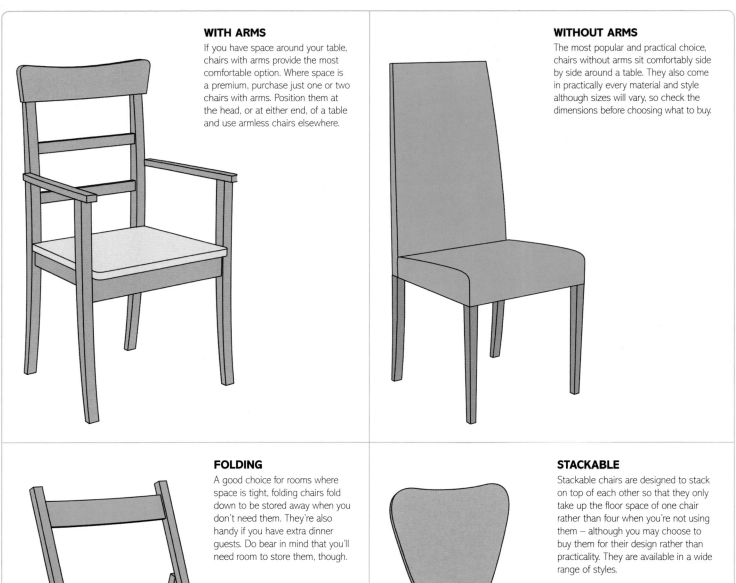

WITH ARMS

If you have space around your table, chairs with arms provide the most comfortable option. Where space is a premium, purchase just one or two chairs with arms. Position them at the head, or at either end, of a table and use armless chairs elsewhere.

WITHOUT ARMS

The most popular and practical choice, chairs without arms sit comfortably side by side around a table. They also come in practically every material and style although sizes will vary, so check the dimensions before choosing what to buy.

FOLDING

A good choice for rooms where space is tight, folding chairs fold down to be stored away when you don't need them. They're also handy if you have extra dinner guests. Do bear in mind that you'll need room to store them, though.

STACKABLE

Stackable chairs are designed to stack on top of each other so that they only take up the floor space of one chair rather than four when you're not using them – although you may choose to buy them for their design rather than practicality. They are available in a wide range of styles.

4 CHOOSE THE MATERIAL

While the material of your table and chairs should match, or at least complement, the look of your kitchen furniture, also think about how durable it will be, how much it costs, if the material is comfortable to sit on, and whether it will age well.

TABLES

WOOD

Medium-priced solid wood lasts for years. If the top is damaged, it can be sanded and refinished. As a natural material there will be variations in the grain and colour.

WOOD EFFECT

Many wood-effect tables have a textured grain effect that looks and feels like real wood. A low-cost option, it costs less than the real thing, but is not as hardwearing.

METAL

Medium-priced metal tables usually have a metal frame and legs and a wooden or glass tabletop for a contemporary look; the brushed metal creates an industrial feel.

GLASS

A medium-cost glass table visually expands a space. Like a metal table, it is usually a combination of two materials: a tempered glass tabletop with wooden or metal legs.

PLASTIC

Available in a range of prices, a plastic table can easily be wiped clean, so is ideal if you have children. Clear acrylic, a type of plastic, is more suited to grown-up dining.

CHAIRS

WOOD

Wood is a practical, medium-cost choice. Wooden chairs can become uncomfortable after sitting on them for long periods of time, so you may want to add seat pads.

UPHOLSTERED

Medium-priced upholstered chairs tend to have a foam-filled seat and back, so feel comfortable. Choose leather or removable washable covers if you have children.

PLASTIC

Low-cost plastic can easily be wiped clean, which makes it a good low-maintenance choice. However, it is not comfortable to sit on for long periods of time.

RATTAN

Rustic-looking, medium-cost, woven rattan is not completely rigid, so is comfortable to sit on. Cheaper versions may unravel over time; if you pay extra, it will last for years.

CHECKLIST

● **Where will the table go,** and how you will use it? A kitchen-diner looks best if the table and chairs co-ordinate with the kitchen units. If the table will be used for more than just eating (doing homework, for instance), ensure the tabletop is hardwearing.

● **Will the table fit?** Lay a newspaper template of the table on the floor to find out. Allow at least 60cm (24in) – and ideally 90cm (36in) – between the table and any walls.

● **Table heights vary,** so if you're buying your dining chairs separately, take careful measurements of the different items to get the correct height.

If space in your kitchen or dining room is tight, or you don't need a large table for everyday use, an extendable dining table that can be made bigger or smaller may give you the flexibility you need. There are many different types available, made to extend and retract in all sorts of different ways; a few of the most commonplace are shown below. Extending tables are available in all the standard shapes you would expect tables to come in, and in a range of sizes and materials, so you won't be limited in your choice.

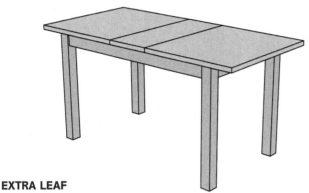

EXTRA LEAF

An extra section (the leaf) in the same material can be added to increase the size of a table. Extra leaves are most commonly kept concealed under the tabletop when they are not in use. Some tables have more than one leaf; four leaves can turn a four-seater table into an impressive 16-seater.

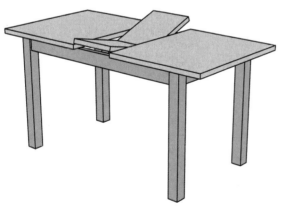

BUTTERFLY EXTENSION

Dining tables with a butterfly extension are similar to those with an extra leaf. The two top panels of the table slide apart to reveal a central "butterfly" extension panel that is pulled up and out – typically enough space to seat two more people.

FLIP TOP

The surface area of a flip-top dining table can be doubled by unfolding the hinged top. In order for the legs to remain central, you either have to slide the top along, or rotate it through 90 degrees.

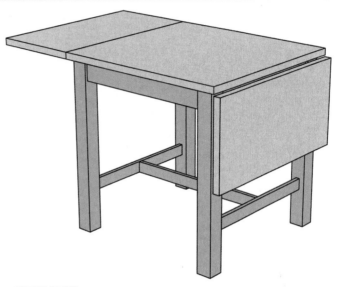

DROP LEAF

A drop-leaf table has a fixed tabletop section in the centre and two folded leaves that be lifted up at one or both sides, depending on how much extra seating you need. The leaves are supported by brackets underneath the table top. A drop-leaf table often also features a concealed drawer in which you can store cutlery.

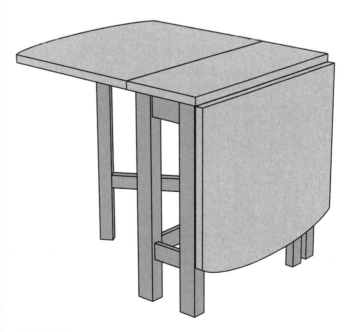

GATE LEG

A variation on the drop-leaf style, a gate-leg table has hinged legs that swing out (like a gate) to support extensions which, when not in use, can be folded down at the side. The sturdy support provided by these gate legs means that the extensions can be quite large, and often these tables convert from something extremely slimline to a table that can comfortably seat several people.

MAKE CUSHIONS
FOR KITCHEN CHAIRS

You can transform plain kitchen chairs, and make them much more comfortable, with colourful cushions. The best way to ensure that these work with your overall colour scheme, and that they fit your chairs snugly, is to make them yourself. These tie-on cushion pads are both simple to create and stylish.

WHAT YOU NEED

- Brown paper
- Scissors
- Pins
- Coloured fabric – use curtain-weight cotton material
- Ric rac
- Needle and thread
- Sewing machine (optional)
- Polyester wadding
- Cover buttons (4 per cushion)
- Button maker (optional)

2 CUT THE FABRIC

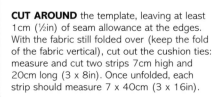

CUT AROUND the template, leaving at least 1cm (½in) of seam allowance at the edges. With the fabric still folded over (keep the fold of the fabric vertical), cut out the cushion ties: measure and cut two strips 7cm high and 20cm long (3 x 8in). Once unfolded, each strip should measure 7 x 40cm (3 x 16in).

1 MAKE A TEMPLATE

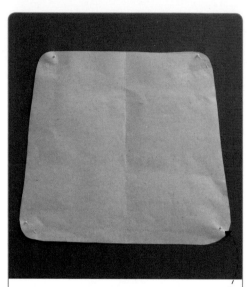

1 MEASURE THE SEAT of one of your kitchen chairs and make a template from brown paper. Place the cutout on the chair seat to check the dimensions are accurate. Trim the template with scissors, if necessary.

2 FOLD THE FABRIC in half (so that you will cut out two fabric shapes) and pin the template onto one end of the fabric.

3 ATTACH THE BORDER

1 LAY ONE of the seat fabric cutouts, face side up, on a flat surface, and pin a length of ric rac in place around all four edges.

2 SEW THE RIC RAC to the edge of the fabric.

4 MAKE THE FABRIC TIES

1 **FOLD OVER THE SHORT** ends of each fabric tie, then fold over the long edges so they meet in the middle.

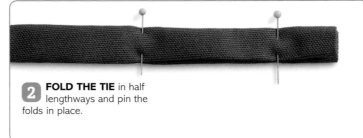

2 **FOLD THE TIE** in half lengthways and pin the folds in place.

3 **SEW ALONG** the outer edges of each tie to make a neat seam.

5 SEW THE SEAT COVER

1 **FOLD THE SEAMED TIES** in half and position them on top of the fabric cutout (with the ric rac face up). The folded ends of the ties should overhang the back of the seat cutout near each corner. Hold each tie in place with a pin at the corners.

2 **PLACE THE SECOND FABRIC** cutout, reverse side face up, over ric rac fabric cutout and ties, and pin the two cutouts together around the edges.

3 **SEW THE FABRIC CUTOUTS** together. Leave a hole at one side of the seat cover that is large enough to pull the cover through it to turn it inside out.

7 WAYS TO
REFRESH A TIRED KITCHEN

If your kitchen is looking a little tired, give it a fresh new look by making some small changes, such as replacing the door furniture or changing the colour of a wall. If you are feeling more ambitious, you can make bigger changes that, though they will require a little more time and effort, can create more impact.

CREATE A FEATURE WALL

Add interest to your kitchen by painting or wallpapering one wall in an eye-catching colour or pattern.

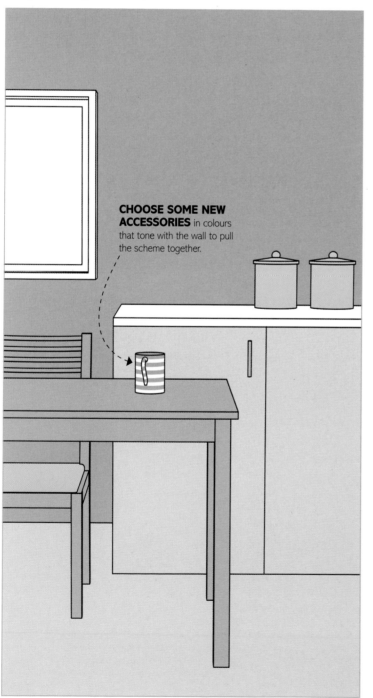

CHOOSE SOME NEW ACCESSORIES in colours that tone with the wall to pull the scheme together.

CHANGE HANDLES

Update the look of your units by adding new handles. The simplest option is to look for designs that will cover existing holes.

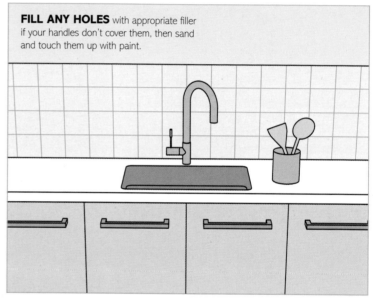

FILL ANY HOLES with appropriate filler if your handles don't cover them, then sand and touch them up with paint.

REPLACE DOORS

For a real transformation, replace cabinet doors and drawer fronts. Ensure the size of the new ones is correct for your units.

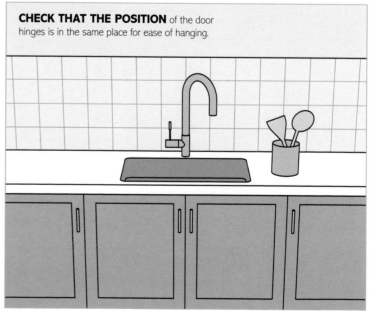

CHECK THAT THE POSITION of the door hinges is in the same place for ease of hanging.

REPLACE SPLASHBACK

A new splashback can make a big difference to the look of a kitchen, especially if you choose a different material to that of your old one.

REPLACE WORKTOP

Replacing your worktops can completely change the look of your kitchen. Swap them for any material your budget can accommodate.

IF YOUR EXISTING WORKTOP is a good fit, lift it out and use it as a template for your new worktop.

REVAMP TILES

Give your existing tiles a makeover using tile paint, which is available in a range of colours, or by adding decorative tile transfers.

CONSIDER RE-GROUTING your tiles if the grout is looking grubby.

CHANGE THE WINDOW DRESSING

Update your window by adding a new blind. If your window overlooks a neighbour's house or the street, add window film.

4 FOLD IN THE CORNERS

1 **FOLD ONE CORNER** of the oil cloth in half to make a triangular shape.

2 **FOLD THE TRIANGLE** diagonally against one side of the table.

3 **TUCK THE END** under the table top.

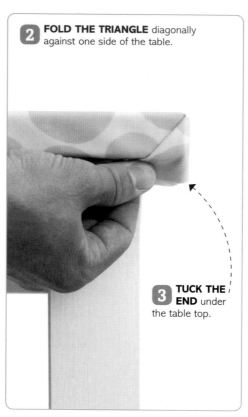

4 **SECURE IT** in place with the staple gun.

ANOTHER WAY TO FOLD

1 **ALTERNATIVELY**, draw the two sides of the oil cloth together at the corner to make a triangular shape with a central fold.

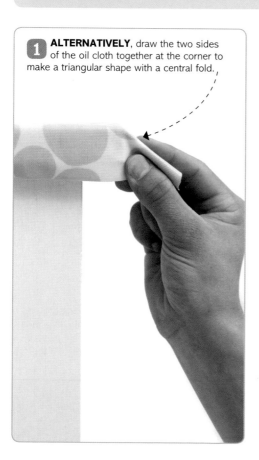

2 **FOLD THE TRIANGLE** straight under the table top.

3 **SECURE IT** in place with the staple gun.

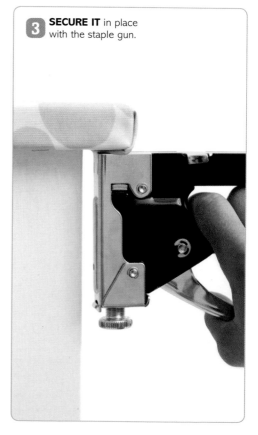

REPAINT
KITCHEN UNITS

To update your kitchen quickly and easily, repaint the doors of your units (if they are wooden) and replace the handles. Ideally, use oil-based paint for this job, as kitchen furniture endures a lot of wear and tear; if you choose a water-based wood paint, add a coat of water-based lacquer over the dried paint.

KITCHEN

78

WHAT YOU NEED

- Screwdriver
- Wood filler
- Fine finishing sandpaper
- Tack cloth
- Kitchen cabinet handles
- Pencil
- Ruler or set square
- Tape measure (optional)
- Drill
- Paint for interior wood
- Paintbrush

1 REMOVE THE DOOR

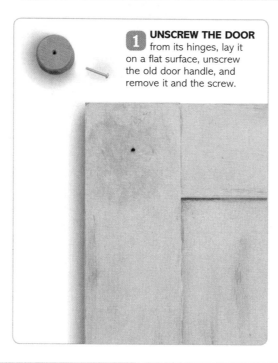

1 UNSCREW THE DOOR from its hinges, lay it on a flat surface, unscrew the old door handle, and remove it and the screw.

2 FILL THE HOLE with wood filler and allow to dry. Then lightly sand the filler with fine sandpaper to smooth its surface.

2 SAND DOWN THE DOOR

1 SAND DOWN the whole door with more sandpaper to get rid of any imperfections in the wood to give a smooth, fine finish, and to provide a "key" for the paint to adhere to.

2 RUB DOWN the wood with a tack cloth to wipe off any loose dust.

3 MARK THE HANDLE POSITION

1 **HOLD** the new handle against the side of the door to see where you would like to position it.

2 **MARK WITH A PENCIL** where the top and the bottom of the handle will be fixed. Draw a horizontal line with the ruler on the wood from each point to the side edge of the door.

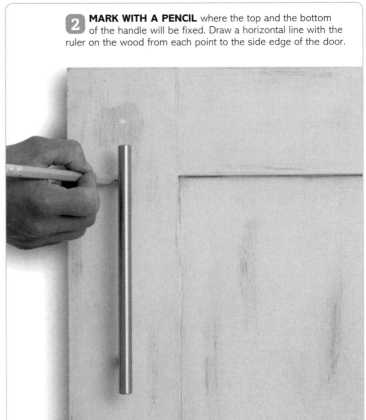

3 **DRAW A VERTICAL LINE** between the two horizontal lines. Use the ruler or a tape measure to ensure the line is straight by measuring the distance from the edge of the door to the top and the bottom of the vertical line.

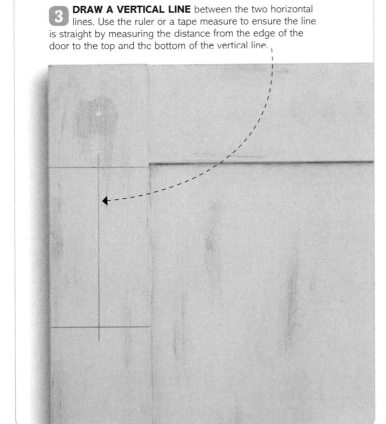

4 **DRILL A HOLE** at each point where the horizontal and vertical lines cross.

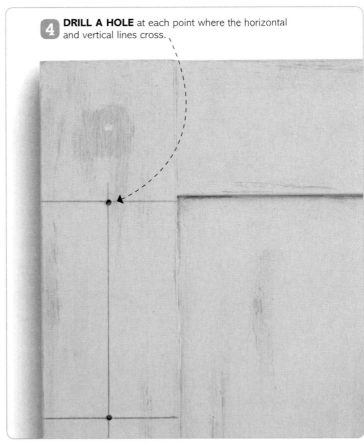

4 APPLY TWO COATS OF PAINT

1 **PAINT THE EDGES** of the door first, following the grain of the wood.

2 **IF YOU HAVE SHAKER-STYLE DOORS**, paint the central panel next, ensuring that you get enough paint into the corners.

3 **PAINT** the horizontal top and bottom edge panels next.

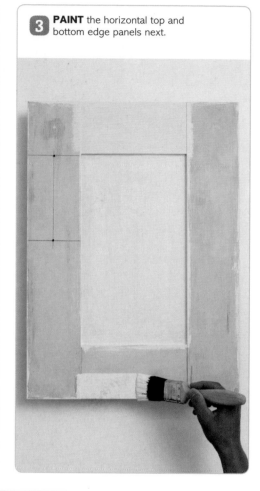

4 **FINALLY, PAINT THE VERTICAL EDGE** panels. This sequence gives a neater finish and highlights the wood grain. Allow the first coat to dry before painting the second coat.

5 ATTACH THE HANDLES

FIX THE HANDLE to the front of the door with screws and a screwdriver, and then screw the door back onto its unit hinges. Repeat the same process with the remaining kitchen unit doors and drawers.

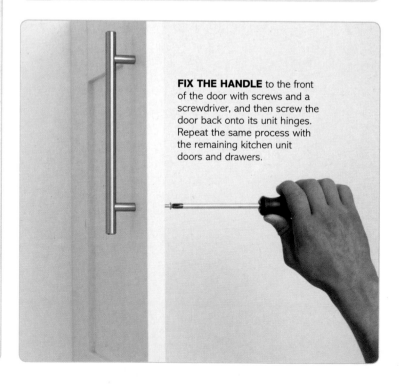

BEFORE

BATHROOM

2 CREATE A MOOD BOARD
FOR YOUR BATHROOM

Making up a mood board before you begin to refurbish a bathroom will not only help you to finalize the design of your layout, it will also encourage you to inject the room with style, personality, and colour, which might otherwise be overlooked in your search for sanitaryware and practical buys like tiles. Here's a guide to follow for creating a useful bathroom mood board.

1 **FIND PICTURES OF BATHROOMS YOU LIKE** in magazines and books, and even on hotel websites. Tear out, take a colour copy, or print out any you like and stick a few favourites to the board; you may want to take different elements from a few images as inspiration for your design. Note down what you don't like about your current bathroom so you don't repeat the same mistakes.

As a starting point, think about whether you would like your bathroom to look contemporary and minimalist or you would prefer a period style, for example.

2 **DO YOU HAVE A KEY ITEM** at the top of your wish list – a freestanding bath, a designer shower, or gorgeous wall tiles, or an ornate sink that you already own, for example – that you really must include? Use this piece as inspiration for the rest of your design.

Your favourite item may influence whether your bathroom will look traditional or modern.

3 **CHOOSE YOUR SANITARYWARE**, starting with the bath, which will dictate the shape and finish of both your toilet and sink, and the taps and shower fittings, too. Before you go any further with your design, you need to finalize your choice of these items.

Stick pictures of sanitaryware that you like to the mood board so you can refer back to them as you build your ideas.

4 **CHOOSE A BACKGROUND COLOUR** for the bathroom: if a large percentage of your bathroom walls will be tiled, pick the tiles first, as they will greatly influence other colours in the room. Your main consideration should be to make the room light and bright enough so that you can see clearly to put on make-up or shave. If your bathroom receives lots of natural daylight or you install effective lighting, you can choose darker wall tiles or paint colours.

Stick a sample tile, or a picture of the tiles, to the mood board as a colour reference.

Select possible colours for any untiled walls, picking either neutral, toning, or contrasting shades.

Buy towels in an accent colour that is a variation of, or a dramatic contrast to, your base colour.

Choose two or three colours to give yourself several options.

5 **INTRODUCING ACCENT COLOURS** to a bathroom needn't be complicated. Ideally, there should be two accent colours and no more than three – with the third as a face flannel, perhaps, or an arrangement of pretty bath bottles. Experiment with the proportions of the colour combinations to see if they work together using tile or paint swatches and floor samples.

6 **CHOOSE STORAGE**, whether you have room for freestanding or fitted furniture or just storage boxes. Bear in mind that any mirrored or reflective surfaces will make your space feel bigger. Shapes and size are important, too: work out whether the pieces you like will be a comfortable fit.

Wicker baskets can be used to store clean towels and bathroom supplies and hide laundry to be washed.

Refer back to your colour palette to decide the colours of your accessories.

7 **ADD FINISHING TOUCHES** such as bath towels, pictures, and bath mats. These items needn't co-ordinate exactly with your main theme, but they need to lift the look of the room and highlight particular areas, such as a stylish sink or shower. These final touches will seal the room's success, and the mood board will help you get this last element right.

3 LAYOUT CONSIDERATIONS IN THE BATHROOM

A bathroom needs careful planning, so before thinking about how you'd like it to look, consider the practical issues – how the room will be used, and which individual components will work best. Will more than one person regularly use the room at the same time? Do you need to make space for double sinks? Should you install a separate shower? How can the room be organized to make it work well for everyone?

BATH

Plan the room's layout and functionality around the bath, since it is the biggest item and you may have little choice about where it will sit. If space is an issue, choose a bath that sits against a wall, and ideally into a corner. If you have a larger room, consider installing a freestanding bath, but check first with your plumber that it won't cause drainage issues. Consider, too, where bath taps will be positioned: freestanding baths, for example, don't usually have taps attached, so they will have to be fixed to the wall or be "floor standing". If your bath is to have a shower above it, the bath should be positioned right against the wall and screened to prevent water spillage.

SINK

Ideally the sink should sit within easy reach of the toilet, and with a solid wall (rather than, say, a window) behind so you can hang a mirror above it. Before choosing a sink and locating the best position for it, give some thought to the storage you'll need. If storage space is tight, consider getting a vanity unit with a sink set into, or sitting on, a shelving unit or cupboard, rather than opting for a simple pedestal sink. This choice may affect your layout, so check the dimensions of the unit carefully first to make sure it will fit into the bathroom plan.

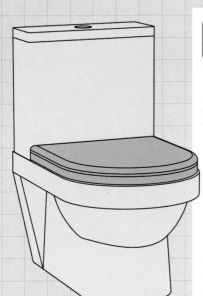

TOILET

Usually, the best place to site the toilet is on or adjacent to an outside wall. This makes drainage much simpler and usually means that the toilet sits beneath a window or extractor fan, too. It should also be either opposite or next to the sink for convenience. If the toilet is to sit adjacent to an outside wall, bear in mind that the size of the soil pipe will mean that boxing-in will be needed to hide it from view, although this boxing-in could be used as extra skirting level shelf space. As with all sanitaryware, there is a range of configurations and sizes for toilets so if space is an issue, shop around before you make a choice.

STORAGE UNITS

Bathrooms benefit from as much storage space as possible. Include shelving for toiletries, towel rails, and hooks for clothes or bathrobes – all within reach of the bath or shower. A wall-hung cupboard for bottles, medicines, and cleaning products is also useful, as are shelves to stack unused towels. Or have storage space built behind a bath panel and accessed via a small door. For a streamlined look, pick vanity units or cupboards below the sink with plenty of storage space.

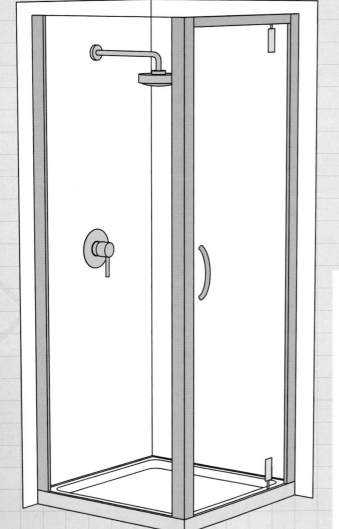

SHOWER

If space allows, install a separate shower, particularly if this is your only bathroom. Sit it along the same wall as the bath and choose a shower tray the same depth for a streamlined look, and to make plumbing and drainage easier. If you have space, a walk-in shower looks luxurious. If your ceiling slopes, put the shower in the tallest part of the room (and take the extra height of the shower tray into account).

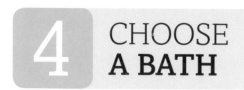

4 CHOOSE A BATH

When it comes to choosing a bath, you need to consider how much space you have, and how you will use it – do you like to spend hours soaking, or prefer to shower? You also need to think of practicalities: a deep bath may look luxurious, but it will take longer to fill and weigh more than a conventional bath.

1 CHOOSE THE SHAPE

The shape of the bath you choose depends on the size and proportions of your bathroom. For example, your awkwardly shaped bathroom may be most suited to a corner bath, or you may only have room for a standard rectangular bath.

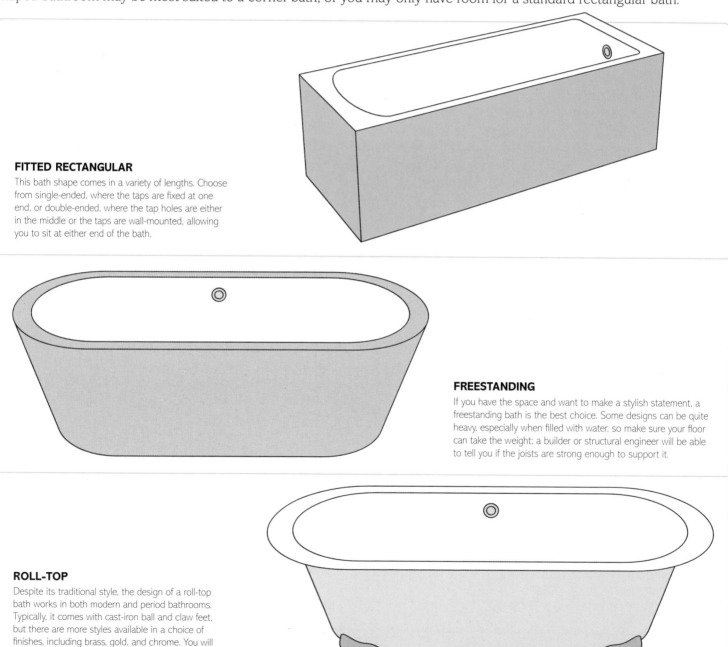

FITTED RECTANGULAR
This bath shape comes in a variety of lengths. Choose from single-ended, where the taps are fixed at one end, or double-ended, where the tap holes are either in the middle or the taps are wall-mounted, allowing you to sit at either end of the bath.

FREESTANDING
If you have the space and want to make a stylish statement, a freestanding bath is the best choice. Some designs can be quite heavy, especially when filled with water, so make sure your floor can take the weight; a builder or structural engineer will be able to tell you if the joists are strong enough to support it.

ROLL-TOP
Despite its traditional style, the design of a roll-top bath works in both modern and period bathrooms. Typically, it comes with cast-iron ball and claw feet, but there are more styles available in a choice of finishes, including brass, gold, and chrome. You will need to check with a builder or structural engineer if your bathroom floor can take the weight.

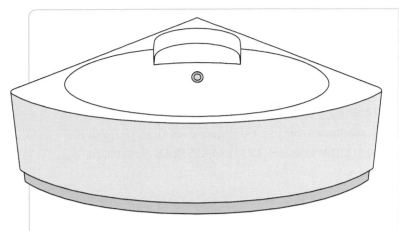

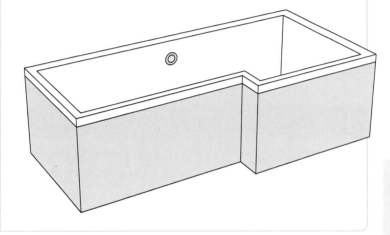

SHOWER BATH

If you are going to have a shower attachment over the bath, consider a shape that provides extra showering space. These baths are either L-shaped or bowed to make one end of the bath roomier.

CORNER BATH

A good option for small, square rooms, this bath doesn't require the long wall that other baths do. However, their triangular shape means they take up more floor space and use more water than a standard bath, and you may not be able to lie down comfortably.

2 CHOOSE THE MATERIAL

If you want to make a style statement, look for a bath in a "stand-out" unusual material and be prepared to pay for it. If practicality and a low budget are higher up on your list, shop for an eye-catching bath shape in a cheaper material.

ACRYLIC

A popular choice, acrylic is warm to the touch, lightweight, and durable, so can be made into a variety of shapes and sizes. It's a relatively inexpensive option.

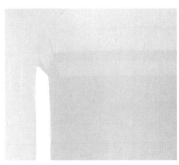

STEEL

Heavy, hard-wearing, medium-cost steel is usually only available in a rectangular shape. Its vitreous enamel surface is impact-, scratch-, and acid-resistant.

CAST-IRON

Medium-priced and heavy, a cast-iron bath is extremely strong, but it cools hot water quickly. It has a hardwearing surface that is impact- and scratch-resistant.

WHIRLPOOL AND SPA BATHS

If you are replacing your bath, look for models with whirlpool or spa systems (or both, known as hydro systems) built in.

Spa baths
● Spa baths have low-profile nozzles set into the base of the bath; these pump air bubbles into the bath water, creating a gentle, fizzing massage effect.

Whirlpool baths
● Whirlpool baths have jets set around the sides of the bath. A powerful pump, usually situated beneath the bath, pushes a mix of air and water through the jets, creating an invigorating massage effect that can be controlled with a turbo or electronic controls.
● Whirlpool baths are easier to keep clean, as a cleaning solution can be passed through the pipework (many spa systems can only be cleaned with a long soak in cleaning solution).
● Putting in one of these baths is as easy as installing a regular bath: the piping is already fitted. However, the switchbox to the power supply must be installed by a qualified electrician.

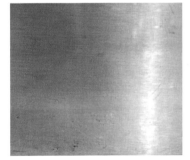

COPPER

Although an expensive option, a copper bath is a style statement. It also heats up instantly when in contact with warm water and retains the warmth for longer.

WOOD

Available in good-looking woods like ash, walnut, teak, and iroko, this expensive option has a finishing coat that strengthens the structure and provides a durable finish.

SOLID-SURFACE MIX

Usually a mix of stone and resin, this high-cost bath is very tough and hardwearing, and can be moulded into any shape. You can also choose from a variety of colours.

6 CHOOSE
A BATHROOM SINK

The size of your bathroom and the suite you choose may predetermine your choice of sink, but with so many different shapes and styles available, where to start? Consider practical issues, such as storage needs and how many people use the bathroom at one time, as well as the look you want to achieve.

CHOOSE THE TYPE

Each of these basic sink types comes in a range of styles, from square, contemporary shapes to curvaceous lines suited to traditional rooms. Sizes vary, too, with big sinks for family use and small sinks for where space is an issue.

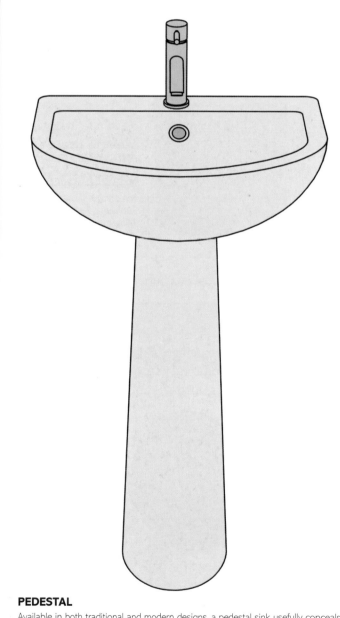

PEDESTAL

Available in both traditional and modern designs, a pedestal sink usefully conceals most common pipework. The base of the pedestal is attached to the floor and the sink, which is fixed to the wall with screws or hidden brackets, sits on top of it.

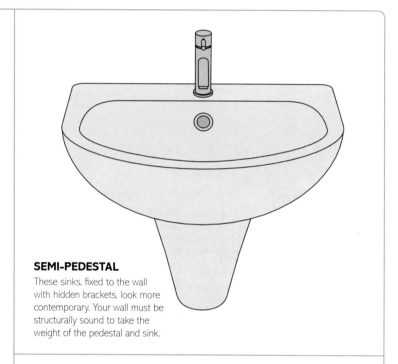

SEMI-PEDESTAL

These sinks, fixed to the wall with hidden brackets, look more contemporary. Your wall must be structurally sound to take the weight of the pedestal and sink.

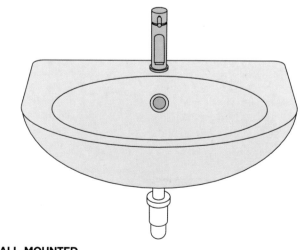

WALL-MOUNTED

Wall-mounted sinks are usually attached directly to the wall using concealed brackets. However, if the wall is not structurally sound enough to take the sink's weight, you may need a mounting frame hidden within the wall itself.

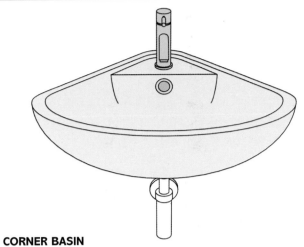

CORNER BASIN

If you're short on space, a corner sink is a good choice, as its shape allows it to sit neatly in the corner of the room and take up less floor space. More often than not, these sinks are wall-hung, although you can find some with pedestals.

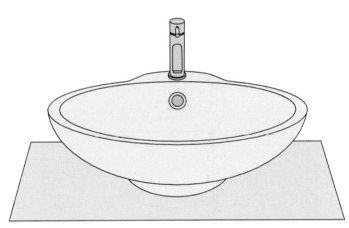

COUNTERTOP

This style of sink sits on top of a piece of furniture – either a cupboard, table, or purpose-made unit. It comes in a wide range of shapes, including round, oval, and square, and a selection of materials such as ceramic, glass, and natural stone.

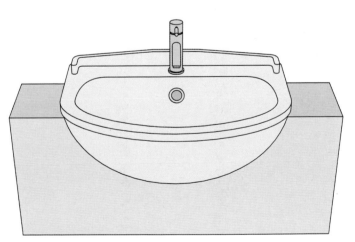

SEMI-RECESSED

Semi-recessed sinks require minimal space on your countertop, making them ideal for smaller bathrooms. They are designed to be fixed into a cavity within a slim worktop or storage cupboard, with the front of the sink overhanging the worktop.

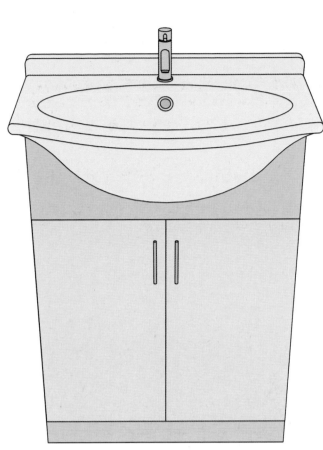

VANITY UNIT

Vanity units sit underneath a sink (which is inset) and act as a pedestal, as well as offering storage of one or two door cupboards or drawers. They are available in a wide range of materials and designs, with floor- or wall-mounted options.

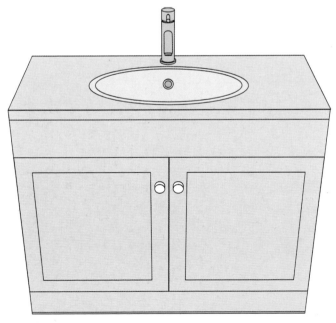

FITTED BASIN UNIT

A fully-fitted sink unit is normally made to measure to make the most of your bathroom's space. Much like a vanity unit in its design, this type of sink can sit on top of the unit or be sunk into the worktop.

7 CHOOSE
BATHROOM TAPS

When choosing taps for your bathroom, style is just one consideration. You should also check that your preferred options will work with your water supply (standard pressure is fine for most modern taps but some require a higher pressure), as well as being compatible with your sink or bath.

1 CHOOSE THE TYPE

Before you choose which type of tap you need, first decide whether it must be – or you want it to be – mounted on the bath or sink, the counter surface, or the wall. (If your sink or bath has pre-drilled holes, your decision is already made.)

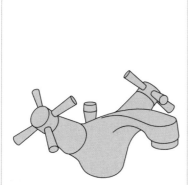

MIXER

Hot and cold water are mixed inside this tap, and its temperature can be regulated by separate controls, which makes it a good choice for a family bathroom.

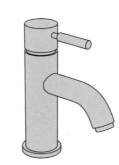

SINGLE LEVER

With a single tap and lever handle that controls the temperature and water flow, single lever taps are easy to control and very neat in appearance.

PILLAR

A pair of pillar taps with crosshead or lever handles will supply hot and cold water separately (this may not be the safest option if you have small children).

WALL-MOUNTED

Wall-mounted taps are ideal for double-ended baths (but do require concealed pipework). Check the spout's length and position is suitable for your bath or basin.

2 CHOOSE THE FINISH

Bathroom taps are available in many different finishes, so what you choose will depend on the colour of your sink or bath and other elements of the bathroom, and whether you prefer a sleek and shiny, or fashionable matt, finish.

CHROME

Shiny chrome suits contemporary and traditional bathrooms, and is relatively easy to keep clean, though water spots do show. It is available in a range of prices.

GOLD EFFECT

Medium to high in cost, and often only available in traditional styles, these taps add a touch of luxury. They work well if teamed with warm natural stone tiles.

BRUSHED METAL

Best in contemporary bathrooms, mid- to high-priced brushed metal taps don't show water marks so easily – a bonus if you live in a hard-water area.

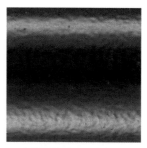

POWDER-COATED BRASS

Black taps to match a black sink create a dramatic feature. Made of powder-coated brass, and low to high in cost, they feature chrome levers or other details.

OIL-RUBBED BRONZE

Prices vary for this dark-coated brass finish. Over time, the yellow brass beneath the coating will start to become visible, giving the fitting a timeworn quality.

CHOOSE
A TOILET

While it might not be the focal point of your bathroom, you should pay attention to the design of your toilet. By doing so, you will ensure that it fits in with the rest of the room's scheme, might save you valuable space if you need it, could be easier to clean, and may help you economize on water usage.

CHOOSE THE TYPE

The type of toilet you choose will largely depend on whether you prefer a contemporary or traditional feel to the room. You will also need to consider where it will be placed, and whether you prefer the look of a one- or a two-piece toilet.

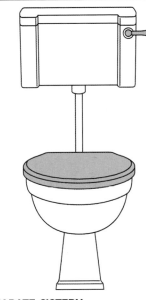

CLOSE-COUPLED

Often the least expensive option, this style is easiest to fit and hides more pipework than other designs. The cistern is fixed to the wall and sits on top of the pan, which stands on the floor. The flush is operated by a push button on top of the cistern.

SEPARATE CISTERN

The pan for this traditional style of toilet is fixed to the floor, while the cistern sits a short distance up on the wall, and has a short flush pipe in between the two pieces. It typically has a lever flush in keeping with its classic design.

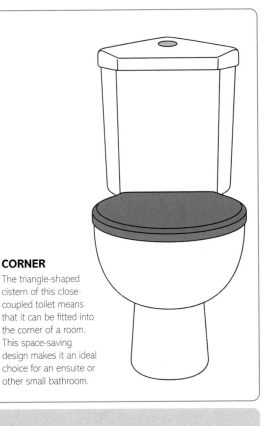

CORNER

The triangle-shaped cistern of this close-coupled toilet means that it can be fitted into the corner of a room. This space-saving design makes it an ideal choice for an ensuite or other small bathroom.

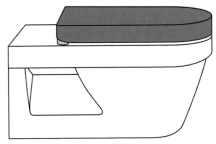

CONCEALED CISTERN

The cistern for this modern, easy-to-clean one-piece toilet is concealed in a false wall behind or inside a purpose-built unit, and is a good choice if you have limited space. Buy a wall-mounted variety (ask a builder if your wall is strong enough first) or one with a pan that stands on the floor.

BIDETS

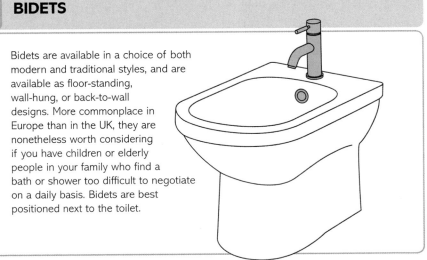

Bidets are available in a choice of both modern and traditional styles, and are available as floor-standing, wall-hung, or back-to-wall designs. More commonplace in Europe than in the UK, they are nonetheless worth considering if you have children or elderly people in your family who find a bath or shower too difficult to negotiate on a daily basis. Bidets are best positioned next to the toilet.

BATHROOM

99

9 CHOOSE FLOORING

One of the most important considerations when decorating your bathroom is the flooring you use. Not only does it need to look good, it should be non-slip, durable, easy to clean, comfortable to walk on in bare feet, and, most importantly, moisture- and humidity-resistant.

1 CHOOSE THE LOOK

Wood, tiles, and seamless flooring can all look contemporary, while the former two are better choices for a period-style room. Tiles and seamless flooring stand up better to moisture; wood is less water-resistant, but is a viable option if you love the look.

TILED

Floor tiles come in a range of materials – including porcelain, ceramic, and vinyl – and colours and sizes. Although tiles may seem like an obvious choice, they are hard and cold underfoot, so might be best if teamed with underfloor heating.

SEAMLESS

Vinyl and rubber sheets are a popular seamless flooring for a bathroom, although poured resin is also a good option. Ideal for small spaces, its lack of joins gives it a neat finish. However, if the floor becomes damaged, the whole floor has to be replaced.

WOODEN

The colour and texture of wood creates a nice contrast to sleek sanitaryware, and gives continuity if wood floors are used elsewhere in the house. If your bathroom gets wet and humid, avoid solid wood and opt for laminate, engineered wood, or vinyl lookalikes.

CHECKLIST

- **If you are laying tiles,** you can tile straight onto concrete or existing tiles (provided they are sound and level), but be aware that doing this will raise the level of your floor significantly, as will underfloor heating. You may have to remove and shave the bottom of the door before rehanging it.

- **A timber floor** must have a sub-floor fitted over it before you can tile. The simplest way to achieve this is to screw down marine plywood boards.

- **Ensure that any gaps** between planks or tiles are well sealed to stop water seeping through to rooms below.

2 CHOOSE THE MATERIAL

What you choose depends on whether you prefer the classic look and feel of tiles or something softer like vinyl or rubber. If you are having underfloor heating installed, check which materials are suitable to use with it first.

TILES

PORCELAIN

Porcelain is a versatile, very hardwearing choice in a range of prices and designs, including mosaic. Seal unglazed tiles before and after grouting.

CERAMIC

Cheap compared to natural stone and porcelain, ceramic tiles are a good choice for larger areas. They are also hardwearing and won't need sealing.

QUARTZ COMPOSITE

Expensive quartz composite has a luxurious look and is available in a wide range of colours, including black, white, grey, red, and blue. It rarely chips or cracks.

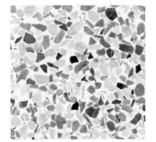

TERRAZZO

High-cost terrazzo (marble chips set into cement with a colour pigment added) comes in many colours and finishes. When wet, this surface may become slippery.

VINYL

Available in a range of effects and prices, vinyl tiles are water-resistant so are ideal for a bathroom. More expensive vinyls are best left to a professional to be fitted.

RUBBER

Medium-priced rubber tiles are available in a huge range of colours and different textures. These tiles are a good choice for family bathrooms.

SEAMLESS

RESIN

Poured resin, available in a range of colours, is highly contemporary. It is laid directly onto concrete sub-floors or specialist marine plywood, but not floorboards.

RUBBER

A practical choice, medium-priced rubber is hardwearing and warm underfoot, and comes in a range of colours and textures. Low-profile textures provide extra grip.

VINYL

Low- to medium-priced modern sheet vinyl comes in a range of designs that reproduce the look and texture of material such as wood, stone, metal, and glass.

LINOLEUM

Made of natural and sustainable ingredients, this medium-priced floor is easy to clean and naturally resistant to bacteria and fungus, so is an ideal choice.

WOODEN

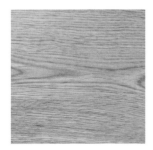

HARDWOOD

A hardwood floor must be installed perfectly, with no gaps for moisture. It is not a good option if the floor will get very wet. It is medium to high in cost.

ENGINEERED WOOD

The construction of this medium-priced wood (layers of hard and softwood boards topped with a layer of hardwood) means it is less likely to warp.

BAMBOO

Medium to high in price, bamboo has moisture-resistant qualities and does not shrink, expand, or warp. It's eco friendly, too. It should be sealed before use.

LAMINATE

Some laminate wood planks are designed for bathrooms and have a moisture-resistant core, though they are still not moisture-proof. It is low to medium in cost.

VINYL

Wood-effect vinyl will give an authentic look, and is easier to care for than real wood. Prices depend on the brand; cheaper versions are self-adhesive.

5 WAYS WITH
TILE PATTERNS

If you want to add pattern and interest to a bathroom, the easiest and most practical way to do it is with tiles. Decide if you want a modern, colourful, retro, or unusual look, and then pick tiles – whether rustic handmade, machine-made, metalic, glass, resin, or mosaic – that will best suit your scheme.

FEATURE WALL

Create a feature behind your bath with a panel of tiles that contrast with the base colour of the room. As in any other room, create just one focal wall while leaving the others plain.

IF YOU WANT TO MAKE colour a dynamic element of the tiled area, limit yourself to no more than three colours.

GRADUATION

Start at the bottom of a wall with a row of dark-coloured tiles and gradually work up the wall using paler shades of the same colour.

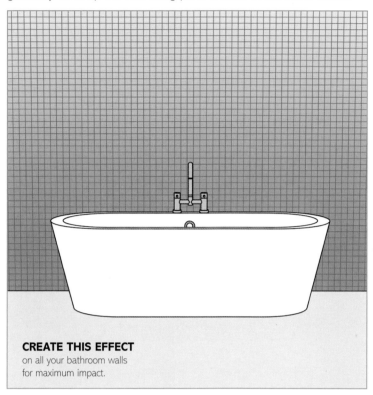

CREATE THIS EFFECT
on all your bathroom walls
for maximum impact.

PATCHWORK

Create a patchwork wall using a mixture of tiles with different patterns. Try to stick to a limited colour palette for the best effect.

STRIPES

Add interest to a painted wall with wide bands of tiles to create a striped effect. The tiled stripes can run vertically or horizontally.

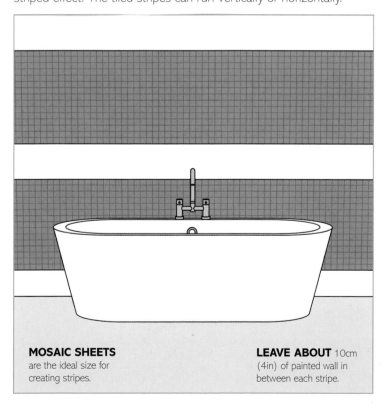

MOSAIC SHEETS
are the ideal size for
creating stripes.

LEAVE ABOUT 10cm
(4in) of painted wall in
between each stripe.

BORDER

Add a border around the top of your tiled wall. Either use a specific border tile with a pattern, or a tile in a different colour.

IF YOU WANT TO CREATE the
illusion of height, add a vertical border
to draw the eye upwards.

11 CHOOSE
BATHROOM LIGHTING

Bathrooms need to be well lit so they feel bright and welcoming and you can see what you're doing if you're shaving or applying make-up. However, bathroom lights also need to cope with the amount of moisture generated, particularly if you have a shower in the room, so ensure you choose suitable fittings.

1 DECIDE ON A STYLE OF LIGHTING

Most bathrooms are fairly compact so you may be limited in your choice of lighting. In this room, your primary focus should be on getting the ambient and task lighting right.

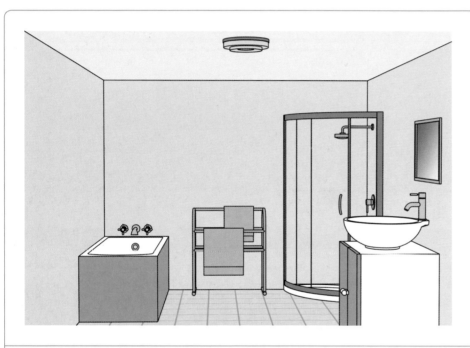

AMBIENT
Your overhead lighting should account for the ambient lighting within the room, and it needs to be bright enough for you to see what you're doing, morning and night. Consider wall lights or candles if you want to lay back and relax in the bath.

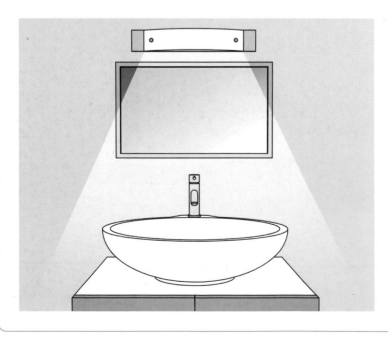

TASK
Task lighting in a bathroom can include strong overhead downlights fixed to the ceiling. Ideally you should situate one task light above the sink, another above the bath, and a third above the shower. Also place a bright light above the mirror over your sink.

2 CHOOSE YOUR LIGHT FITTINGS

There's nothing worse than a weakly lit bathroom – it makes the room feel cold, unwelcoming, and smaller than it really is. So, ensure you get a good combination of lighting types within the room, space and budget permitting.

CEILING LIGHTS

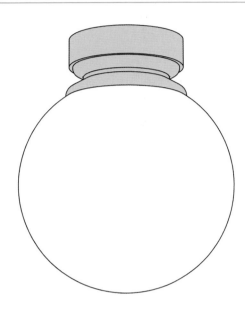

CEILING LIGHT

A central ceiling light, provided it is used in combination with other types of lighting, will give good levels of ambient lighting in a bathroom. For safety reasons, the light itself must be enclosed or flush. A prominent fitting is not the best choice if your bathroom has a low ceiling.

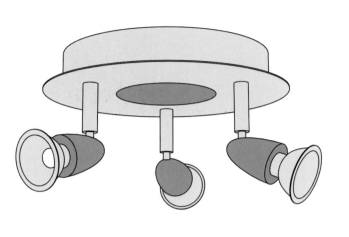

SPOTLIGHTS

Spotlights are good for providing both task and accent lighting in a bathroom; their adjustable heads mean you can direct the light exactly where you need it. Choose from individual heads, or bars or plates with two to four heads that can be adjusted independently of each other.

FLOOR LIGHTS

RECESSED DOWNLIGHTS

Recessed downlights offer high levels of practical lighting in a bathroom, and their unobtrusive design means that they're perfect for a small or low-ceilinged bathroom. If you are using these lights over a shower or bath, you will need to purchase sealed downlights.

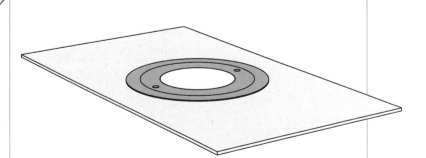

RECESSED UPLIGHTS

Highlight your bathroom walls using recessed floor uplighters. Fit them close to the wall around the edges of the room to create subtle shafts of light that will illuminate your chosen wallcovering. A dimmer switch will also allow you to vary the height the light travels and create different moods in the room.

WALL-MOUNTED LIGHTS

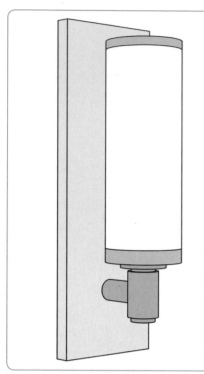

WALL LIGHTS

Used in addition to a central ceiling light or downlights, wall lights can provide a soft atmospheric light and also add interest to your room's decorating scheme. Fit them in alcoves, either side of a mirror, or even above a bath.

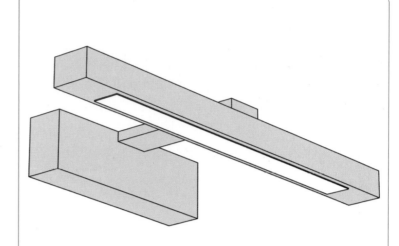

OVER MIRROR LIGHT

These lights provide bright task lighting. The design is often long and slim with a shaver socket in one end. They typically work independently to other lighting in the bathroom. Some bathroom mirrors have lighting built into them which works in the same way.

SAFETY ZONES

When it comes to bathroom lighting, it's safety first. You need to ensure that your light fittings are appropriate, safe to use, and correctly located. Electrical equipment must be protected against the inevitable condensation, humidity, and sprays of water.

Although a qualified electrician must do the work itself, knowing the rules will help you when it comes to choosing your lighting.

A bathroom is divided into three "safety zones" that dictate which lights can be safely used where. The zones are ranked from 0 to 2, with 0 being the wettest:

- **Zone 0**: the actual area inside the shower basin or bathtub.

- **Zone 1**: the area immediately above the bath or shower, up to a height of 2.5 metres, and within a radius of 1.2 metres from the tap or shower head.

- **Zone 2**: the area outside zones 0 and 1, for a distance of 0.6 metres horizontally and 2.25 metres vertically. This should also include the area around any washbasins or windowsills situated next to a bath.

- **Non-Zoned**: the area of the bathroom outside of Zone 2. This will include the area underneath a bathtub or shower basin, if it's enclosed and can't be accessed without using a tool.

Bathroom light fittings have an IP or ingress protection rating, which indicates how water resistant they are. These are rated from 0 (no protection from liquids) to 8 (protected against immersion under pressure for extended periods). Comparing zones with IP ratings will tell you which lights can go where. Obviously, the use of anything

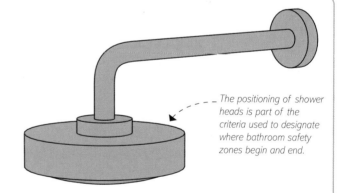

The positioning of shower heads is part of the criteria used to designate where bathroom safety zones begin and end.

electrical in Zone 0 is heavily controlled. Any fittings here can only be 12V maximum, and have a minimum IP rating of 7 (protected against immersion in water).

- **Zone 1** is similarly tightly regulated. A minimum IP rating of 4 is required (protection against water sprayed from all directions), but 240V light fittings are allowed, as long as they meet the IP requirements, and have had a 30ma residual current device (RCD) fitted.

- **In Zone 2** an IP rating of at least 4 is also required.

- **In the Non-Zoned area**, any light fittings are permitted, and there is no minimum IP rating, but apart from shavers all electrical items such as lamps, extension leads, and hairdryers are forbidden. In addition, the main lights should only be switched on and off by a cord, or a switch outside the bathroom.

12 CHOOSE WINDOW TREATMENTS

Above all, the window treatment you choose for your bathroom needs to offer privacy and insulation. Pick a design that allows you to open and close the window easily to let steam escape, is resistant to moisture itself, and looks good, too.

1 CHOOSE THE TYPE

The size of your bathroom and window will largely determine the type of window dressing you choose, and whether you want a purely practical or more decorative option. Choose a material that is washable or, at the very least, can be wiped easily.

BLINDS

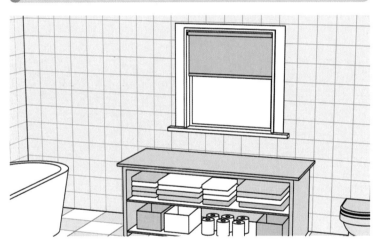

Blinds will give your windows a neat, streamlined look, and are a good choice for smaller bathrooms. Ensure that the material – whether wood, faux wood, or fabric – is resistant to moisture and easy to clean. Also ensure that its fixtures block as little light as possible.

CURTAINS

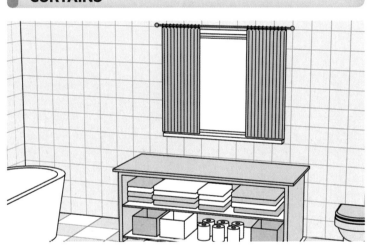

Only really suitable for large or well-ventilated bathrooms, curtains should be made from a machine-washable fabric and washed often to prevent mould caused by hot, humid surroundings. Use a curtain pole that's wider than the window to pull the curtains back fully.

SHUTTERS

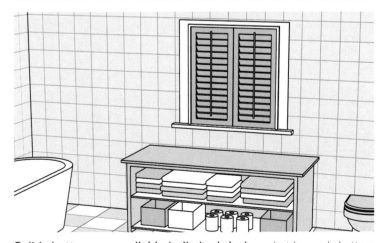

Solid shutters are available in limited designs, but louvred shutters can be designed with two or three panels in a choice of styles including full-height and tier-on-tier. Louvred shutters are ideal for bathrooms as they can be tilted open and shut for light, privacy, and insulation.

FILM

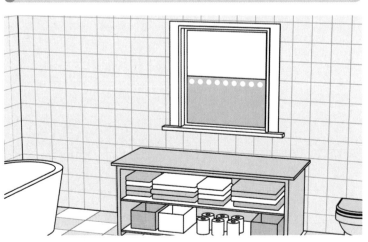

Window film offers complete privacy without blocking out all natural light. It can be bought by the metre or made to measure, and is fixed to interior windowpanes with a water and detergent solution. Choose from plain frosted or coloured film.

2 CHOOSE THE STYLE

What you choose for your bathroom window is dictated to some degree by the size of your room: the smaller the room, the simpler the window treatment – and any pattern on it – should be. It should complement the look of your sanitaryware, too.

BLINDS

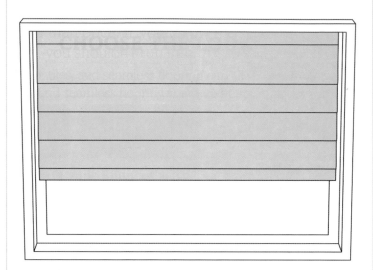

ROMAN

Unless your bathroom is very well ventilated, a Roman blind should be made from a fabric that is not susceptible to mildew in hot and humid rooms. The benefit of choosing a fabric blind is that it allows you to add pattern to a room that might otherwise be fairly plain – although keep the fabric plain if your bathroom tiles are patterned.

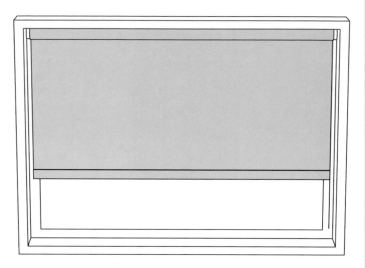

ROLLER

Roller blinds are a fairly inexpensive option, and, providing you're a competent DIYer, are easy to fit. You can have roller blinds made to measure, although most ready-made blinds can be cut to size. Choose blinds that are made from moisture-resistant fabrics.

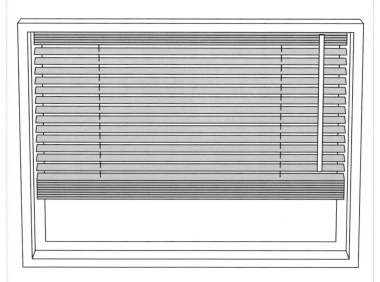

VENETIAN

Made from metal or wood, the adjustable slats of a Venetian blind allows you to control the amount of light coming through the window, as well as providing privacy. They are available in a choice of materials, colours, and slat widths.

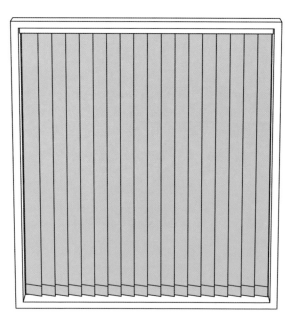

VERTICAL

More suited to modern bathrooms with larger windows, vertical blinds are made up of long strips of fabric that can be tilted or drawn. They're available in a wide range of colours and fabrics; look for those that are resistant to moisture and mould.

SHUTTERS

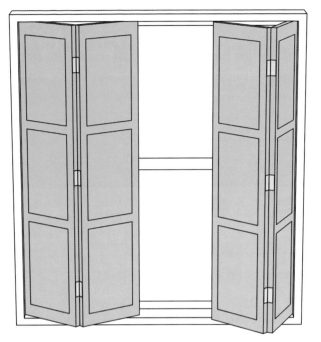

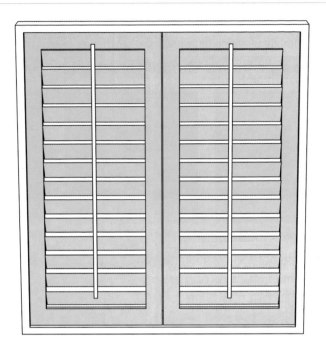

SOLID

Solid shutters are designed to be closed shut at night and folded back against the wall during the day. As well as full-height shutters, you can choose half- or three-quarter height, which can be kept closed at all times for privacy while still letting in light.

LOUVRE

The adjustable slats of louvred shutters make them a good choice for bathrooms. The best options are tier-on-tier shutters or full-height shutters with a mid-rail so you can control the top and bottom sections independently. They are available in a wide choice of wood or paint finishes.

CURTAINS

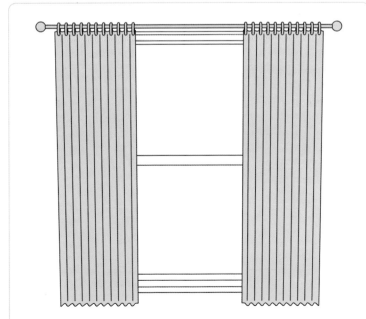

SILL LENGTH

Slimline sill-length – or just below sill-length – curtains in a washable cotton can be used to introduce a decorative theme to your bathroom. For example, a flower design will give your bathroom a country feel, while blue and white stripes can lend a nautical flavour. You may need to team them with a blind or window film to offer some privacy.

FILM

PLAIN OR PATTERNED

If your bathroom window looks directly into a neighbour's house, use a plain or coloured film that completely obscures the window. For upstairs bathrooms that aren't overlooked, you can choose film with a cut-out design such as spots, stars, or a nautical motif to add a decorative touch.

LIVING ROOM

2 CREATE A MOOD BOARD
FOR YOUR LIVING ROOM

A living room is generally regarded as the most public space in a house, as it is the room that most visitors will be invited into. So it pays to get your colour scheme absolutely spot on. The best way to get the look right first time is to create a mood board filled with colours, textures, and items that really suit the proportions, orientation, and atmosphere of your living room.

1 **FIND PICTURES OF ROOMS YOU LIKE** and stick one or two of your favourites to your mood board. Be realistic about recreating the same look – the layout, light, and proportions of your room may be very different to those in the picture you prefer.

Pick pictures of living rooms that reflect something of your personality, and not just current trends.

2 **DO YOU HAVE A KEY ITEM** that you absolutely love and want to include in the room as your starting point for the scheme? It might be a picture, a rug, or even a keepsake. Or perhaps you have an existing piece of furniture such as a sofa that has to be included in the design? Use this as your starting point instead, either as inspiration for colours, patterns, or shapes, or as something to build a theme around.

Using a favourite item as a starting point for your inspiration will give your living room character and individuality.

3 PICK A BASE COLOUR

for your walls or floors, as these areas will form the largest block of colour in your room. Paint the best tester pot colour or pin your favourite wallpaper sample onto the mood board, ensuring it's in proportion to how it will be used in the room (so, if you're painting all four walls, paint the whole board in your test colour). If you like the effect, use that as the starting point for your colour palette.

When you choose your background colour, consider whether a lighter tone might be easier to live with in the long term.

Choose two, or a maximum of three, accent colours and stick or paint the samples on top of your base colour to see if they all work together.

4 INTRODUCE ACCENT COLOURS

that are subtle variations of your base colour or a dramatic contrast to it (or both). One colour will be your main accent shade, used, perhaps, in a wallpaper design on a chimney breast, or as a sofa cover. A second accent colour should be used less, in cushions, lampshades, or vases. A third colour might just be a shade variation visible in the pattern of a cushion.

A contrasting colour, if needed, should be used minimally in a scheme.

5 ADD PATTERN & TEXTURE,

which can be as subtle or as overt as you like. No room absolutely has to include pattern, but those that do tend to be more interesting. If pattern is not your thing, introduce texture with items like a wooden table and a faux fur throw arranged over the back of a chair or across a sofa.

Add images of patterned items like cushions to the board to see if they lift and complement your scheme.

If you want to add texture with a carpet, rugs, or throws, stick samples to the board to check they look right visually.

6 CHOOSE FURNITURE

that you'd like to include (assuming you are replacing existing pieces). Here, colour comes into play – use the tricks you've learnt above to pick the right shade of fabric or type of wood. When it comes to shape, revisit the colours and patterns on your mood board. Will a traditional piece of furniture with curvaceous lines sit more comfortably in your scheme than a contemporary piece?

7 ADD FINISHING TOUCHES

such as cushions, lampshades, vases, and ornaments. These items will help to personalize your room and make it individual to you. These subtle touches can make or break a room's success, and the mood board will help you plan this effectively: collect ideas for what you'd like to add and stick pictures to the board to see if they match your theme, design, and colour palette.

Items like lamps can pull the look of a room together – particularly a large through room.

Your accessories needn't match perfectly, but they do need to suit the style of the room.

CARPET

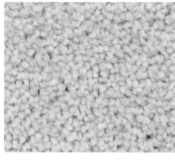

TWIST PILES
Medium-priced twist piles have a coarse, rugged appearance, are hardwearing, come in plains, heathers, or patterns, and are made from wool or man-made fibres.

VELVET PILE
Despite its luxurious appearance, this medium- to high-cost carpet is surprisingly hardwearing, and its dense, low-cut pile gives a soft smooth appearance.

LOOP PILE
This low- to medium-priced option is a popular alternative to coir and sisal floors with its similar looks, but has the warmth, comfort, and durability of natural wool.

SAXONY
A deep, dense pile that feels soft and smooth underfoot and gives a classic look. It is best used in rooms with low foot traffic, and is medium to high in price.

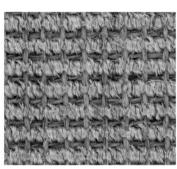

COIR
The surface of hardwearing, low-cost coir is non-slip, so is a good choice if you have children who like to run around indoors. However, it can feel rough underfoot.

SISAL
Sisal is hardwearing, has a fine texture and a subtle sheen, is averagely priced, and is available in a range of weaves and colours so adds both colour and texture to a room.

JUTE
With its flat woven designs, jute is a smart-looking, medium-priced option for living rooms. It is softer than other natural floor coverings, though not as hardwearing.

SEAGRASS
Medium-priced woven seagrass has a chunky appearance. Its natural waxy texture makes it stain-resistant, so it's a good choice for a busy room.

SEAMLESS

CONCRETE
Although expensive, poured polished concrete gives a stylish, contemporary look and is extremely durable. Choose from a range of shades, including red and green.

RESIN
High-cost poured resin flooring is very contemporary. Its seamless matt or gloss finish suits both large open-plan living rooms and awkward spaces.

LIGHT-COLOURED FLOORING combined with a darker colour on the walls can make a room feel narrower and taller.

STAIN
A WOODEN FLOOR

If you want to give inexpensive pine floorboards the look of rich mahogany or walnut wood, or you want to disguise a well-worn floor, use a wood stain. To prepare the room, tape up doors so the dust won't penetrate the rest of the house, and open all the windows to allow for as much ventilation as possible.

WHAT YOU NEED

- Hammer
- Wood filler (optional)
- Face mask
- Professional sanding machine
- Vacuum cleaner or broom and dustpan
- Protective gloves
- Old cloth
- Methylated spirits
- Masking tape

- Wood stain or wood dye
- Large paintbrush
- Clear wood varnish

1 PREPARE THE FLOOR

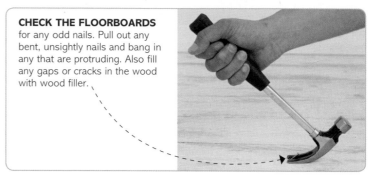

CHECK THE FLOORBOARDS for any odd nails. Pull out any bent, unsightly nails and bang in any that are protruding. Also fill any gaps or cracks in the wood with wood filler.

2 SMOOTH THE FLOORBOARDS

SAND THE FLOOR with a professional sanding machine, wearing a suitable mask over your face to protect your lungs from the dust. Follow the grain of the wood as you sand, moving the sander back and forth along the length of the floorboards to get a clean finish.

3 CLEAN WITH SPIRITS

HOOVER UP THE DUST with a vacuum cleaner, or sweep it clean with a broom. Then put on protective gloves and wipe down the floorboards with a piece of cloth soaked in methylated spirits.

4 PROTECT WITH TAPE

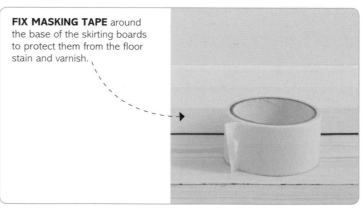

FIX MASKING TAPE around the base of the skirting boards to protect them from the floor stain and varnish.

5 STAIN THE WOOD

APPLY THE STAIN with a cloth, working in short sections across the floor. If your boards are very light, or relatively new, stain the very edges of the floorboards with a paintbrush first and wipe off the excess stain quickly with a cloth. Then apply the stain across the rest of the floor in the usual way.

6 APPLY THE VARNISH

DEPENDING ON THE DEPTH OF COLOUR you want, or if the floor looks a little patchy, repeat the staining process. Then apply a couple of coats of clear varnish (see the manufacturer's instructions) to the boards. Use a paintbrush for corners and small areas, or a mop with an applicator pad for large areas.

5 CHOOSE WALL COVERINGS

You needn't limit yourself to one type of wall decoration for a living room – a combination of two or three types will give a plain, boxy room a much more interesting look. Choose something that both suits the period of your home in terms of material and design, and one that you can live with for the long term.

1 CHOOSE THE MATERIAL

Your living room will be subject to a certain amount of wear and tear, especially if you have children, so look for the toughest finishes you can find: pick a paint or wallpaper that can be wiped down easily, or cladding that can be easily filled and repaired.

PAINT

The wide choice of paint colours available means you can create almost any look fairly quickly and inexpensively. Your walls will need to be in good condition for paint to look its best, as it won't hide cracks or any uneven surfaces. Apply two to three coats.

WALLPAPER

Wallpaper is sold in a range of colours, plains, patterns, and finishes. Plain wallpaper gives a tougher surface than painted plaster. Patterned wallpapers add interest to plain walls, and textured wallpapers (left white or painted) are good for imperfect walls.

CLADDING

Cladding can give your walls a range of looks, from traditional style panelling made from solid wood or MDF to simple tongue-and-groove cladding or flat wood veneer panels for a retro look. All but the veneers can be stained, varnished, or painted to suit a scheme.

CHECKLIST

● **Prepare your walls properly.** Whether they are being painted or papered, cracks and holes need to be filled and sanded back and any unevenness needs to be smoothed.

● **Have you got enough wallpaper?** Buy an extra 10% as a contingency, and ensure that it's all from the same batch so the colours match perfectly. If you use a patterned wallpaper, ensure you have enough extra paper to match the pattern repeat.

● **If you are fixing** any panelling to your walls, use a pipe and cable detector to check whether there are live wires or pipes behind the plasterwork.

2 CHOOSE THE TYPE

Paint is sold in various formats, each giving a different effect, and wallpaper is available in a variety of finishes and textures. If you've chosen to clad your walls, pick something that's going to be practical as well as give the right look.

PAINT

MATT

Water-based non-reflective matt emulsion suits modern- and traditional-style living rooms, and is available in an endless choice of colours. Prices vary greatly.

SILK OR SHEEN

Silk and soft sheen paints are a good medium-priced choice for family rooms, as marks can be wiped off easily. The subtle sheen can help to reflect light in the room.

METALLIC

Medium-priced metallic emulsion paints bring a touch of luxury and come in a range of colours. Try using metallic paint on a feature wall like a chimney breast.

SUEDE EFFECT

Suede-effect medium-priced emulsion has miniscule grains that give a brushed suede effect. Apply it in short random brush strokes to achieve the textured finish.

WALLPAPER

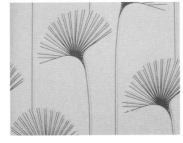

PLAIN OR PATTERNED

Use plain wallpapers as an alternative to paint on walls with fine surface cracks. Patterned paper comes in a huge range of designs and colours; prices vary hugely.

FLOCK

With its raised velvet texture, this medium- to high-cost paper is typically available in rich and opulent colours to add drama. It is more expensive than other wallpapers.

METALLIC

Patterned wallpapers with a metallic sheen help to reflect light around a room, so are ideal for smaller and darker living rooms. They range in price from medium to high.

TEXTURED

Medium-priced textured wallpapers are available in a choice of raised designs. Some embossed wallpapers also have a coloured pattern.

CLADDING

TONGUE & GROOVE

Cheap or averagely priced, this cladding is usually made of pine, but you can buy MDF designs. Typically fixed to the lower half of a wall, you can also fit it full height.

FLAT WOOD VENEER

If you like the mid-century look, medium to expensive wood veneer panels are the ideal choice. Iron-on wood veneer on a thin sheet of MDF is the best option.

WAINSCOT PANELLING

Medium-priced wainscot panelling works equally well in contemporary or country-style rooms. Paint it in a soft sheen that matches your skirting boards.

PAINT
WALLS

The technology behind modern paints makes them vastly superior to old-fashioned paints (which had to be applied in one direction and then another), so it is now easier to achieve the best finish. You may need to apply several coats depending on the quality and colour of the paint and the original colour of your wall.

WHAT YOU NEED

- Dustsheets
- Masking tape
- Wall filler and sandpaper (optional)
- Sugar soap
- Sponge
- Wall paint
- Small- or medium-sized paintbrush
- Roller and tray

1 PREPARE THE AREA

LAY DOWN dustsheets to cover the floor and any furniture. Cover the tops of the skirting boards with masking tape. Fill and sand any holes or imperfections to ensure that the walls are smooth enough to paint.

2 CLEAN THE WALLS

IF YOU HAVE TAKEN down wallpaper, apply sugar soap to the walls to get rid of residual wallpaper paste. If left on, the paste will "craze" the paint and prevent a smooth finish.

3 PAINT THE EDGES OF THE WALL

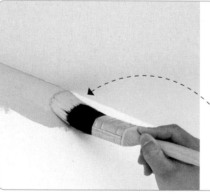

1 CAREFULLY PAINT along the upper edge of the wall where it meets the ceiling with a paintbrush. Paint at a fairly steady speed (not too slowly), so the paint goes on smoothly and your hand doesn't wobble.

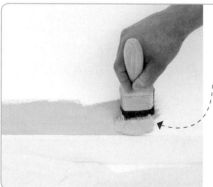

2 PAINT ALONG THE BOTTOM of the wall where it adjoins the skirting. The masking tape will protect the skirting from any excess paint brushed over it.

3 PAINT THE CORNERS and sides of the walls next, using the same brush to work the paint right into the crevices and down the edge of each wall.

1 **USE A THICK PILE ROLLER** to cover the remaining area of the wall. This type of roller will ensure that the paint goes on thickly and smoothly, and gives a slight textural effect.

2 **TURN THE ROLLER SIDEWAYS** to paint the uppermost and lowest areas of the wall. Check the manufacturer's instructions for how much time to allow the paint to dry, then apply a second coat.

LIVING ROOM

141

6 WAYS WITH
FEATURE WALLS

Every room, and a living room in particular, needs a focal point. One way to do it is to create a feature wall that will help to make your room's scheme more cohesive. If you have a particular theme, period, style, or colour scheme for the room, use this as a starting point for your wall feature.

WALLPAPER

Use a patterned wallpaper to create a stunning panel or wall in a colour that tones with the predominant colour of your other walls.

MIRRORS

Add interest to slim wall spaces by hanging mirrors vertically. Use odd numbers for a more pleasing look.

A SIMILAR EFFECT can be created with pictures, too.

STICKERS

Stylish wall stickers can be used to change the look of your room fairly quickly and do not require you to be creative.

FOR LARGER DESIGNS, you will need an extra pair of hands to help you press the stickers onto your wall.

PLATES

Hang plates with different styles, shapes, and designs. Make the display cohesive by sticking to a colour palette of three or four shades.

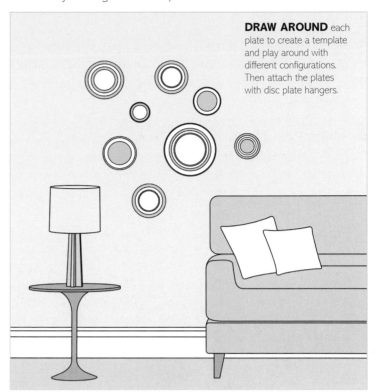

DRAW AROUND each plate to create a template and play around with different configurations. Then attach the plates with disc plate hangers.

PHOTO WALL

Create a picture gallery with different-sized frames that match in style or colour. Choose black and white photos for a really unified effect.

WOOD PANELS

Cover squares or rectangles of MDF with iron-on wood veneer or paint and fix them to the wall to create a modern patchwork design.

FOR A MORE INTERESTING design, use panels of different sizes.

10 WAYS WITH
ART

You've probably invested plenty of money on your pictures and photos, so why not put some proper thought into how you should hang them? Achieving the right look can create a much more effective display. Decide which of these ten options will best suit your own artworks and home.

MIXTURE OF FRAME SHAPES

Group together a mixture of pictures in differently sized and shaped frames for an eye-catching effect. Keep the display as symmetrical as possible so that each picture stands out in its own right.

CREATE A UNIFIED LOOK by keeping your display tightly spaced.

GROUPING

Hanging a group of four pictures of exactly the same size in a tight group gives the illusion of one larger picture.

ONE LARGE PIECE

Make the most of a large expanse of wall by hanging one large picture centrally for dramatic effect.

THE SIZE OF YOUR ARTWORK shouldn't be wider than the piece of furniture it hangs above.

OFFSET

You don't always have to hang pictures in a straight line; hanging them slightly offset to one another gives a less formal look.

THIS EFFECT WORKS BEST if the frames match in terms of proportion, if not shape.

TRIPTYCH

Hang a triptych – where one picture is divided into three sections, which are framed and fixed to the wall next to each other.

FILL A WALL

Fill a whole wall with a collection of pictures and paintings. The frames and picture styles needn't match,
but a cohesive theme – whether colour or subject matter – will turn it into a more successful design.

ON A SHELF

For a more relaxed display, sit pictures on a floating shelf or picture rail, allowing them to lean against the wall.

USE A MIXTURE of sizes and shapes, but find a cohesive colour theme for best results.

TALL PIECE

One tall picture, or a line of smaller pictures hung vertically, will draw the eye upwards and add a feeling of height to a room.

LIGHT IT UP

Illuminate your artwork with a picture light. Attach the picture light directly to the frame or to the wall immediately above the picture.

TONAL TO ROOM COLOURS

If you position a picture at a focal point within a room, make sure it contains at least one colour that matches your decorating scheme.

HANG
A PICTURE FRAME

A framed picture usually looks best if it is hung centrally on a wall, although if you hang it above a fireplace, it works best visually if the picture is centred vertically as well as horizontally. You may need someone to help you position the picture correctly on the wall before you mark where it should hang.

WHAT YOU NEED

- Tape measure
- Pencil
- 2 picture rings and plates, or screw eyes
- Bradawl
- Screwdriver
- Picture wire
- Pliers (optional)
- Spirit level (optional)
- Picture hook and head pin or screw (size depends on weight of the frame)
- Hammer (or drill if fixing a screw)

1 ATTACH THE PICTURE RINGS AND PLATES

1 PLACE THE PICTURE FRAME face down on a flat surface, and measure a third of the way down on either side of the frame from the top with a tape measure. Mark each point with a pencil.

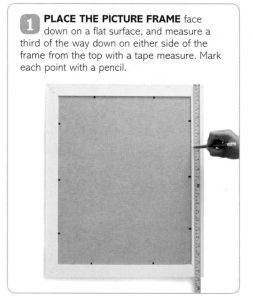

2 IF YOU ARE USING a picture ring and plate, place the plate against the pencil mark and make holes in the frame through the two circles in the plate with a bradawl. If you are using a screw eye, make a hole with the bradawl at the point of each pencil mark.

3 ATTACH THE PICTURE PLATE to the wooden frame with screws, using a screwdriver, or insert the screw eyes.

2 ATTACH THE WIRE

1 LOOP ONE END OF THE WIRE through one of the plate rings or screw eyes and wind the end around the length of wire. Use pliers, if necessary, to wind the wire.

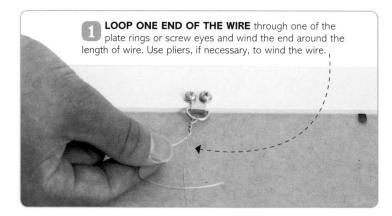

2 REPEAT ON THE OTHER SIDE, keeping the length of picture wire taut as you wind the end around it.

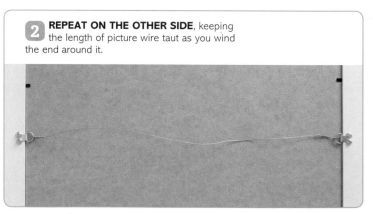

1 **HOLD THE PICTURE** up to the wall where you want to hang it. Make sure it is centered and then mark the central point of the top of the frame on the wall with a pencil.

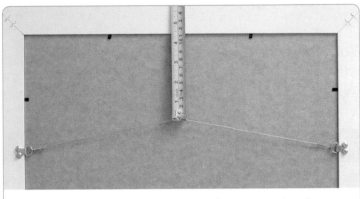

2 **PLACE THE FRAME** face down on a flat surface again, pull the picture wire taut in the centre, and measure the distance from the top of the taut wire to the top of the picture frame with a tape measure.

3 **MEASURE THE SAME DISTANCE** below the mark on the wall, making another pencil mark at the lower point. Use a spirit level, if necessary, to ensure that the second mark is directly below the first mark.

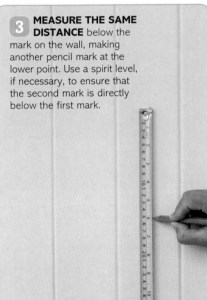

4 **PLACE THE BOTTOM** of the picture hook where the pencil mark is (as the hook is where the wire hangs from), hammer the head pin into the wall, then hang the picture. If the frame is heavy, use a screw and a drill instead.

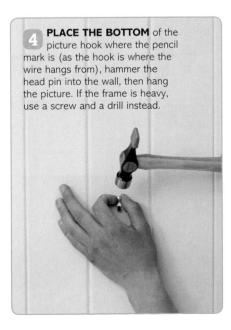

3 CHOOSE THE MATERIAL

The material you choose for your sofa doesn't just dictate its look, it also affects its price, longevity, and maintenance. So, before you fall in love with a particular fabric, find out whether it is an affordable and practical choice.

LEATHER

Medium-priced leather comes in a whole range of finishes, from soft and polished to distressed for an antique feel. Avoid placing a leather sofa next to a radiator or window.

100% COTTON

Cotton is durable and strong, but fades and can stain easily, wrinkle, or stretch. Premium-grade cotton keeps its looks for longer. It is a medium-priced choice

FORMAL VELVET

Although expensive, velvet is luxurious and soft. It is made from natural fibres such as silk or cotton, which drape better and will last longer, or synthetics such as rayon.

CHENILLE

This very soft medium-priced textured fabric is either 100% polyester or a blend of cotton, rayon, and polyester. Deep pile chenille is susceptible to crushing.

MICROFIBRE

A very fine but hardwearing polyester fibre, low-cost microfibre has the look and feel of velvet or suede. Its advantage is that it can be wiped easily with a damp cloth.

FAUX SUEDE

A cheap option, faux suede is 100% polyester, but feels and looks similar to the real thing. It is easy to clean and is more resistant to spillages than other leathers.

WOVEN DESIGNS

Woven designs come in a huge range of weaves and weights, so they vary greatly in price and durability. Designs include stripes, checks, florals, and damasks.

FAUX LEATHER

This medium-priced man-made material is treated to look like leather, but doesn't age so well. However, it is easier to clean and is pretty durable.

NUBUCK

This expensive type of leather is similar to suede, but is durable – a good alternative to classic leather upholstery. It can be dyed and pre-treated to protect it from stains.

WOOL/FELT

This material, available in a range of solid colours, may be 100% wool or a mix of wool and polyester; prices vary depending accordingly. It has a smart, flat appearance.

LINEN

Ideal for informal sofas and loose covers, linen has similar properties to cotton, but doesn't fade and is less resilient. It ages well but is expensive and tends to wrinkle.

SOFA BEDS

A sofa bed may be your best option and a useful investment if you want to put up guests in relative comfort, but don't have rooms to spare. Points to consider include how big the bed can be without having to buy a conspicuously large sofa, whether it's more important to have a good sofa or a good bed, and whether you will need to move the sofa in order to convert it to a bed, making weight an issue. There are many types available, with a range of ingenious mechanisms; below are four of the most common options.

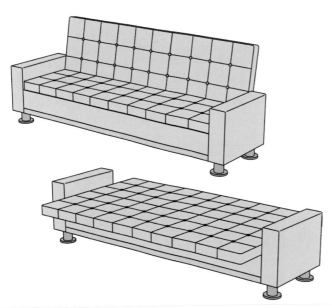

BENCH STYLE

The simplest of sofa beds, bench-style models have a mattress-like base and back, the latter of which folds down to create an instant bed. Of all the models, this type is the one model that can be as comfortable as any normal bed and, if you're likely to only occasionally fold the bed back into a sofa, it's the best choice.

PULL-OUT

The most common type of sofa bed, this model looks like a standard sofa and is available in a range of styles. The bed frame and mattress, which are folded and concealed inside the sofa base, are pulled up and outwards to form the bed. It may include storage space to store a quilt and pillows, and is usually very heavy.

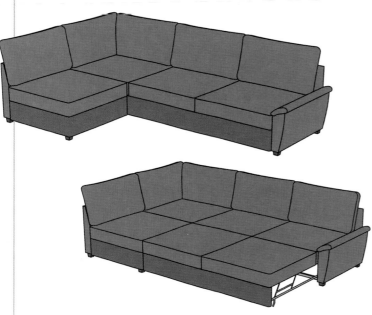

CORNER

Corner sofa beds typically comprise a two-seater sofa and a chaise which forms the corner unit. The bed section comes out from the base of the sofa section, either with a pull-out action (see above right) or as a pop-up truckle. These sofa beds also sometimes feature storage space, which is useful for storing bed linen.

FUTON

A futon-style sofa bed usually has a frame that is made of wood or metal and a choice of mattress thicknesses and materials. The two basic types are bi-fold (shown above), which fold back like bench-style sofa beds, and tri-fold, whereby the mattress is folded into three sections to make a more compact sofa.

FIT
WALL SHELVES

Before you fit your wall shelves, it's worth attaching the brackets to the shelf before checking where you want to position the shelf against the wall (rather than holding up just the brackets). In this way you can space the whole piece visually first to ensure the best result.

WHAT YOU NEED

- Wooden shelves (your choice of wood and thickness)
- Brackets
- Tape measure
- Pencil
- Bradawl
- Screwdriver
- Spirit level
- Drill
- Wall plugs (for plasterboard or brick, depending on your wall; size should correspond to the size of the screws)
- Screws

1 ATTACH THE BRACKETS

1 PLACE THE BACK OF THE SHELF on a flat surface and butt the shelf brackets up against the underside of the shelf. Judge by eye where the brackets should be positioned.

2 MEASURE THE DISTANCE of each bracket from the edge of the shelf with a tape measure to check each is equidistant from the end. The top and base of the brackets must also be parallel.

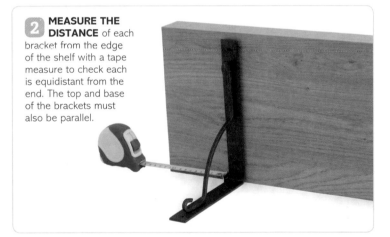

3 MAKE LIGHT PENCIL MARKS for the bracket holes on the underside of the shelf. Attaching the brackets in this "side on" position ensures that they sit flush with the back of the shelf.

4 USE A BRADAWL to make holes in the underside of the shelf over the pencil marks. If necessary, turn the shelf, face side down, onto a flat surface to do this.

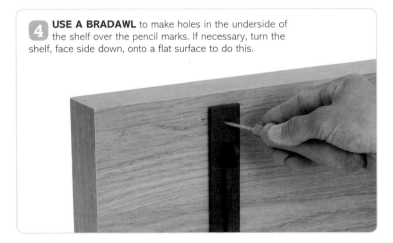

5 INSERT THE SCREWS through the brackets into the holes, and screw the brackets to the underside of the shelf.

2 MARK THE POSITION

1 **HOLD THE SHELF** (with the brackets attached) up to the wall to see where you want to position it. Place a spirit level along the length of the shelf to make sure it is level.

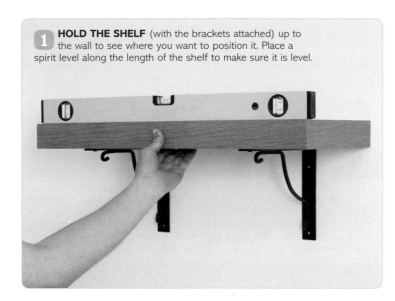

2 **MARK THE BRACKET** holes on the wall with a pencil.

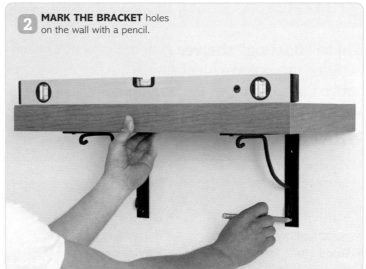

3 MOUNT THE SHELVES

1 **DRILL HOLES INTO THE WALL** over the pencil marks. Select the drill bit that corresponds to the size of the wall plugs.

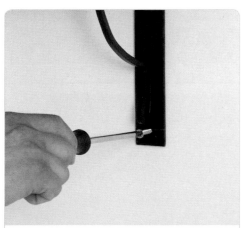

2 **INSERT THE WALL PLUGS** and attach the shelf to the wall with the screws using a screwdriver.

WALL-MOUNTED LIGHTS

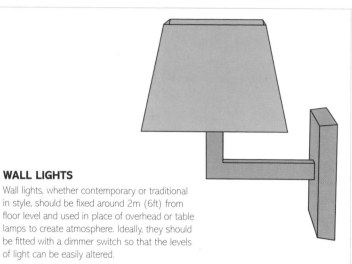

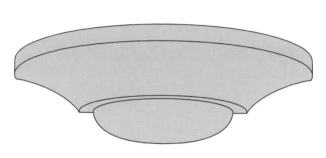

WALL LIGHTS

Wall lights, whether contemporary or traditional in style, should be fixed around 2m (6ft) from floor level and used in place of overhead or table lamps to create atmosphere. Ideally, they should be fitted with a dimmer switch so that the levels of light can be easily altered.

WALL UPLIGHTERS

Wall uplighters, like fixed wall lights, are used to create softer pools of light than overhead lighting would and can be combined with table lamps to create a relaxing space. They also play a part in improving the proportions of the room – the light from them is thrown upwards, making a ceiling seem higher that it really is.

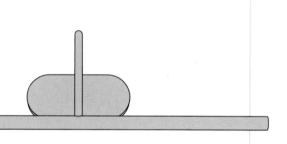

PICTURE LIGHTS

The living room is the one place where you're likely to have a favourite piece of art to display, and the best way to show it off is with a picture light, which should sit just above or below it. Look for a fitting that matches the others in your room in terms of material and finish for the best effect.

SINGLE SPOTLIGHTS

Single spotlights are typically used to highlight areas of a room or things in it – from architectural details to pieces of art. Limit yourself to no more than one spotlight per room (or per zone in a very large room), otherwise the drama you may be hoping to create will be dampened.

LAMPS

FLOOR LAMPS

Floor lamps usually sit comfortably behind an armchair to provide task lighting for reading or craft projects. However, contemporary buys can also be bought for decorative effect and look just as good lighting up a dark corner. Experiment with different shades before you buy to ensure the light thrown around is right for your space, both in terms of colour and strength.

FLOOR UPLIGHTERS

Just as wall uplighters project light upwards to the ceiling, floor uplighters perform the same trick in enhancing the space in a low-ceilinged room, or showing off the proportions of a room with a high ceiling. Choose one with adjustable light levels for the best effect.

TABLE LAMPS

Table lamps are a must-have in a living room, however contemporary, because they allow you to take the light down to the lowest level and create soft pools of relaxing light. Dot the lights evenly around so the whole room can be adequately lit by them, and switch off all the overhead lights.

10 CHOOSE WINDOW TREATMENTS

Of all the rooms in your house, the living room is the one room where you may want to introduce luxurious fabrics to make a stylish, individual statement and heighten the sense of comfort and relaxation. However, if you want a more contemporary, understated look, choose something more subtle.

1 CHOOSE A TYPE

It may be that you want to put more than one type of dressing on your living room windows. Doing so will introduce a layered look to the room. But which should you match up, and which should you hang on its own?

BLINDS

If you prefer a streamlined look, or you have a small living room, blinds are a neat choice. Roller and Roman blinds are available in a wide choice of colours and designs, and Venetian blinds in a choice of materials and colours. Team with curtains for a layered look.

CURTAINS

A classic choice for living rooms, curtains are available in a wide range of fabrics, patterns, styles, and headings so they can be used in both traditional and modern homes. Curtains can be matched with blinds and also shutters, if chosen carefully.

SHUTTERS

A smart choice for modern rooms, solid shutters are available in limited designs. Louvred shutters can be designed with either two or three panels and in a choice of styles including full-height, café-style, and tier-on-tier. They are also ideal for bay and arched windows.

CHECKLIST

● **Is your living room** overlooked? If so, consider using a translucent fabric such as muslin, voile, or lace net that offers privacy while still letting in light.

● **Think about the amount** of space around your window and ensure that you will be able to pull back curtains fully or open shutters – by doing so you can make the room seem larger and let in more light.

● **If you live on** a busy road, consider curtains made from a heavy-weight fabric such as velvet, which can help eliminate street noise.

MAKE
LONG CURTAINS

Making your own curtains is a sure-fire way to ensure they are the perfect size and material for your room. These tab-top curtains loop directly on to the pole for a modern look that doesn't require curtain hooks. Make them floor length or, for a more luxurious feel, longer so that they pool on the floor.

WHAT YOU NEED

- Tape measure
- Fabric – use curtain-weight cotton material (see page 384 for quantity)
- Scissors
- Sewing machine, or needle and thread
- Iron
- Pins

1 MEASURE AND CUT

1 TAKE A MEASUREMENT from the bottom of the pole to the floor. (If you want the curtains to finish just above the floor, use this measurement as your starting point; if you want the curtains to pool on the floor, add on an extra 20–30cm/8–12in).

2 CUT THE FABRIC to length, adding an extra 25cm (10in) for hem and top edge allowance.

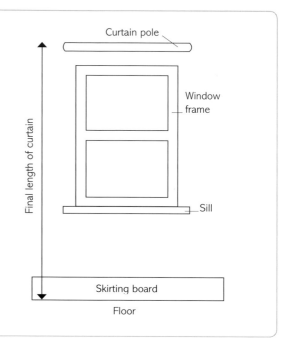

Curtain pole

Window frame

Final length of curtain

Sill

Skirting board

Floor

2 JOIN THE FABRIC

JOIN TOGETHER lengths of fabric to make up the necessary width (for these curtains to hang nicely, the width of each should be approximately half to three-quarters the length of the pole). To join, place the lengths together, right side to right side, and sew a seam along one edge. Then open up and lay flat, right side down, and press the seam open with an iron.

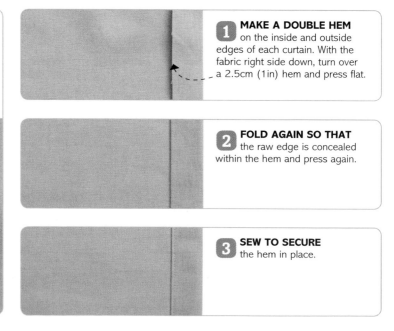

3 HEM THE SIDES

1 MAKE A DOUBLE HEM on the inside and outside edges of each curtain. With the fabric right side down, turn over a 2.5cm (1in) hem and press flat.

2 FOLD AGAIN SO THAT the raw edge is concealed within the hem and press again.

3 SEW TO SECURE the hem in place.

4   HEM THE BOTTOM

1   **TURN UP THE BOTTOM** of the curtains in a similar way but with a 10cm (4in) hem. Fold over and press, then fold and press again, and sew in place.

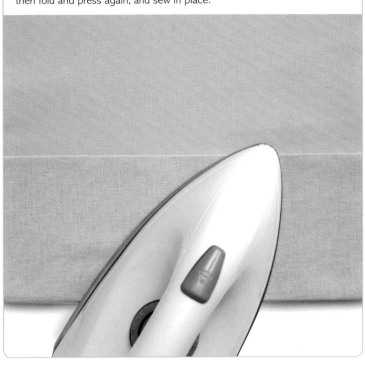

2   **SEW THE SIDES** as well so that the hem space is completely enclosed.

5   MAKE THE TABS

1   **TO MAKE THE TABS** that will attach the curtains to the pole, cut lengths of fabric that are 20cm (8in) wide and long enough when doubled over to wrap all the way around the pole, with some space for movement, as well as a seam allowance of 1–2cm (½–¾in). If in doubt, make them slightly longer than you need – the excess will be hidden when the curtain is finished.

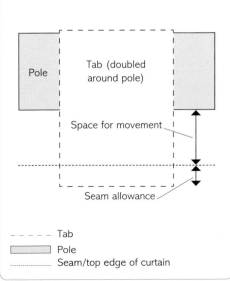

Pole

Tab (doubled around pole)

Space for movement

Seam allowance

- - - - -   Tab

Pole

Seam/top edge of curtain

2   **FOLD EACH TAB** in half lengthways, right side to right side, and stitch along the raw edge to make a tube.

3   **TURN EACH TUBE** the right way round and, with the seam centred, press flat.

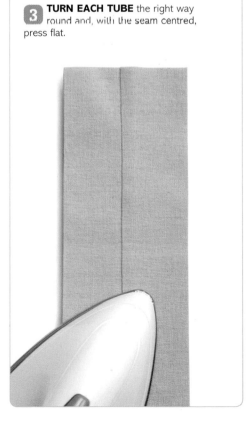

6 POSITION THE TABS

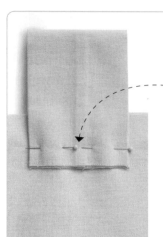

1 **PIN THE TABS** in place along the top edge of the curtain. Position one at each end, one in the middle, and the remainder at 20–30cm (8–12in) intervals.

2 **MEASURE THE DISTANCE** from the top of the tabs to the bottom of the curtain and check it corresponds to the desired final length of the curtain as determined at step 1.

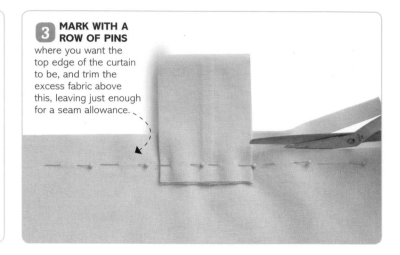

3 **MARK WITH A ROW OF PINS** where you want the top edge of the curtain to be, and trim the excess fabric above this, leaving just enough for a seam allowance.

7 SEW ON THE TABS

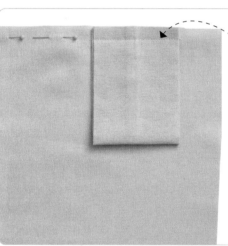

UNPIN AND INVERT the tabs so that the round end of the loop now faces downwards. Ensure that the distance between the round end of the loop to the row of pins remains the same. Sew the tabs in place.

8 PREPARE THE BACK PANEL

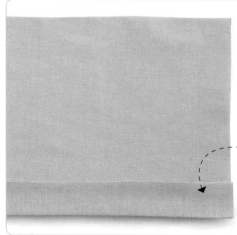

CUT LENGTHS of fabric, measuring 25cm (10in), for the back of the curtain. Cut as many as you need to make up the width and join together as at step 2. At the bottom, make a 3.5cm (1½in) fold (wrong side to wrong side) and press flat.

9 JOIN THE FRONT AND BACK PANELS

1 **POSITION THE BACK PANEL** against the top of the main piece of fabric, right side to right side, with the folded edge at the bottom. The shorter piece should overhang the longer piece slightly at the inside and outside edges. Pin in place.

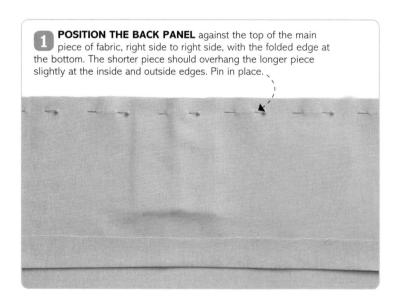

2 **SEW ALONG THE ROW** of pins to attach the back panel.

10 SEW THE BACK PANEL

1 FLIP THE BACK PANEL over so that the fabric is wrong side to wrong side and the tabs are exposed. Press with the iron.

2 PIN THE BACK PANEL in place and then sew to join.

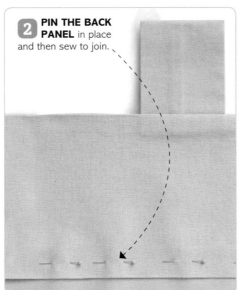

3 AT THE SIDES, neatly fold the overhanging fabric inside and sew the sides as well.

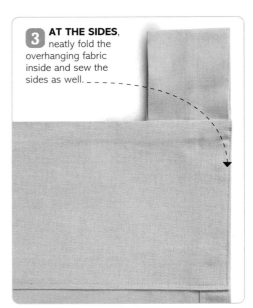

11 HANG

PASS THE CURTAIN POLE through all the loops and secure back in the brackets.

11 CHOOSE A FIRE

Before buying a fire for your living room, ask a professional to assess whether you have a working chimney or flue and what condition it is in, the type of fuel you can use, and the required heat output. Armed with this information, you'll be able to choose from the various types of fire that are available.

CHOOSE THE TYPE

Start by deciding whether you want a traditional fire or stove set into an existing or faux chimney, or to create a more contemporary look with a modern fire that's set into or mounted on the wall.

STOVE

More efficient than open-fronted fires, stoves can either be free-standing on a hearth, inset into the fireplace opening, or – provided the stove has an external flue – sited centrally in the room to create a focal point. Traditionally found in country homes, stoves are also becoming increasingly popular in contemporary houses.

INSET

Inset fires sit neatly inside a fireplace opening behind the hearth. Most can be installed into a standard-sized fireplace opening, although this may need enlarging for a bigger fire. They are typically placed within a stone or wooden mantel, or flush against a tiled, stone, brick, or other non-combustible surface.

WALL-MOUNTED

Wall-mounted fires are contemporary and don't take up any floor space. Depending on the type of fuel used, the fire can either be installed fully inset into an existing or false chimney breast or hung directly on the wall. They are available in portrait, landscape, and square formats.

OUTSET

Outset fires are fitted on the hearth in front of the fireplace opening of a working chimney. These tend to be fairly traditional in design, with a glass front and black surround and quite often with brass detailing. Outset fires are only available as gas fires.

MASONRY HEATER

These can be the primary heaters in houses up to 185m square (607ft square) in size. Made of brick- or stonework, they store heat while the fire burns, then slowly and evenly release the heat over the next 12 to 24 hours. Some versions combine the main heating function with a smaller stove for cooking, and even built-in heated benches. They require a chimney.

FUEL TYPES

The type of fuel you want to burn is fundamental to the style of fire you choose. Here are some points to consider before you buy:

● **Solid fuels** include wood, coal, smokeless fuels, and wood pellets. Many fires and stoves are multi-fuel, so they can burn any of these alternatives. If you do choose a solid-fuel fire, you will need to have somewhere dry to store the fuel.

● **Many gas fires** require a traditional flue and need to be inset into an existing chimney breast. If you don't have a chimney or flue, a balanced-flue gas fire can be positioned on, or ducted to, an outside wall.

● **Electric fires** can be positioned anywhere in a room with a power point. More expensive fires are very realistic and may have an optiflame mirror effect, hologram, or even a built-in smoke machine to give a more authentic appearance.

5 WAYS WITH
LIVING ROOM DISPLAYS

Displaying your accessories and personal possessions in a creative way will give your living room a neat, stylish look. Pick out objects that look attractive (rather than those that are purely functional) and follow these tips to work out how to display your collections in the best possible way.

GROUPING OF VASES

A good way to display vases is in a grouping of three or five. Use colour-coordinated vases of varying heights and arrange them into a loose pyramid shape.

ALTERNATIVELY, you could arrange the vases so they ascend in height.

COLOUR-CODED BOOKSHELF

A prominently placed bookshelf will look more ordered if you limit it to books where the colours suit your decorating scheme.

MEMENTOS ON BOX SHELVES

Open box shelves provide a narrow shelf on which to display collections and mementos, and create a neat border around them.

BELL JARS

Use a glass bell jar to show off a small collection. Choose mementos or even delicate dried flowers for your visual displays.

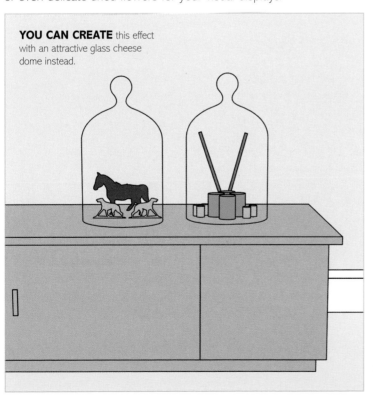

YOU CAN CREATE this effect with an attractive glass cheese dome instead.

SHELVING UNIT ARRANGEMENT

Balance your shelf displays by placing larger accessories in the corners of alternate shelves to create a zigzag pattern.

POSITION SMALLER OBJECTS at the other ends of the shelves.

5 WAYS WITH
CUSHIONS AND THROWS

Cushions and throws on a sofa shouldn't be arranged haphazardly or left to chance. There are many ways – from formal to relaxed – to dress a sofa so that it looks different every time. Choose a look that suits the style of your living room, or change the arrangement according to your mood or the occasion.

BOHO

For an eclectic, informal look, cover the seat cushions of your sofa with an animal print throw, tucking it in underneath and around the sides, and add cushions in bright colours and prints.

LOOK FOR SCARVES and fabric remnants that you can use to cover your seat pads if you don't want to use an animal print throw.

NEAT – TWO THROWS

Cover each seat pad of a two-seat sofa with a small plain throw, then add a single striped cushion to each seat.

CHOOSE POLYESTER PADS, which are firm and keep their shape, for a more formal look, or squishy feather cushions for a more relaxed vibe.

SMART – SINGLE THROW

Team a single light-coloured wool throw with luxuriously covered plain cushions (all of the same size) for a uniform look.

FOR INTEREST, add one cushion in a patterned fabric.

VINTAGE CHIC

A checked picnic-style blanket with cushions in a mix of floral and striped designs will give your sofa a vintage look.

MAKE SURE the cushions you choose are in proportion to your sofa.

JUST CUSHIONS

Use cushions of different sizes, but in similar colours and prints, to make an interesting visual mix.

FOR A SMART LOOK, keep your cushion arrangement symmetrical.

12 CHOOSE RUGS

Rugs come in a variety of sizes, materials, and shapes, and can be used to add texture, colour, and pattern to otherwise plain rooms. Adding a rug to an area of the house with exposed floorboards will help to minimize draughts and make any rooms with hard flooring look and feel warmer and more inviting.

1 CHOOSE THE SHAPE

The rug you choose largely depends on the shape and look of the area or room in which you place it. For contrast, try a round or natural-shaped rug (made from animal hide) in an angular room. If you are in doubt about the size, bigger is usually better.

ROUND

Incorporating a round rug is a good way to soften hard edges in a room if the furniture has lots of sharp angles. Adding a couple of small, colourful round rugs is also a fun way to brighten a child's bedroom.

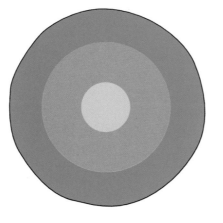

SQUARE

Square rugs work well in small square rooms, where they can act as a great focal point underneath a square coffee or dining table, for example. Try using two or three square rugs to break up the space if you have a long rectangular room.

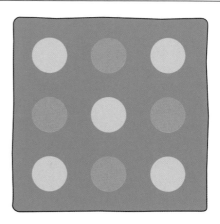

RECTANGULAR

These rugs are the most popular option and can be positioned in the middle of a room in front of a sofa, or practically right up to the edges of a room to give the impression of a fully carpeted space.

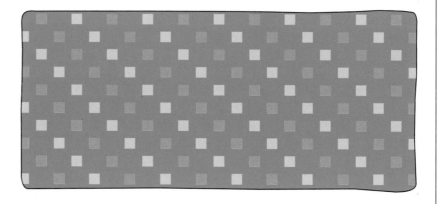

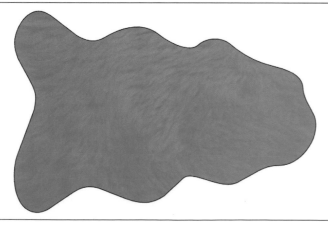

NATURAL/ANIMAL

Rugs made from natural hide or sheepskin are often left in their natural shape, giving them an authentic look. They are ideal for living rooms and bedrooms, and particularly enhance wooden or stone floors. Sizes and shapes vary, so be prepared to be flexible.

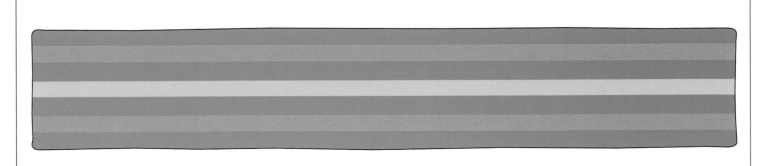

RUNNER

Mostly found in hallways, runners are long, thin, rectangular rugs available in a variety of lengths and widths, and often striped. They can add colour and texture while protecting your floor, and also tend to make a space look longer.

2 CHOOSE THE MATERIAL

The fibre and weave you choose for your rug really comes down to personal preference and where you will use it. Long pile is good for creating a cosy ambience, while leather and sheepskin are perfect for modern interiors.

LONG PILE

Medium-priced long pile rugs add texture, comfort, and warmth. They come in a range of materials, from wool to hardwearing synthetics, but have a tendency to shed.

FLAT WOVEN

Flat-weave rugs are made from wool or synthetic fibres such as polypropylene or polyester, hence their wide range of prices. They are suitable for use in all rooms.

NATURAL FIBRES

These medium-priced rugs made from natural fibres such as seagrass, sisal, and jute add texture, but do not have the same warmth and softness as other materials.

CARING FOR YOUR RUG

With a little care and attention, you can keep your rug looking its best for years.

● If your rug is in a room that receives direct sunlight, prevent uneven fading by rotating the rug regularly; turning it every six months or so should be adequate.

● To prevent the fibres from being crushed, avoid having sharp castors or narrow legs placed directly on your rug, or at the very least, move the furniture from time to time so that the pressure is on a different point.

● New rugs with long pile yarns and those made of wool are likely to shed fibres when you first lay them down. This should reduce during the first few weeks of use with the help of light vacumming. However, some rugs will continue to shed throughout their life cycle.

● Clean up any spills immediately, scraping up solids and blotting up liquids (never rubbing) with a clean damp cloth.

● If you cannot remove a stain yourself, it may be worth consulting a specialist cleaner – they can often work wonders. Professionals may also be able to repair burns and holes.

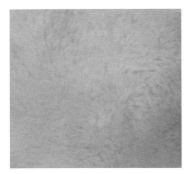

SHEEPSKIN

Sold in a choice of shades and sizes (which can be sewn together), these rugs are averagely priced; the pricier rugs are thicker and heavier with denser wool.

LEATHER & HIDE

Medium to high in price, a rug of natural leather or hide is unique in its markings, colour, and size. Shaggy, patchwork leather, and hide rugs are usually cheaper.

PEBBLE

Designed to look like pebbles, these expensive modern textured rugs made of pure wool stitched in various configurations are soft and comfortable underfoot.

5 WAYS WITH
RUGS

Rugs can be used to great effect in a living room, whether to add colour or pattern, provide a focal point, or create an optical illusion. They can also make a room look more inviting and comfortable, or define a particular area if you have a large through room. Decide which of these looks will suit your room.

AREA RUG

Place a large rectangular or square rug in an open-plan space and group your furniture around it or on it to help define the living or relaxing area of the room.

DON'T LIMIT YOURSELF to just one rug in a large space, but do ensure that your rugs at least complement one another if they don't match exactly.

ROUND RUG

If you have a contemporary living room and modern furniture with sleek, sharp angles, use a large round rug to soften these lines.

ROUND RUGS create a less formal look; they can be used effectively in traditional spaces, too.

THREE SLIMLINE RUGS

If you can't find one rug to occupy your space, lay three slimline rugs next to one another to fill the desired area.

HALL RUNNERS are a good buy for this type of effect. For a more relaxed look, don't line up any patterns exactly.

GROUPING OF DIFFERENT RUGS

For a really laid-back look, use a combination of different-sized patterned rugs to fill the space.

FOR THE BEST EFFECT, make sure the rugs share the same colour palette.

STRIPED RUG

Make a small room appear larger with a striped rug. Horizontal stripes will make the room feel wider; vertical stripes will make it look longer.

NEUTRALLY COLOURED stripes will give a more subtle effect than bright, bold colours.

5 WAYS TO
REFRESH A LIVING ROOM

A living room sometimes just needs refreshing rather than completely renovating and redecorating. This needn't cost a fortune and can be achieved within a matter of hours. Make some or all of these changes to lift the look of your living room and make it appealing again.

ADD NEW CUSHIONS

New cushions will change the look of your sofa instantly. Change all the cushion covers, or just add two or three new cushions in a pattern or colour that complements your sofa fabric.

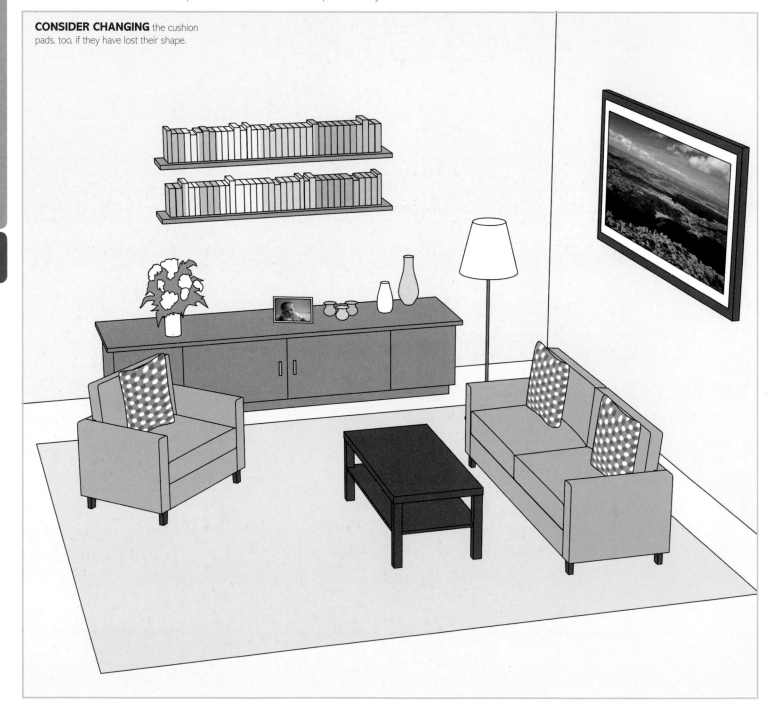

CONSIDER CHANGING the cushion pads, too, if they have lost their shape.

CHANGE A LAMPSHADE

Lamps are easy to update: change the size, shape, and colour of the lampshade to give your lamp a completely different look.

MAKE SURE that the shade is in proportion to the size of the lampstand: if it's too big or small, the overall effect will look unbalanced.

REARRANGE FURNITURE

By simply moving your sofa and coffee table to new positions, you can give your sitting room a fresh feel and outlook.

IN SUMMER MONTHS, position the sofa so that it faces the windows, and in winter turn it towards a fireplace.

RE-COVER YOUR SOFA

Pick new sofa covers, whether unfitted or made-to-measure, or cover individual seat and back cushions with large fabric remnants.

SWAP ACCESSORIES

Change your accessories: why not swap smaller items such as vases, candles, and picture frames for versions in a new colour or shape.

LOOK IN OTHER ROOMS for accessories that you can borrow to use in this room, too.

BEDROOM

1 WHAT TO DO WHEN REVAMPING YOUR BEDROOM

When redoing your bedroom, or any other bedroom in your house, it's essential to schedule the work in a certain order. By doing so, you'll save time, money, and the prospect of having to redo certain jobs that you might have already tackled. Follow these steps to get all the timings right.

1 DEVISE YOUR BUDGET

How much do you have to spend? Once you've decided your budget, it's vital to use it effectively. So, if the walls need plastering, don't spend the majority of your budget on a new bed. Always allow yourself a contingency of at least 10 per cent, too, especially if yours is an old property that might have hidden problems.

2 PLAN THE LAYOUT

Draw a scale floorplan of the room and include all doors, windows, and radiators. Work out where the furniture will be placed and use this as a guide to position electrical sockets, ceiling and wall lights, light switches, and a TV aerial point if needed.

3 REVIEW THE HEATING

Look at how the room is heated and consider whether it would be beneficial to make changes – for instance, could you gain useful wall space by moving the radiator? Would a larger radiator be more suitable for the room?

4 BOOK TRADESPEOPLE

Contact an electrician, carpenter, heating engineer, plasterer, and decorator for quotes. If you're not moving walls, now is a good time for a joiner to quote for fitted wardrobes. Ask if other tradespeople's work will affect the job so you can get each person in at the right time.

5 ORDER YOUR MATERIALS

Once your quotes are in, order any flooring, woodwork, doors, radiators, and windows. Furniture, wallpaper, paint, carpets, and lights can be ordered once the main jobs are under way.

6 STRIP THE ROOM

Remove old wallpaper to see if the walls and ceiling need replastering or patching before painting or repapering. Rip out old woodwork, damaged mouldings that can't be repaired, and old or unsatisfactory flooring, and remove old electrics and pipework for heating.

7 FIT NEW HEATING – FIRST FIX

If you are having new pipework laid for new radiators, have this done first, as it may stop other trades progressing.

8 INSTALL THE ELECTRICS – FIRST FIX

The electrician's first fix will include laying cabling beneath the floors and into the walls and ceiling to provide channelling for light switches. If you are having recessed lighting in the room, the electrician can begin the necessary work for these lighting fixtures now. Ensure that cabling for any phone and TV aerial points is installed now, too.

9 FIT NEW WINDOWS

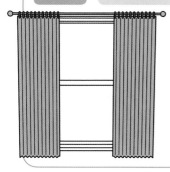

This task can be worked into your schedule once the room is gutted and before plastering. If the windows are being renovated, prepare them for painting now. While this is being done, book the plasterer.

10 PLASTER THE WALLS AND CEILING

Plastering is best done by a professional, and once the work is complete it will need at least two weeks to dry out before decorating can start. Now is the time to have any plaster mouldings repaired, or purchase new mouldings.

11 LAY THE FLOORING

While the plastered walls and ceiling are drying out, you can lay hard flooring, such as wood, or a sub-floor if you are having a carpet laid later.

12 HAVE WARDROBES FITTED

If you are having fitted wardrobes hand-built or have bought them from a high street retailer, have them fitted now before any new skirtings and mouldings are installed.

13 TACKLE THE WOODWORK

Once the plaster is dry, start fitting any new wood mouldings – skirting boards, architraves, doors, door frames, and picture rails – ensuring first that the carpenter or joiner knows the position of any underlying pipework and wires.

14 DECORATE

Fill any fine cracks, then paint the ceiling, walls, and woodwork, and finally put up wallpaper if you are using it.

15 ORGANIZE THE SECOND FIX

With the decorating complete, the electrician and heating engineer can return to fit the radiators and fix the light fittings and electric sockets.

15 ADD FINISHING TOUCHES

Put up curtain poles or blinds, attach the door furniture, and lay a carpet if you are having one.

2 CREATE A MOOD BOARD
FOR YOUR BEDROOM

A bedroom is a private sanctuary, a place where you should really feel at peace and be able to relax properly. So choosing the right style for your bedroom isn't just about selecting a decorative scheme or experimenting with colours and patterns, it's about finding a look that will allow you to completely unwind and feel comfortable. With that priority in mind, you can begin to build ideas using a mood board.

1 **FIND PICTURES OF BEDROOMS YOU LIKE** by looking through books, magazines, and on the internet and either tearing them out, printing, or colour-copying them. You should soon find that a theme begins to emerge or a specific style or colour scheme appeals to you. Edit the pictures you've selected down to a manageable number to act as a starting point for your scheme. If you are redecorating, it's worth noting what you don't currently like about the room so you don't repeat the same mistakes.

Select a picture or two that you like, or you want to take elements from, to stick to your board as inspiration.

2 **PICK A FAVOURITE ITEM**, which could be something you absolutely must include in the room – a beautiful bed, picture, or cushion, for example. Use it as a starting point for colours, patterns, shapes, or a theme.

If you're wallpapering the room, use colours within the wallpaper design as the basis for your accent colours.

3 **PICK A BACKGROUND COLOUR** early on, since your walls are the biggest area to decorate. Consider how you'll use the room: should it be light so you can dress and apply make-up, or do you want a cosy, calm setting? Pin wallpaper samples and paint colours onto the mood board, keeping them in the same proportions they'll be used in the room.

Use a third accent colour, if required, minimally in the room's scheme.

Choose one colour as your main accent shade and aim to use the second colour fractionally less.

4 **INTRODUCE ACCENT COLOURS**, which can either be a subtle variation of your base colour or a dramatic contrast to it (or both). Choose at least two colours, but no more than three. Play around with colour combinations using swatches and samples to see if they work together successfully, then pin your favourites to the board.

5 **CHOOSE NEW FURNITURE** that you'd like to include in the room. Use the same approach as you did for choosing your colour scheme to pick the right shade of fabric for a headboard or the best type of wood for wardrobe doors or a chest of drawers. To work out if the pieces will sit comfortably in the space, plot the dimensions of the room on graph paper and draw the furniture to scale.

Shape and size is an important consideration in a bedroom, especially if you want to buy a new bed.

Think about whether you'd like any beside furniture to be the same style and material as, or a complete contrast to, that of your bed.

6 **ADD PATTERN AND TEXTURE** to provide visual interest and a dimension of comfort. If your wallpaper is patterned, you can still use other patterns in the room, providing the colours are the same tones as those of the wallpaper. Or introduce texture with a rug, fitted carpet, bedspread, or cushion covers so the room doesn't feel too plain and unwelcoming. Add samples or pictures of your preferences to the mood board.

A chunky knitted throw or bedspread over the bed is an easy way to include texture in your bedroom.

If you choose a carpet or deep pile rug to add texture and extra comfort, check that it complements or tones with your mood board colours.

Accessories should either match your restricted palette or be in colours that you find calming and restful.

7 **ADD FINISHING TOUCHES** such as cushions, bedside lamps, pictures, and rugs. These items needn't necessarily match perfectly, but they should be cohesive in terms of colour (this is where you'll use your accent colours), style, or theme if the room is to work well. These subtle touches can make or break a room's success, so use the limited colour palette and design scheme of your mood board to help you make your final choices.

3 LAYOUT CONSIDERATIONS IN THE BEDROOM

Your bedroom is inevitably a room that takes the overflow from other parts of the house, so you will need to include as much storage as you can to accommodate everything you use daily. Add to that the fact that it also has to fit in the largest pieces of furniture you'll probably own – a bed and wardrobes – and you'll realise you've got a challenge on your hands. Follow these tips to make the most of your space.

BED

Firstly, work out the position of your bed; assuming it's a double bed, both sides should be accessible (so don't push the bed against a wall). If the ceiling slopes, check there's enough headroom at either side of the bed. Also ensure that the bedroom door doesn't open on to the bed, and that you can open wardrobe doors or drawers easily. If space is tight, avoid a high bed with footboards or posts; a low, minimally furnished bed makes a room feel bigger. If you can pick a bed with drawers beneath for extra storage to free up floor space in the room, so much the better.

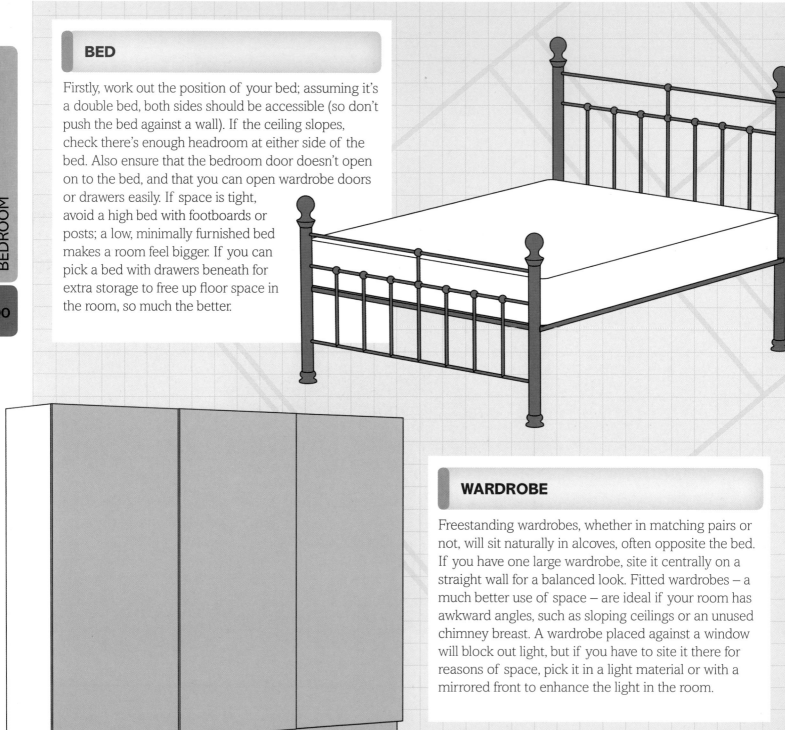

WARDROBE

Freestanding wardrobes, whether in matching pairs or not, will sit naturally in alcoves, often opposite the bed. If you have one large wardrobe, site it centrally on a straight wall for a balanced look. Fitted wardrobes – a much better use of space – are ideal if your room has awkward angles, such as sloping ceilings or an unused chimney breast. A wardrobe placed against a window will block out light, but if you have to site it there for reasons of space, pick it in a light material or with a mirrored front to enhance the light in the room.

BEDSIDE TABLES

Bedside tables are all about creating a balanced look and should always come in pairs – they needn't match exactly, but they should be similar in size. If you think you only have room for one bedside table, try sliding the bed across slightly and fitting in two mini tables or table-height shelves instead so that you don't unbalance the look of your bedroom.

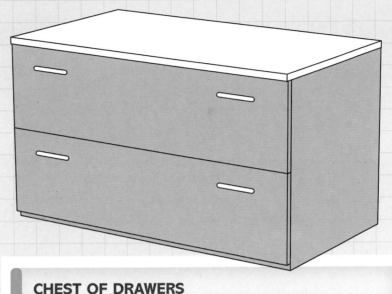

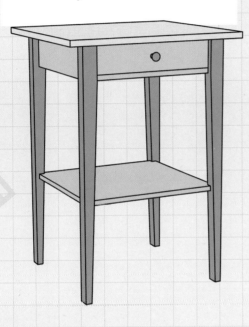

CHEST OF DRAWERS

If your bedroom is large, think about buying matching chests of drawers to sit either side of the bed in place of bedside tables. This option will give you plenty of storage for lamps, books, and clothes that don't need hanging. If there's only room for a single chest of drawers, site it centrally on an empty wall and put a mirror above it to make a focal point. It can also double up as a dressing table, but without a chair. If it has to share a wall with a wardrobe, buy one that matches the depth and style of the wardrobe for a streamlined feel. Or, for a sleek look, place it within a run of fitted wardrobes.

DRESSING TABLE

If your bedroom is big enough to comfortably hold all the essential furniture you require and you still have plenty of floor space, a dressing table is a real luxury item to include. Ideally, it should be placed where the natural daylight is good – in a bay window (with a stand-alone mirror) or at right angles to a flat window (with a wall-hung mirror), for example. Ensure that there's room to comfortably sit in a chair at the dressing table and there is sufficient space for a partner to move around behind it.

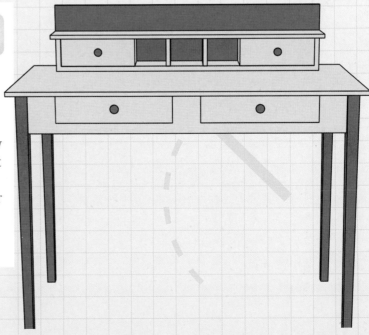

4 CHOOSE FLOORING

Comfort is likely to be high up your wish list when you choose the flooring for your bedroom. However, you should also consider what part it will play in your decorating scheme; the floor is often referred to as the fifth wall in a room. It's worth thinking, too, about how easy it will be to keep clean.

1 CHOOSE THE LOOK

If you want a cosy, relaxing look, carpet is an ideal choice, and a good way of introducing colour to a room. Tiles or wooden flooring give a sleek look and can be used in either a contemporary or a rustic-looking bedroom.

TILED

Tiles are a good choice for any bedroom, helping to keep a room cool in summer and, when teamed with underfloor heating (which is strongly recommended), warm in winter. They are also practical. Opt for large-format tiles, and consider using pale colours.

WOODEN

Wood can create a contemporary or traditional look depending on the finish and tone you choose. There are various choices: plank floors (boards that are 15–20cm/6–8in wide); strip floors (narrow boards), and parquet (laid in blocks or a herringbone design).

CARPET

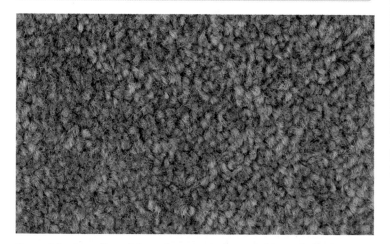

Carpet feels soft and luxurious underfoot, and is available in a range of colours and designs. Solid colour carpets will show more marks than flecks or patterns. Natural floor coverings like sisal are not as soft underfoot, but are an aesthetically pleasing alternative.

CHECKLIST

● **Concrete sub-floors** must be clean, dry and flat. Correct any errors using a self-levelling compound, ensuring it is completely dry before laying any flooring over it.

● **If you are laying tiles over floorboards**, overlay the boards with hardboard, smooth side up. Timber treated with wood preservatives is not suitable as a sub-floor.

● **Carpets are best laid** over an even surface such as plywood or chipboard. Anything with grooves creates marks in the carpet. A good-quality underlay will also ensure that it looks its best, as well as making it more comfortable underfoot.

2 CHOOSE THE MATERIAL

A bedroom doesn't have as much foot traffic as the rest of the house, so you can choose the flooring almost on looks alone, if you wish. However, since you're likely to be walking about barefoot, consider comfort underfoot both in summer and in winter.

TILED

PORCELAIN

Porcelain flooring comes in both glazed and unglazed finishes. It is highly durable and easy to keep clean, but it can feel cold and hard underfoot. Prices vary.

CERAMIC

Low-cost ceramic tiles are less expensive than natural stone and porcelain. They won't stain, don't need sealing, and are available in many styles, shapes, and colours.

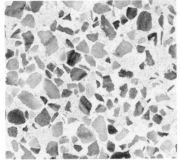

TERRAZZO

Made of marble chips in cement with a colour pigment added, terrazzo has a highly polished finish. It is expensive, and must be fitted by a professional.

TRAVERTINE

Made from natural stone, high-cost travertine has either a sleek polished finish or a natural tumbled look with soft edges and a sponge-like appearance.

LIMESTONE

Limestone tiles are available in a highly polished gloss or rough, matt finish and a range of colours. Although expensive, their good looks make them worth it.

WOODEN

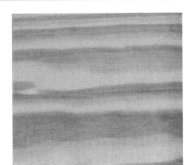

HARDWOOD

Medium to high in price, hardwood floors withstand lots of wear and tear, and can be re-sanded many times over to restore their natural beauty.

SOFTWOOD

If you want to paint your wood floor, softwood is a cheap or medium-priced option. Only use specialist packs dried in a kiln so shrinkage is kept to a minimum.

ENGINEERED WOOD

Medium-priced engineered wood has the look and feel of a solid wood floor. It can be fitted as a floating floor with an underlay – a good choice for uneven floors.

BAMBOO

Medium- to high-cost bamboo flooring, which looks like wood, can be fitted as a floating floor or glued or nailed down, making it suitable for most level sub-floors.

LAMINATE

Cheaper than hardwood and engineered woods, laminated planks comprise a decorative wood effect image fixed onto a base of compressed fibreboard.

BEDROOM

203

CARPET

TWIST PILE

Low- to medium-priced twist piles are extremely affordable, which makes them a popular choice. They have a coarse, rugged appearance and are very hardwearing.

VELVET PILE

This medium- to high-priced carpet has a dense, low-cut pile and a soft, smooth appearance like suede. Its plush, luxurious finish makes it ideal for a bedroom.

LOOP PILE

A medium-priced loop pile carpet has level, uniform loops, or loops of different heights for a textured appearance. It looks like coir and sisal flooring, but has added comfort.

SAXONY

Medium- to high-priced saxony carpet is woven in loops and then sheared to make an even surface. Its deep, dense pile feels soft and smooth underfoot.

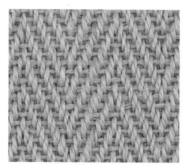
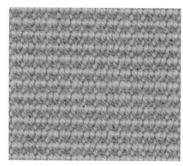

COIR

Low-cost coir, made from coconut husk fibres, has a highly textured finish that can feel rough underfoot, but it is extremely hardwearing and non-slip.

SISAL

Medium-cost sisal has a fine texture and a subtle sheen. It is available in a range of weaves as well as a choice of colours – either used as blends or solid tones.

JUTE

Medium-priced jute is comprised of flat woven designs, which give it a smart appearance. It is softer than other natural floor coverings, but not as hardwearing.

SEAGRASS

Medium-priced natural seagrass grows in coastal meadows on river banks. When woven, it has a chunky appearance and a waxy texture, making it stain-resistant.

ADDING A RUG

If you have opted to use hard flooring, such as wood or tiles, in your bedroom, you should consider placing a rug beside – or either side of – your bed.

● **Choose a deep pile** for a feeling of luxury in a colour that complements the room's scheme.

● **Ensure the rug** is weighty enough that it won't move or crease when you walk on it, causing a trip hazard.

● **Before you finalize your decision,** check that the rug will be the right size by measuring and cutting a template out of newspaper and placing it on the floor where the rug will go.

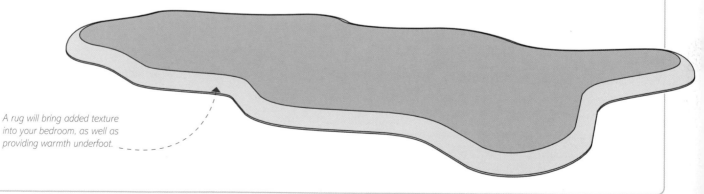

A rug will bring added texture into your bedroom, as well as providing warmth underfoot.

THE PARALLEL STRAIGHT LINES of a wooden floor can help create the visual effect of a longer or wider room.

5 CHOOSE WALL COVERINGS

When choosing what to cover your bedroom walls with, your main priority should be the look you want to create; you don't need to worry so much about paint or wallpaper being hardwearing in a bedroom. So, unless your walls are very badly cracked or uneven, you have free reign to use your imagination.

1 CHOOSE THE MATERIAL

As well as creating the right visual effect in a bedroom, you also need to consider the condition of your walls. If they are newly plastered, do whatever you choose, but if the walls are old and uneven, wallpaper or panelling may be a more practical choice.

PAINT

Painting your walls is a fairly quick and inexpensive way to decorate a bedroom, but don't underestimate the amount of paint you will need – between two to three coats. Light colours stretch the sense of space; deeper, rich colours create a cosy, cocoon-like feel.

WALLPAPER

If the paper you've fallen in love with is particularly expensive, or you don't feel brave enough to paper all the walls, paper a feature wall (normally the wall behind or facing the bed). Patterned wallpaper has a pattern repeat, so calculate the amount you need first.

CLADDING

Wainscot panelling, which has a picture frame-like effect and is made from solid wood or MDF, gives a traditional feel, simple tongue-and-groove cladding creates a nautical or country effect, and flat wood veneer panels give a contemporary look.

CHECKLIST

● **When buying wallpaper** it is worth getting an extra 10% as a contingency. Ensure that it is all from the same batch, so that the colours match perfectly, and that you will have enough paper to match up the repeat pattern of a patterned wallpaper.

● **Have you prepared** your walls properly? Whether you paint or paper the walls, fill and sand any cracks and holes and smooth uneven areas.

● **Tester pots allow you** to check the finish of paint as well as the colour; where possible, avoid matt paints that are chalky, as they will not wipe down well if they become marked.

2 CHOOSE THE TYPE

The type of paint, wallpaper, or cladding you choose will have a dramatic effect. Paint is sold in various finishes, each giving a different look, wallpaper is available in a variety of styles and textures, and cladding comes in a wide range of looks.

PAINT

MATT

Matt emulsion is a non-reflective water-based paint that minimizes imperfections on uneven walls. It suits both modern and traditional bedrooms. Prices vary greatly.

SILK OR SHEEN

A good choice for small or dark bedrooms, silk and soft sheen medium-priced paints have a subtle sheen that reflects light. These paints are durable, too.

METALLIC

For a touch of luxury, use a medium-cost metallic emulsion paint. Or buy metallic shimmer paints that can be painted over a matt colour to create a subtle sheen.

SUEDE EFFECT

Suede-effect medium-priced emulsion, available in a range of rich colours, has miniscule grains that give a brushed look. Apply it with random brush strokes.

WALLPAPER

PLAIN OR PATTERNED

Use plain paper as an alternative to paint, or use patterned paper for a decorative effect. Machine-printed paper is cheap; hand-printed designs cost much more.

FLOCK

Flock wallpaper has a velvet texture and is available in rich colours, so it can be used to create a dramatic look. It is more expensive than other wallpapers.

METALLIC

Medium to high in price, metallic wallpaper comes in a variety of patterns, including contemporary florals and retro geometric designs, and plain and textured finishes.

TEXTURED

Medium-priced textured wallpapers are thicker than other papers and are typically white with a choice of raised patterns. Use it left white or painted on uneven walls.

CLADDING

TONGUE & GROOVE

Cheap- or medium-cost tongue-and-groove panelling can give a nautical, country, or retro look. The boards are usually made of pine – or buy ready-made MDF panels.

FLAT WOOD VENEER

Cover a wall in medium- to high-priced veneer panels to create a mid-century look. Iron-on wood veneer on a thin sheet of MDF that is then fixed to the wall is best.

WAINSCOT PANELLING

This medium-priced panelling can add interest to plain walls in a traditional or contemporary room. Consider wallpapering inside the panelled frame itself.

6 WAYS WITH
HEADBOARDS

Make a statement in your bedroom with a decorative headboard. Whether it's made of fabric or painted directly onto the wall, a headboard creates impact by making your bed look more substantial and inviting. It can be as high as you like, but keep its width the same as, or just slightly greater than, that of the bed.

FABRIC STRETCHED OVER A FRAME

Make your own headboard using a favourite fabric stretched and stapled onto a wooden frame the same width as the bed.

YOU NEEDN'T STICK TO PLAIN FABRICS for a headboard: if your bed linen is mostly plain, you can use the headboard to bring a patterned element into the room.

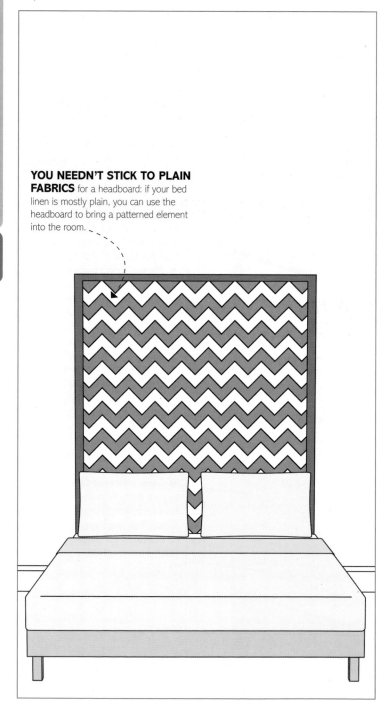

DECORATIVE PANELS

Fretwork, or cutwork, panels create an unusual backdrop to your bed. Use different-sized panels to form a rectangular shape.

FOR GLAMOROUS APPEAL, spray the panels with metallic paint before fixing them in place.

CLASSIC

For a classic look, choose an upholstered headboard with button detailing. This will give your bed a smart, boutique hotel feel.

DON'T ALWAYS OPT for a flat fabric – choose a textured velvet if you want to create a luxurious feel.

WALLPAPER

You can create a decorative headboard effect on the wall itself – hang lengths of patterned wallpaper where the bed will be situated.

FABRIC-COVERED PANELS

Cover foam rectangles in fabric to make two individual headboards. Leave a gap of approximately 10cm (4in) between panels.

FIX THE HEADBOARDS directly onto the wall, using battens beneath them to give extra support.

PAINTED PANELS

If you're not brave enough to decorate your walls with a bright colour or pattern, painted MDF panels fixed to the wall are a good alternative.

5 ATTACH THE TIES

1 PIN THE TIES to the inside edges of the fabric. Pin four ties along each side, plus two along the top and two along the bottom.

2 ENSURE THE TIES are positioned correctly so that when the cover is folded in half, each tie aligns with one on the other side.

3 SECURE EACH TIE in position with a square seam, which will help to reinforce the join.

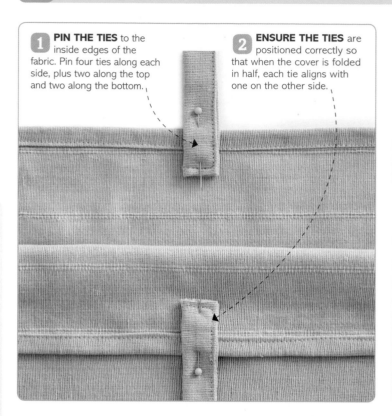

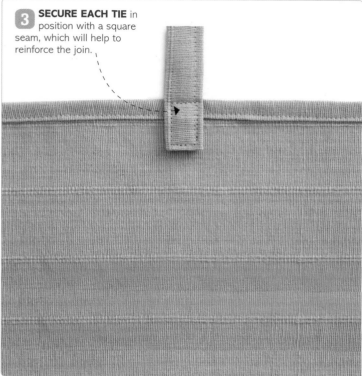

6 COVER THE HEADBOARD

PLACE THE FABRIC COVER over the headboard and secure each pair of ties in a bow.

MAKE
BED CUSHIONS

Accessories can be easily added to a bedroom to lift the atmosphere from plain and simple to cosy, relaxing, or luxurious. If your bedroom needs freshening, or you want to make it feel a little more inviting or sumptuous, make cushions in a fabric (or fabrics) of your choice to scatter over the pillows on the bed.

WHAT YOU NEED

- Coloured fabric
- Iron
- Pins
- Sewing machine, or needle and threads
- Buttons
- Buttonhole cutter (optional)
- Cushion pad or pillow

1 MEASURE AND CUT THE FABRIC

FOR EACH BED CUSHION, measure and cut a piece of fabric: use the following dimensions (right) to cover a 60 x 40cm (24 x 16in) cushion pad, or adjust these measurements if your cushion pads or pillows are a different size. The upper and lower sections of fabric identified by the dotted lines (2 x 30cm/12in) will be folded over each other to make an "envelope" front to the cushion.

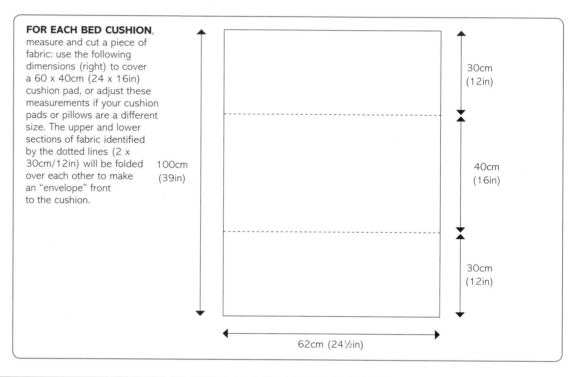

100cm (39in)

30cm (12in)

40cm (16in)

30cm (12in)

62cm (24½in)

2 STITCH THE HEM

1 FOLD AND IRON the shorter ends of the fabric.

2 FOLD THE SAME ENDS over again, iron them once more, and secure the hem in place with pins.

3 SEW THE SEAM. This will make the front of your cushion, so make this seam as neat as possible.

3 FOLD THE FABRIC

1 **LAY THE FABRIC** out flat, right side up, and measure the distances 30cm (12in) and 70cm (28in) from the top of the fabric. Mark each point in the centre of the fabric with a pin.

2 **FOLD THE TOP** of the fabric over at the point of the top pin, then fold the bottom of the fabric on top of it at the point of the bottom pin (the fabric is folded like this initially to identify where to place the buttonholes).

4 MAKE THE BUTTONHOLES

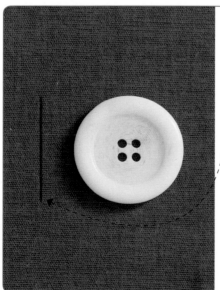

1 **MEASURE FOUR EQUIDISTANT POINTS** along the length of the bottom flap of fabric. Make a short mark with a pen at each point. The mark should be the same length as the buttons you have chosen.

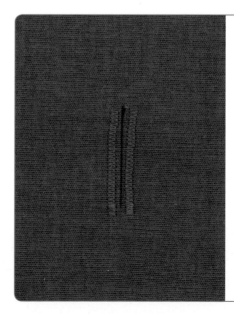

2 **SEW ALONG** either side of the marked line. If you are using a sewing machine, make this a zig zag stitch with a width of 3 and a length of ½ stitch.

3 **NOW SEW EACH END** of the buttonhole. If you are using a sewing machine, use the maximum stitch width and hold the fabric still while you sew. Make sure you catch the sides in with this stitch to secure them.

4 **CUT ALONG** the marked line, using a specialist buttonhole cutter if available. Cut carefully, making sure you don't cut the stitching.

5 SEW THE SEAMS

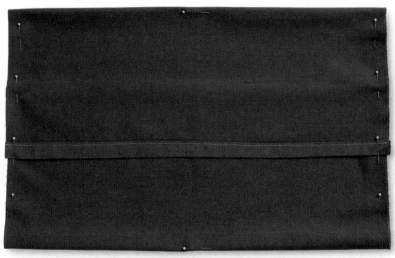

1 **REFOLD THE FABRIC,** this time with the top flap covering the bottom flap (hiding the buttonholes), then pin the fabric together at the sides.

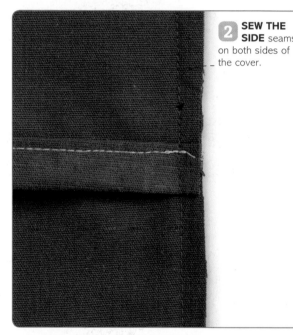

2 **SEW THE SIDE** seams on both sides of the cover.

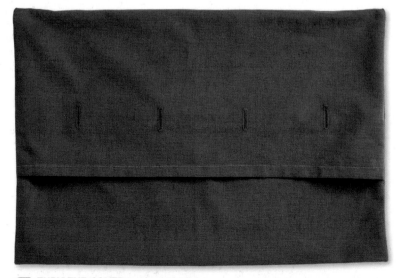

3 **TURN THE COVER** inside out so it is the right way round and lay it out flat.

4 **SEW ON THE BUTTONS** with a needle and thread, then insert the cushion pad or pillow.

7 CHOOSE
A WARDROBE

As it is one of the largest pieces of furniture in your bedroom, you will want your wardrobe to be as attractive as possible. However, the size of the wardrobe and its storage options should be your most important considerations, or you may end up with a beautiful piece of furniture that isn't at all practical.

1 FITTED OR FREESTANDING

When considering whether to choose fitted or freestanding wardrobes, ask yourself which look you prefer, which would suit the style of your home, which would be more space efficient for the shape of your room, and what your budget will stretch to.

FITTED

Fitted wardrobes are more space efficient, so are an ideal choice if you need lots of clothes storage or if your room is an awkward shape. They can be made to measure, or at least to your specification, so you can get what you need without compromise.

FREESTANDING

Available in a wide range of materials, designs and styles, freestanding wardrobes offer a versatile choice of looks. They tend to come in standard sizes, so you should search for one that best suits the space you have available.

2 CHOOSE TYPE OF DOOR ACTION

The type of door action you choose may be a style choice, but there are also practical considerations. If you're short on space, sliding doors may be best, as you won't need quite the same amount of space you would require to open hinged doors.

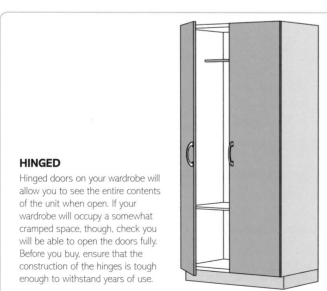

HINGED

Hinged doors on your wardrobe will allow you to see the entire contents of the unit when open. If your wardrobe will occupy a somewhat cramped space, though, check you will be able to open the doors fully. Before you buy, ensure that the construction of the hinges is tough enough to withstand years of use.

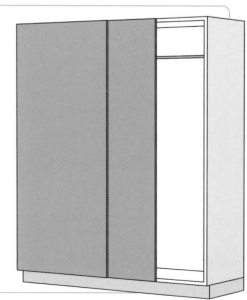

SLIDING

Many larger or fitted wardrobes come with full-height (often floor to ceiling) sliding doors. Two- or three-door combinations are usual. Bear in mind that with these doors you won't be able to see all of your clothes at once – one section will always be hidden by a door. Always ensure that the sliding action is well constructed.

3 CHOOSE THE SIZE

Choose your wardrobe according to how much space you have and how many clothes you want to hang (if you own more clothes that need folding than hanging, a greater amount of drawer space will prove more valuable).

SINGLE DOOR
The most slimline option, a single-door wardrobe will offer limited storage but may be the only choice in a small room. Check the depth of the door to make sure that you have enough space to open it fully.

TWO DOOR
Two-door wardrobes are a classic freestanding choice. This design often comes with a drawer, or set of drawers, at the bottom, although check they are deep enough to be practical.

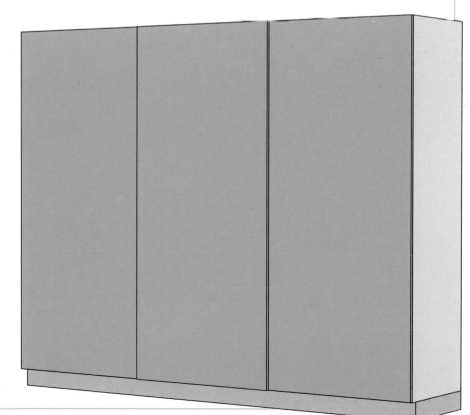

THREE OR MORE DOORS
Larger wardrobes with three or more doors provide plenty of space to include storage options such as shelving, drawers, or shoe racks alongside your hanging space. This allows you to keep all your clothing in one place, without the need for additional chests of drawers or other storage.

4 INTERNAL STORAGE OPTIONS

Your wardrobe's internal storage is every bit as important as its external appearance. Consider all your storage needs, weighing up how much hanging space – long and short – and how much shelf and drawer space you need.

FULL-LENGTH HANGING ONLY

If you want to hang long items, such as dresses, trousers, and coats, choose a full-length wardrobe so the clothes can hang without obstruction. With this option, you will need other furniture, such as a chest of drawers, to store any clothes that you do not want to hang.

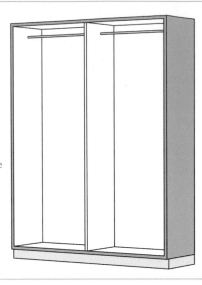

MULTIPLE-HEIGHT HANGING

Multiple-height hanging combines a full-height rail for long clothes with half-height rails for items such as shirts. Bear in mind that the interior of a man's wardrobe will look very different to that of a woman, who is more likely to need more full-height space for her clothes.

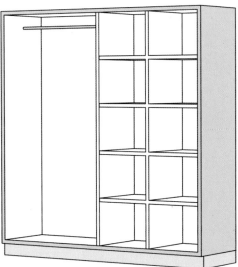

HANGING AND SHELVES

A combination of hanging space and open shelves caters for clothes that you need to hang and those that you prefer to keep folded. Make sure the shelves are wide enough for the items you plan to store, and ensure that they are adjustable so you can arrange them to suit your needs.

HANGING AND INTERNAL DRAWERS

If you don't have space in your bedroom for a separate chest of drawers, look for a wardrobe which includes an integral one. Choosing one with different-sized drawers will allow you to store everything from scarves to chunky jumpers.

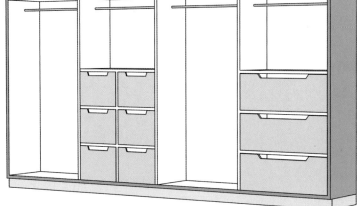

ALL STORAGE TYPES

Some wardrobes, especially fitted options, come with all types of storage: multiple-height hanging, shelves, and drawers. Consider carefully whether you have the right combination for the type of clothes you own and how you would like to store them.

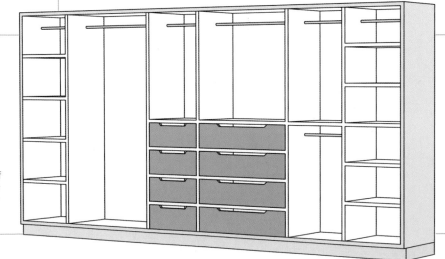

CHOOSE THE HANDLES

A wardrobe with sliding doors may have just a groove or rail for your fingers rather than handles, but if it does need handles, choose ones that are in proportion to the piece of furniture and will complement its look.

T BAR

These angular handles come in various lengths and different finishes, the most common being stainless or polished steel. T-bar handles best suit very contemporary wardrobes and chests of drawers or dressing tables.

D

These handles are similar to a T-bar handle, but are curved at the corners for a softer shape. Available in a range of lengths and finishes, they also suit contemporary furniture, but are a better match for pieces with curves within their design.

BOW

Shaped as a single smooth, streamlined curve, bow handles are simple and elegant. They can be narrow or wide, round or flat, so they can suit a variety of different furniture styles. They are available in a variety of finishes.

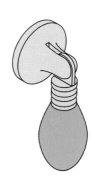

TEARDROP

The design of this classic handle shape gives a neat look to your furniture. It is available in a wide range of metal finishes; the teardrop is usually made from the same metal as the rest of the handle, or from ceramic.

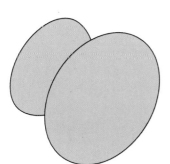

KNOBS

Knobs are available in a huge selection of sizes, materials, and shapes. For traditional-style bedrooms, choose a wooden or porcelain finish, or for a more modern room, choose brushed or polished metal.

DECORATIVE HANDLES

If you want to have a bit of fun with the design of your bedroom handles, look for something that is designed to look like a flower for grown-up bedrooms, or footballs or fairies for children's rooms. These handles are made from a range of materials, from plastic to metal.

WARDROBE ORGANIZERS

If you are designing your wardrobe interior from scratch, you will find it easy to ensure all your storage needs are catered for. However, you may find the storage offered by your wardrobe is less than ideal if you have picked it primarily for its outward appearance or you have revamped an existing wardrobe. If so, there are ways to remedy the situation: various organizers are available that enable you to use the space in your wardrobe differently.

● A hanging organizer (right) can be fastened to a hanging rail to provide soft shelving for folded clothes, shoes, and accessories. A typical organizer has six compartments and measures 30cm (12in) wide. Narrower versions specifically designed to store shoes are also available.

● An organizer with three or more rows of storage pockets that hangs against the inside of the wardrobe door can be suspended from the top of the door on hooks. These over-the-door organizers are useful for storing flat shoes, belts, scarves and other small items and accessories.

● Wire cube organizers are another good way to divide up your wardrobe space. Their modular design means that you can create a framework of cubes to suit the space. Sit the framework inside the wardrobe to create extra shelving.

PLAN THE PERFECT
WALK-IN WARDROBE

If you have a box room or an otherwise unused, awkward space in your bedroom, fitting it out as a walk-in wardrobe will use space efficiently, help you to organize your clothes properly, and allow the bedroom itself to be a space reserved purely for relaxation and rest. Follow these tips for the best results.

BEDROOM

230

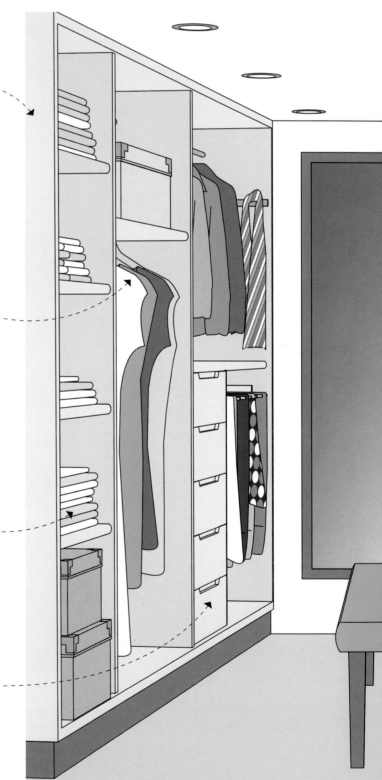

USE FITTED FURNITURE

Professionally fitted furniture allows you to maximize your storage space from floor to ceiling and work around any awkward angles and sloping ceilings. If your budget is low, try high street modular furniture, but plan it down to the last detail. Avoid having doors on the units: your clothes will be concealed by the box room door, or you can use a screen or curtain if your wardrobe area is within another room.

INCLUDE HANGING SPACE

Assess your current wardrobe and try to gauge how much hanging space you need, and of what type. Allow room for long garments, shorter clothes such as shirts and skirts, and consider including slide-out trouser hangers. The hanging rails needn't all be together; it makes more sense to group clothes according to type and season (all winter clothes together, all skirts together, all shirts together, and so on).

INSTALL OPEN SHELVING

Open shelving is useful for clothes that you wear regularly and that do not require hanging, such as T-shirts, vests, and light sweaters. Also install highline open shelving above head height for items you rarely need to access.

FIT DRAWERS OR BASKETS

Whether you choose drawers in which to store bulky sweaters that don't need to be hung or baskets for lighter items such as underwear, you will find them a useful addition. If you can, create a dressing table by incorporating a drawer for make-up at tabletop height, with legroom beneath and a mirror above.

INSTALL GOOD LIGHTING

Effective lighting is a must. Install lights within units with deep hanging spaces and above or around a dressing table. Also ensure the room is well lit, if not by daylight then by recessed downlights (which give a daylight-like effect) or overhead spotlights.

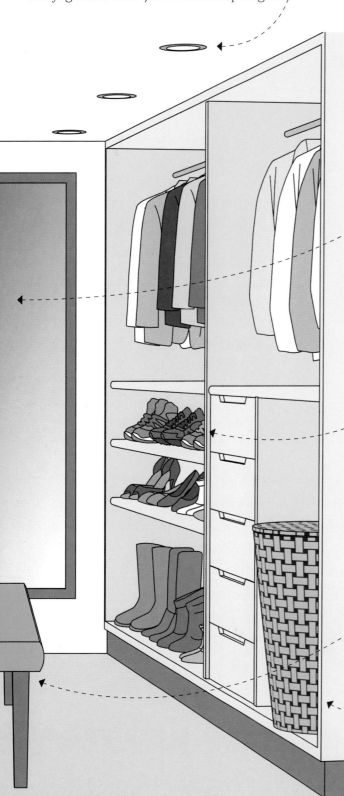

COMPARTMENTALIZE YOUR SPACE

If you share a wardrobe with your partner, it makes good sense to divide it in two and design each half separately. This will help you to make better use of space, prevent you mixing up your clothes, and create a more organized wardrobe overall.

HANG A MIRROR

A full-length mirror is a must in a walk-in wardrobe. Fix it to an empty wall or to the front or the back of a door. If you have ample floor space, opt for a free-standing mirror in one corner. Ensure that the light around the mirror is good, and if you will be applying make-up at a dressing table, add a second mirror above your make-up drawer.

MAKE ROOM FOR SHOE STORAGE

Divide your shoe storage into separate sections for sports shoes, everyday and evening shoes, and boots. Install sloping shelves for shoes (or shelves with a rod for the arch of each shoe to rest on) and open shelves for boots with space above. Never underestimate how much shoe storage you need.

MAKE SPACE FOR SEATING

It is always helpful to have somewhere to sit in a walk-in wardrobe, and especially important if you have included a dressing table. A simple stool, that you can approach from all sides, is a practical choice. Alternatively, consider a bench running down the centre of the space, or one built into a run of storage units against the wall.

ADD A LAUNDRY BASKET

If you will be undressing in the walk-in wardrobe, include a laundry basket in your scheme. It should be lidded to keep the space smelling fresh and looking neat. To save space, it could even double up as a bench with a lift-up lid and storage within.

REVAMP
A WARDROBE

If you have wooden furniture that is still good but won't suit your new decorating scheme, consider whether you could revamp it rather than replacing it. This sequence shows you how to transform an old pine wardrobe, giving it an aged, antique look.

WHAT YOU NEED

- Medium-grade sandpaper
- Tack cloth or general-purpose cloth
- Knotting solution
- Basecoat wood paint
- Two tones of interior wood paint (one lighter, the other slightly deeper or a subtly contrasting colour)
- Paintbrushes (including a pure bristle brush)
- Fine-grade sandpaper (wet-to-dry)
- Clear lacquer

1 PREPARE THE WOOD

1 SAND ALL THE WOODEN surfaces of the wardrobe (including the insides of the doors if you want to paint them) to get rid of as much old varnish as possible and create a "key" for the paint to adhere to.

2 WIPE DOWN THE WOOD with a tack cloth or a slightly damp general-purpose cloth.

3 PAINT OVER ANY KNOTS in the wood with knotting solution and allow to dry (see the manufacturer's instructions).

1 **APPLY A LAYER** of basecoat paint to the wardrobe and allow it to dry (see the manufacturer's instructions).

2 **APPLY AN UNEVEN COAT** of coloured paint using a pure bristle brush with loose bristles. Drag the paint roughly over the wood in any direction. Keep the brush as dry as possible by dabbing any excess paint from the brush with a cloth.

3 **BUILD UP THE TEXTURED LAYERS** of paint until you are happy with the colour. The more layers of paint you apply with the bristle brush, the deeper the colour and the stronger the texture. Allow to dry.

4 **PAINT A DEEPER** or subtly contrasting colour into the recesses and corners of the wardrobe using the same rough, dry-brush technique. Allow to dry.

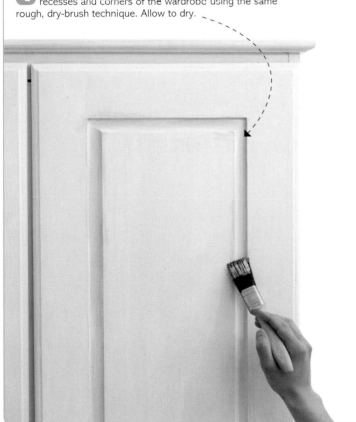

5 **APPLY ANOTHER LAYER** of basecoat using the dry-brush technique so that the layers of coloured paint beneath still show through. Allow to dry.

3 SAND DOWN THE WARDROBE

1 **LIGHTLY SAND** areas of the wardrobe with fine-grade sandpaper to create the impression of ageing.

2 **PAY ATTENTION TO CERTAIN AREAS** – in particular, along the edges and corners of the wardrobe frame and the panels of the doors – as you sand.

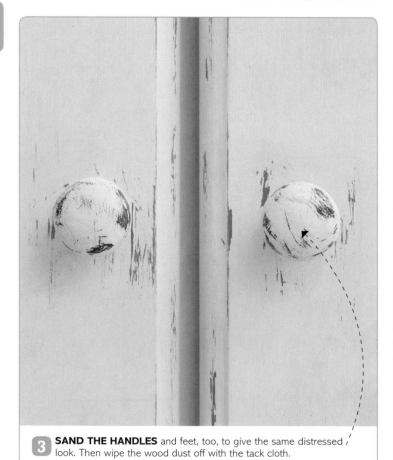

3 **SAND THE HANDLES** and feet, too, to give the same distressed look. Then wipe the wood dust off with the tack cloth.

4 COAT WITH LACQUER

APPLY A COAT or two of lacquer to protect the surfaces of the wardrobe, if you wish.

BEFORE

8 CHOOSE
BEDSIDE UNITS

Usually bought in pairs for double bedrooms, bedside units come in modern and traditional styles and a variety of materials, including wood, acrylic, and mirrored glass. Whether you match them to your other bedroom furniture or go for an eclectic, contrasting style, ensure they suit your storage needs.

CHOOSE THE TYPE

When considering which type of bedside unit you want, think how you will use it and whether it has to provide you with storage. Bedside units are available in many different designs, from simple tables to those with open shelving or drawers.

TABLE
If you only want something on which to stand a lamp and an alarm clock, go for a neat, streamlined table. Many such units have a single drawer or shelf to provide limited storage.

DRAWERS
Bedside units with drawers are a good option for small bedrooms where other storage space is limited. They will also help an otherwise cluttered space feel more streamlined.

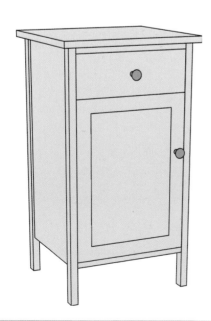

CUPBOARD
A cupboard unit allows you to store larger items that may not fit easily into a drawer. Remember though that cupboard space is more difficult to organize than drawer space.

SHELVING
In a contemporary, streamlined room, open shelving within a bedside unit is a good choice, assuming you can keep the contents neat. Or use the unit as a mini bookcase.

9 CHOOSE
A DRESSING TABLE

A dressing table can be a useful addition to a bedroom: as well as providing a place to get ready in the morning, it can also free up valuable storage space in the bathroom, and can even double as a spot where you can sit and do some home administration.

CHOOSE THE TYPE

If your dressing table is purely to provide a place where you can do your hair and makeup, most types will be suitable; however, if you need it to double up as a desk, check there is adequate table space and ensure you can keep it free from clutter.

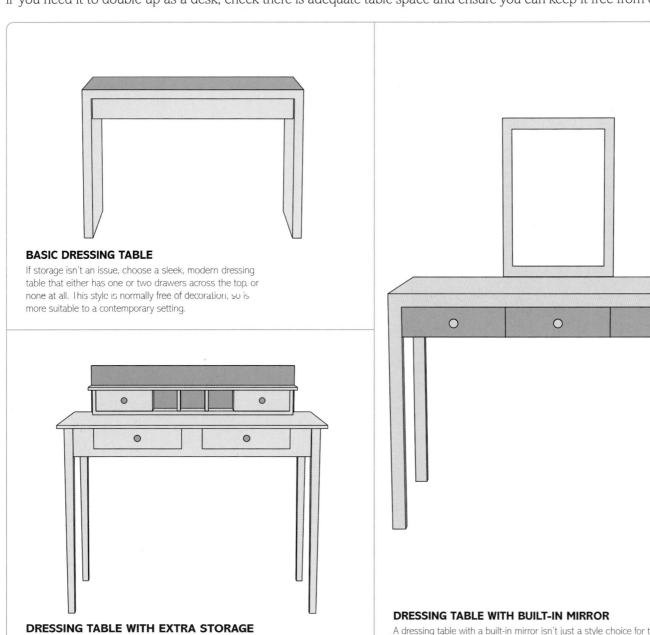

BASIC DRESSING TABLE

If storage isn't an issue, choose a sleek, modern dressing table that either has one or two drawers across the top, or none at all. This style is normally free of decoration, so is more suitable to a contemporary setting.

DRESSING TABLE WITH EXTRA STORAGE

To minimize clutter, a dressing table with drawers, cupboards, or a combination of the two will allow you to keep beauty products and accessories close at hand, but out of sight.

DRESSING TABLE WITH BUILT-IN MIRROR

A dressing table with a built-in mirror isn't just a style choice for those who like a classic boudoir look, it's also a very practical buy because it allows you to keep both hands free while doing your hair and make-up. For the best possible view of yourself, choose one with a triple mirror.

5 WAYS WITH
BEDSIDE LIGHTING

Good bedside lighting is essential for both practical and decorative purposes. From a decorative point of view, low-level lighting is vital for making a bedroom feel welcoming; from a practical angle, a bedside light to read by – or save you having to get out of bed to turn off an overhead light – is a must-have.

ANGLEPOISE

An anglepoise lamp, either a small version that stands on the bedside table or a large version that stands on the floor, gives you lots of scope to adjust the angle and height of the beam.

RETRO-STYLE anglepoise lamps are available in a range of colours, so choose one that suits the look of your bedroom.

TABLE LAMPS

Table lamps are a classic choice for bedside lighting. Look for ones that will complement the style of the other lights in the room.

THE SIZE of the lamps you choose should be in proportion to the size of your bedside tables.

CLIP ON

If you have a tall headboard or a shelf behind your bed, clip-on lighting provides a versatile solution that can easily be moved.

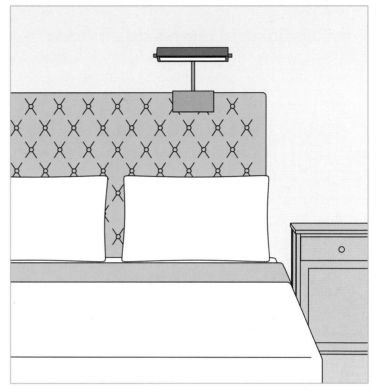

PENDANT

Pendant lighting over bedside tables creates a contemporary look. Ensure that the size of the shade doesn't dwarf the table below.

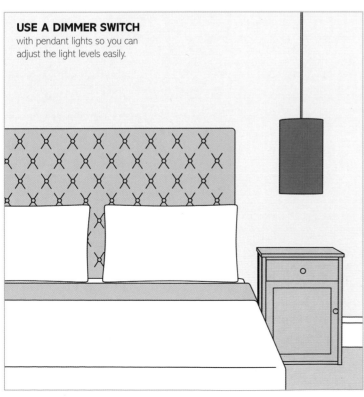

USE A DIMMER SWITCH with pendant lights so you can adjust the light levels easily.

WALL LIGHTS

Wall lights won't take up any space on your bedside table, and in small rooms they won't dominate the space.

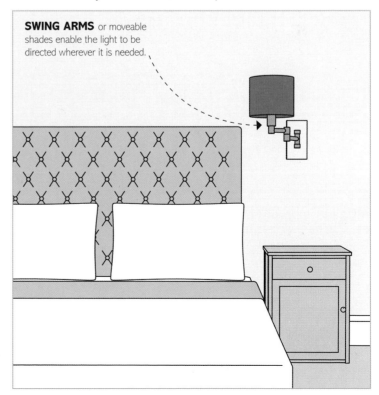

SWING ARMS or moveable shades enable the light to be directed wherever it is needed.

10 CHOOSE LIGHTING

Whether you spend time in your bedroom during the day or not, you will need good lighting first thing in the morning – ideally natural daylight, or at least effective task lighting – and soothing lighting at night. You might also want your lights to improve the room's proportions, and naturally you'll want them to look good.

1 DECIDE ON A STYLE OF LIGHTING

Just as in other rooms, aim for a combination of lighting styles that can achieve a variety of moods in the room at any given time. If you apply make-up, do your hair, or dress in the room, you'll also need good task lighting to see what you're doing.

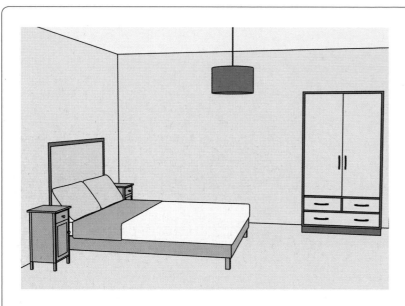

AMBIENT

Ambient lighting is vital in a bedroom. Particularly in the evenings, you will undoubtedly want to dim the lights to help you unwind before bed. Lamps and overhead lights are usually the primary sources of ambient lighting; make sure you include a dimmer switch for adjusting the latter.

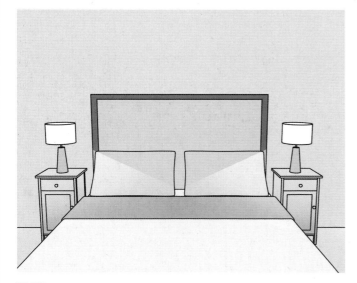

TASK

Task lighting in a bedroom may be a lamp that you use for reading in bed or an over-mirror light that allows you to see yourself clearly close-up. In the mornings, daylight is often the best source of light so don't ignore this in favour of artificial light if you can arrange your room in such a way as to use natural light effectively.

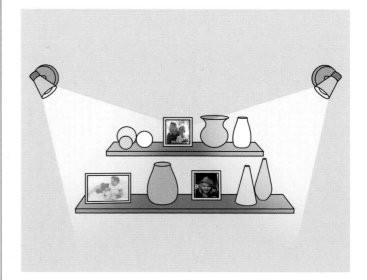

ACCENT

Accent lighting is typically used to show off a piece of art or sculpture, or perhaps illuminate a focal point such as an architectural detail. In a bedroom, you can also use it to illuminate a bookshelf or a favourite collection. You won't need a high level of accent lighting in a bedroom, so use it sparingly.

2 CHOOSE YOUR LIGHT FITTINGS

An average-sized double bedroom may only have two or three lights, so ensure they work together design-wise and provide the right levels of light. You needn't go for coordinating pieces, just ensure they don't compete with each other for attention.

CEILING LIGHTS

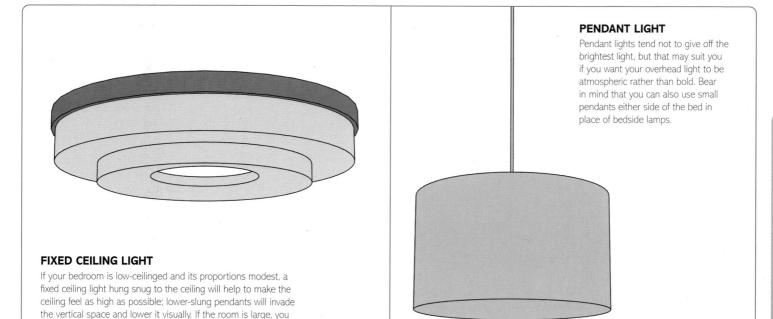

PENDANT LIGHT

Pendant lights tend not to give off the brightest light, but that may suit you if you want your overhead light to be atmospheric rather than bold. Bear in mind that you can also use small pendants either side of the bed in place of bedside lamps.

FIXED CEILING LIGHT

If your bedroom is low-ceilinged and its proportions modest, a fixed ceiling light hung snug to the ceiling will help to make the ceiling feel as high as possible; lower-slung pendants will invade the vertical space and lower it visually. If the room is large, you can afford to go for a show-off fitting that hangs lower down.

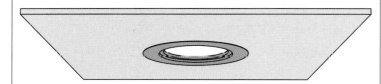

STATEMENT LIGHTING

If you have a large bedroom, choose a statement light as your centrepiece and ensure it can be used with a dimmer switch. Otherwise, you'll find that you only switch it on occasionally. Match it with bedside lamps in a similar style, but that don't compete for attention.

RECESSED DOWNLIGHTS

A contemporary bedroom that's north facing or has a low ceiling will benefit from recessed downlights, especially on dark mornings when you'd really prefer natural daylight. However, don't use recessed downlights as your only source of bedroom lighting – team them with some lamps and fit a dimmer switch so that you can adjust the light levels as you wish.

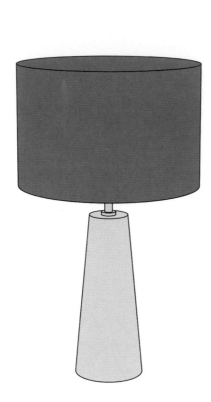

TABLE LAMPS

Just as table lamps in a living room create soft pools of relaxing light, bedside lamps conjure up a similar atmosphere. Bear in mind when installing them that they need to be fixed, or sit, at the right height so that when you lie in bed reading, the light illuminates the space but doesn't shine right into your eyes.

FLOOR LAMPS

If you have room in your bedroom for an armchair, a floor lamp standing next to it makes a nice decorative feature, but it may also encourage you to sit and read there or spend time doing craft projects. Ensure the shade isn't too large for the room and that it provides you with decent task lighting if you will be using the light in this way.

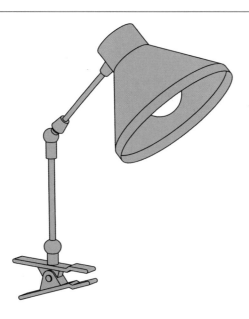

CLIP-ON LIGHTING

Clip-on lights, attached to a headboard or a shelf above the bed, are a good lighting solution in bedrooms where there isn't the space for a bedside table and lamp. You could also consider including them, regardless of what other lighting you have, if you need an extra light source for discreet late-night reading.

WALL-MOUNTED LIGHTS

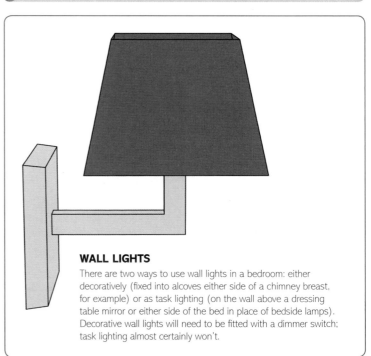

WALL LIGHTS

There are two ways to use wall lights in a bedroom: either decoratively (fixed into alcoves either side of a chimney breast, for example) or as task lighting (on the wall above a dressing table mirror or either side of the bed in place of bedside lamps). Decorative wall lights will need to be fitted with a dimmer switch; task lighting almost certainly won't.

11 CHOOSE WINDOW TREATMENTS

There are two considerations to think about when choosing how to dress bedroom windows. Firstly, will the combination of dressings keep out light, noise, and cold efficiently? Secondly, does your choice work decoratively to help you create a scheme that's comfortable and relaxing?

1 CHOOSE A TYPE

The style of your room – contemporary and pared back, or traditional and layered – will help you choose whether to opt for more than one type of dressing, such as blinds with curtains, or stick to a single, subtle treatment such as sleek shutters.

BLINDS

Fabric roller and Roman blinds are a good choice if you want to introduce layering, colour, and pattern to a bedroom. Their design means you can pull them fully up or down, or anywhere in between. Venetian blinds are typically left down with the slats open or closed.

CURTAINS

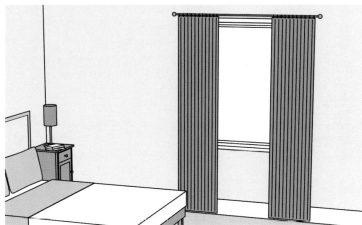

Curtains, whether full- or sill-length, are a good way of adding colour, pattern, and texture to your room's scheme and, depending on the fabric and curtain heading you choose, can be used in both traditional and modern homes.

SHUTTERS

Shutters are a popular choice for period homes, but they look smart in modern homes, too. Solid shutters are available in limited designs. Louvred shutters can be designed with either two or three panels and in styles including full-height and tier-on-tier.

CHECKLIST

- **To keep out as much** street lighting as possible at night, consider adding blackout roller blinds under curtains, or buying blackout-lined Roman blinds.

- **If your windows** are not double-glazed, heavy, lined curtains will help prevent heat loss. They can also give the room a visual warmth.

- **Consider the amount of space** around your window and ensure that you will be able to pull back curtains fully or open shutters. By doing so you can make the room seem larger and let in more light.

2 CHOOSE A STYLE

Each type of window dressing can look traditional or modern depending on its materials, its pattern or design, and what it's matched with – bed linen, wall coverings, and flooring. Base your choice on these other elements so that they all work together.

BLINDS

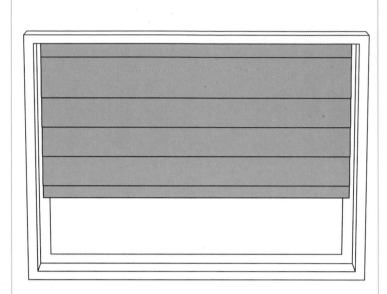

ROMAN

Roman blinds have soft pleats that hang flat against the window when lowered and fold neatly together when raised, which gives them a more layered look than other blinds. Available in a wide choice of fabrics, they are particularly attractive when matched with curtains.

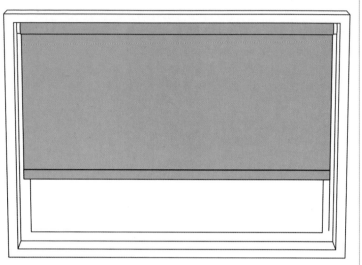

ROLLER

Roller blinds are a fairly inexpensive option and, providing you're a competent DIYer, are easy to fit. Blinds are made from stiffened fabric and available in a wide range of colours and designs, and can be pulled up or down to block out or let sun in. Many ready-made roller blinds can be cut smaller to fit your window exactly.

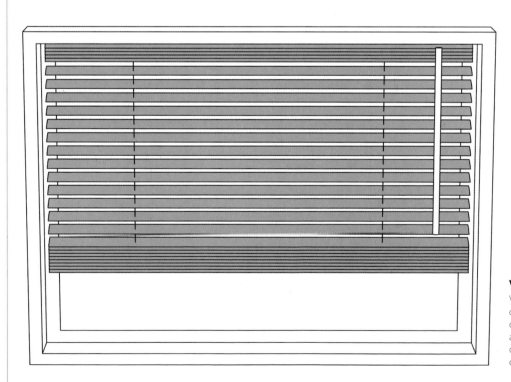

VENETIAN

Venetian blinds have adjustable slats that you can open and close, allowing you to control the amount of light coming through the window. The angled slats also mean they are good for windows that may be overlooked by neighbours. They are available in a choice of materials, colours, and slat widths.

CURTAINS

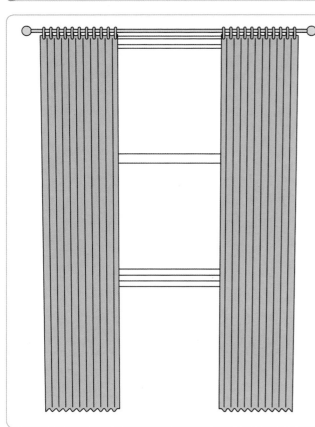

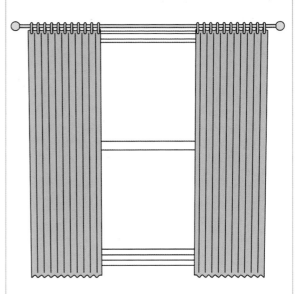

FULL LENGTH

Full-length curtains should typically finish 1 cm (½in) from the floor, but if you want a more luxurious finish, have them made longer so that they drape – or pool – onto the floor. Lined curtains hang better than unlined, and the lining also improves both the insulation and the appearance of the top fabric.

SILL LENGTH

For small windows, or country-style bedrooms, sill-length, or just below sill-length, curtains may be a more practical choice, as they sit neatly at your window. These curtains are also worth considering if your radiators sit directly below a window. This curtain length can look old-fashioned, however, so pick your fabric carefully.

SHUTTERS

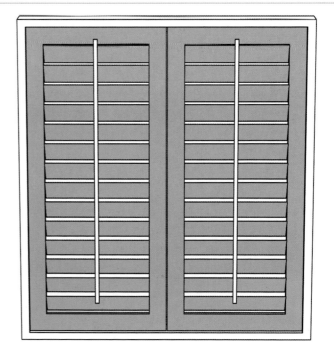

SOLID

Made from solid wood, solid shutters can assist in reducing noise levels, so they are a good choice if you live on a busy road. Designed to be closed shut at night and folded back against the wall during the day, this style of shutter particularly suits tall, thin windows, but is also good for bay windows.

LOUVRE

Louvred shutters suit both modern and traditional bedrooms. The best options are tier-on-tier or full-height shutters with a mid-rail, which allows you to control the top and bottom sections independently, so you can close the bottom half for privacy and leave the top slats open to let in light.

MAKE
BLACKOUT CURTAINS

Curtains lined with a blackout lining will keep unwanted light out of a bedroom, helping you get a peaceful night's sleep. The curtains made in this sequence are just below sill-length with a pencil pleat heading that can be used with any kind of pole or track.

WHAT YOU NEED

- Tape measure
- Fabric – use curtain-weight cotton material (see page 384 for quantity)
- Blackout lining (see page 384 for quantity)
- Scissors
- Sewing machine, or needle and thread
- Iron
- Pins
- Pencil pleat tape
- Curtain hooks

1 MEASURE AND CUT

1 DETERMINE WHAT LENGTH the finished curtains need to be by measuring from the top of the curtain track or pole to just below the sill.

2 CUT THE FABRIC to length, adding an extra 25cm (10in) for hem and top edge allowance.

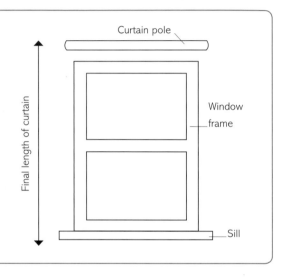

Curtain pole

Window frame

Final length of curtain

Sill

2 JOIN THE FABRIC

JOIN TOGETHER lengths of fabric to make up the necessary width (for these curtains to hang nicely, the width of each should be roughly equivalent to the entire length of the track or pole). To join, place the lengths together, right side to right side, and sew a seam along one edge. Then open up and lay flat, right side down, and press the seam open with an iron.

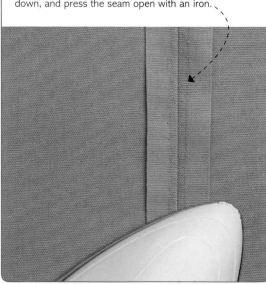

3 HEM THE FABRIC

1 MAKE A DOUBLE HEM at the bottom of each curtain. With the fabric right side down, turn over a 10cm (4in) hem and press.

2 FOLD AGAIN so that the raw edge is concealed within the hem, and press again.

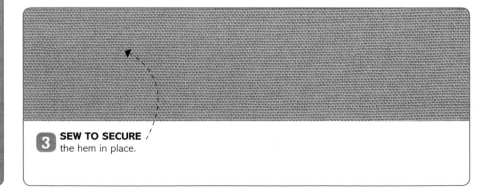

3 SEW TO SECURE the hem in place.

4 JOIN THE LINING

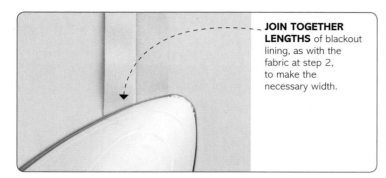

JOIN TOGETHER LENGTHS of blackout lining, as with the fabric at step 2, to make the necessary width.

5 HEM THE LINING

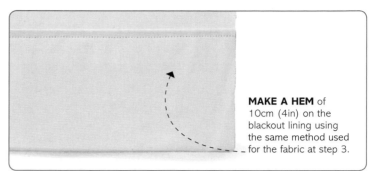

MAKE A HEM of 10cm (4in) on the blackout lining using the same method used for the fabric at step 3.

6 JOIN THE FABRIC AND LINING

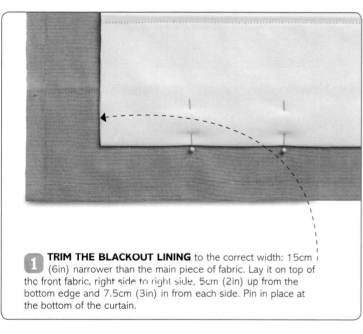

1 **TRIM THE BLACKOUT LINING** to the correct width: 15cm (6in) narrower than the main piece of fabric. Lay it on top of the front fabric, right side to right side, 5cm (2in) up from the bottom edge and 7.5cm (3in) in from each side. Pin in place at the bottom of the curtain.

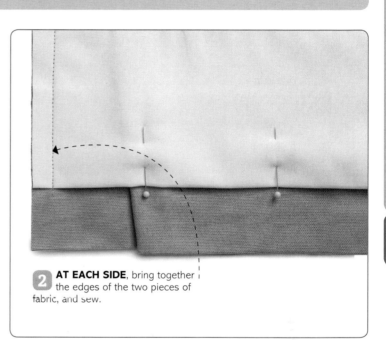

2 **AT EACH SIDE**, bring together the edges of the two pieces of fabric, and sew.

7 SEW THE CORNERS

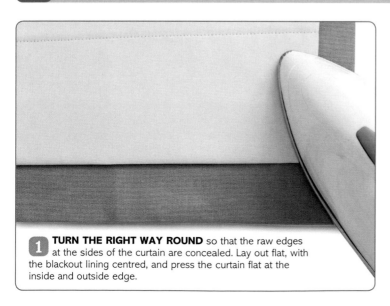

1 **TURN THE RIGHT WAY ROUND** so that the raw edges at the sides of the curtain are concealed. Lay out flat, with the blackout lining centred, and press the curtain flat at the inside and outside edge.

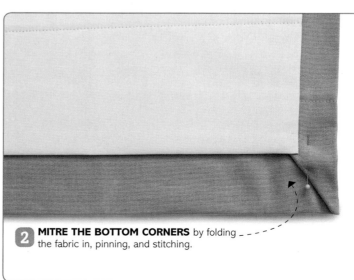

2 **MITRE THE BOTTOM CORNERS** by folding the fabric in, pinning, and stitching.

PLAN THE PERFECT
CHILD'S BEDROOM

Planning a child's room takes real thought, as it needs to accommodate activities such as playing and homework as well as sleeping, and it also needs to be able to evolve over time as your child grows. The following pages 250–267 are all about bedrooms for younger members of the family.

MAKE CLOTHES ACCESSIBLE

From the time children are about four – and often before they can even dress themselves – they want to select their own clothes to wear, so it makes sense to store their clothes in an accessible place. Look for versatile wardrobes with hanging space and shelves that can be slotted in to cope with your child's growing needs. Arrange everyday clothes in the lower drawers of a chest or wardrobe and save the top of the wardrobe for less well-used or out-of-season items. Fix any tall pieces of furniture to the wall so they can't be pulled over accidentally.

WORK IN STORAGE SPACE

When investing in storage, don't be tempted by anything themed or with a particularly fussy finish. Ideally, large pieces of furniture shouldn't have to be replaced – their style should endure and appeal for years. They should also remain as useful as when you first bought them: buy a changing table that can become a teenager's chest of drawers; a bookshelf of story books that can in turn hold CDs and study folders; and a wardrobe with shelves for small child's outfits that is easy to convert into hanging space for an adult-sized teen's clothes.

PROVIDE A STUDY SPACE

Once children start to get homework, they need a dedicated, quiet space to study. Look for a desk that's adjustable so it can be used by both a 10-year-old and an 18-year-old. Ensure that it has enough built-in storage, too, to hold stationery, exercise books and files.

CHOOSE FLEXIBLE FURNITURE

Your best option is to choose furniture that grows with your child. The bed will be your biggest buy, so consider one in a neutral colour that can be lengthened as the years pass. Or, pick a cot that can be transformed into a cot bed. If you can buy a bed with built-in (or underbed) storage, do so – the amount of storage space a baby requires can't begin to compare with that of a teenager. Whatever you buy, ensure it's stable, of a good enough quality to withstand the wear and tear of being in a child's room, and is easy to clean.

CREATE ZONES

However small your child's bedroom is, structure it so that there are defined areas for sleeping (the bed), playing (a rug and toy box or play table) and reading (a chair) or homework (a desk). Ensure that each area has its own, very functional, piece of furniture and handy storage nearby so that the areas don't become confused. Zoning the room like this will help to make it feel tidier and will make it easier for your child to keep it neat, too.

MAKE SPACE FOR PLAY

If you want to encourage your child to play in his or her bedroom, it's important to devote some floor space to this activity. Small children may want a table to colour at or an accessible toy box next to a comfortable rug; older children will appreciate a cosy corner with a beanbag or chair near a bookshelf for reading. If space is tight, you might have to furnish the room cleverly – with a bed on stilts and a play area beneath, for example.

1 CHOOSE FLOORING

When choosing the flooring for your child's bedroom, comfort is likely to be high up your wish list. However, you may also want to consider what part it plays in the decorating scheme and how easy it is to clean if the bedroom is used for activities other than sleeping.

CHOOSE THE MATERIAL

Children's bedrooms are likely to be subject to more wear and tear than an adult's bedroom, so you will need to choose something that is hardwearing and easy to clean. Softness underfoot and noise-reducing properties are also worth considering.

TILED

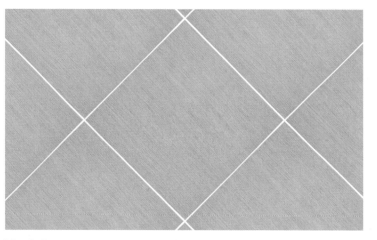

Vinyl tiles are an inexpensive floor covering and come in various colours and designs suitable for kids' rooms, including wood and metal treadplate. Rubber tiles are more expensive, but are hardwearing and are available in a huge range of colours and textures.

WOODEN

A wooden floor is a good choice for a child's room, as you can update the rest of the décor around it. Engineered wood can be fitted with an acoustic underlay, so is ideal for teenage bedrooms. Softwood, laminate, and wood-effect vinyl are cheap yet practical options.

CARPET

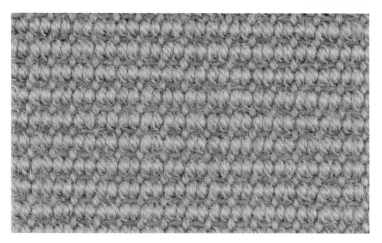

Carpet is soft underfoot and is available in a wide range of colours and designs, such as stripes, that are suitable for kids' rooms. If opting for a solid-colour carpet (which will show marks more easily than one with a fleck or pattern), look for an easy-to-clean material.

SEAMLESS

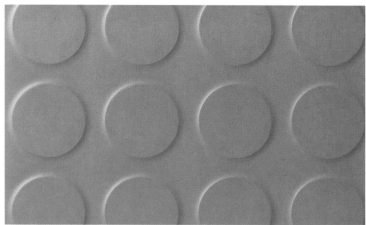

Vinyl, linoleum, and rubber sheet flooring are soft underfoot and any spills are easy to clean. Seamless floors, whether textured, plain, or patterned, are particularly good for small spaces, as the lack of joins give a neat finish.

2 CHOOSE
WALL COVERINGS

You can really have some fun decorating your child's bedroom walls. However, don't get too carried away with using a favourite theme throughout the room – your child is sure to grow out of it before too long and you may face the prospect of having to redecorate again.

CHOOSE THE MATERIAL

When choosing how to decorate your child's bedroom, your main concern should be how it looks. Just remember to also make sure that it has a surface that can simply be wiped clean, or touched up or repaired easily.

PAINT

The cheapest and quickest of choices, paint is available in a variety of finishes, but you are best off using silk or soft sheen paints, which are more durable than matt emulsions, and any marks can be wiped off without damaging the paint.

WALLPAPER

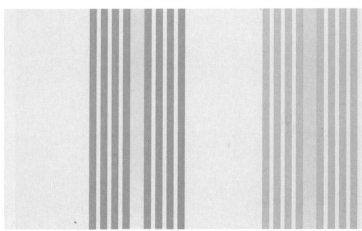

There are endless designs of patterned wallpaper available, although choose a design your child won't grow out of too quickly. It's also best if you pick a wallpaper that can easily be wiped clean of grubby fingerprints.

CLADDING

Tongue-and-groove cladding works well, as it's hardwearing and can be painted any colour you choose. The boards are usually made of pine (although you can buy pre-formed, routed MDF panels), and fixed vertically between the dado rail and skirting board.

CHECKLIST

● **If you choose a paint with a matt finish,** use a tester pot first and check the finish is not too chalky; if it is, it won't wipe down well if you need to remove marks or scuffs.

● **Have you got enough wallpaper** to decorate the whole room? It's worth buying an extra 10% wallpaper as a contingency, but ensure it's all from the same batch so the colours match perfectly.

● **Prepare your walls properly.** Whether your walls are being painted or papered, any cracks and holes need to be filled and sanded back and any unevenness needs to be smoothed.

MAKE AND APPLY
A WALL STENCIL

If you have chosen a theme for your child's bedroom, a wall stencil may help to pull the scheme together. This sequence uses a simple frog shape, a template for which can be found on page 386. Stippling (see step 3) is not essential, but it does help to give the image a little more depth and interest.

WHAT YOU NEED

- Paper (optional)
- Pen or pencil (optional)
- Acetate sheet
- Marker pen
- Craft knife
- Masking tape
- Wall paint
- Small sponge roller
- Stippling brush
- Acrylic varnish
- Paintbrush

1 MAKE THE STENCIL

1 DRAW AN IMAGE onto a piece of paper (skip this step if you are copying your image from an existing source).

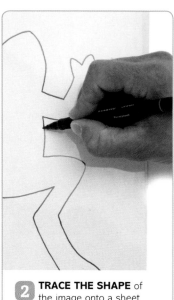

2 TRACE THE SHAPE of the image onto a sheet of acetate using a marker pen.

3 CUT OUT THE SHAPE with a craft knife. Discard the cutout and use the sheet of acetate as a stencil.

2 APPLY THE PAINT

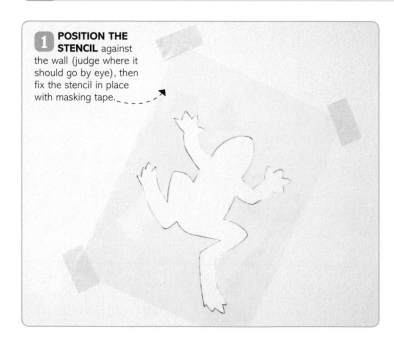

1 POSITION THE STENCIL against the wall (judge where it should go by eye), then fix the stencil in place with masking tape.

2 USING A SMALL SPONGE ROLLER, apply paint over the stencil onto the wall. Allow the paint to dry thoroughly (see the manufacturer's instructions).

3 ADD A STIPPLING EFFECT

1 TO CREATE A STIPPLING EFFECT – a dry-brush technique that gives a fine additional layer of paint – dab a slightly darker hue of paint over one half of the stencil with a dry stippling brush. Use a cloth to dab excess paint from the brush to keep it as dry as possible.

2 REMOVE THE MASKING TAPE and lift the stencil off the wall gently. Place it elsewhere on the wall to repeat the process.

4 VARNISH THE WALL

IF YOU WANT TO PROTECT the stencils (they may prove tricky to touch up later), apply a thin coat of acrylic varnish over the whole wall with a paintbrush.

3 CHOOSE A CHILD'S BED

Children's beds aren't always chosen as carefully as adult beds. Consider how comfortable it will be, now and in the future, and also how the bed can help you make good use of space in what is often a smaller room. Think, too, about its longevity and how soon your child might outgrow it.

1 CHOOSE A BASIC TYPE

Each type of child's bed has its own benefits, whether it be storage, accessibility, or additional floor space beneath. If you want the bed to last, opt for a wood or painted finish that will work with different decorating schemes.

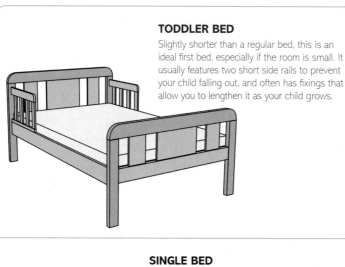

TODDLER BED

Slightly shorter than a regular bed, this is an ideal first bed, especially if the room is small. It usually features two short side rails to prevent your child falling out, and often has fixings that allow you to lengthen it as your child grows.

SINGLE BED

Single beds that will see a child through from toddler to teens are available in a wide choice of finishes, styles, and with or without headboards and footboards. If you are happy to buy for the short term, you can also opt for themed bed frames, such as racing cars or fairytale castles.

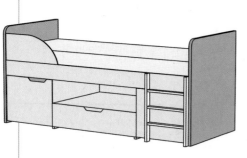

CABIN BED

This type of bed has built-in storage beneath it, making it a good choice for rooms that are short on space. There is a huge range of storage combinations available, including shelving, drawers, wardrobes, and desks.

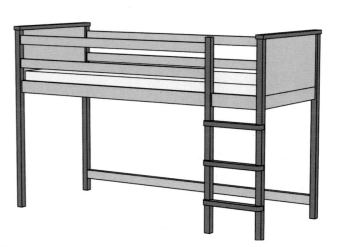

HIGH SLEEPER

If a bedroom is short on floor space, a high sleeper is a practical option for children of five years and over. The bed is raised much higher than a standard bunk bed (often high enough for an adult to stand beneath) allowing space below that can be used for other furniture or simply as a play space.

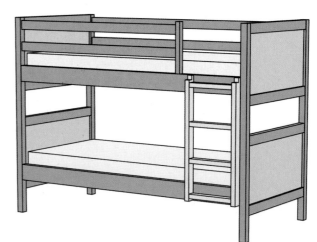

BUNK BEDS

Where children share a room, or a spare bed is needed for when guests stay, bunk beds are an ideal solution. As well as the classic single-over-single bunk beds, there are also options available, such as a larger bed on the bottom, with storage drawers, or a pull-out truckle that provides even more sleeping space.

CONSIDER ADDITIONAL FEATURES

There are many ways in which a child's bed can offer extra functionality. In a small bedroom, this can help compensate for limited storage space, play space, or workspace elsewhere in the room.

BEDS THAT CONVERT

If you're buying a cot, consider one that converts into a toddler bed to extend its life by another three years. The sides usually detach and the mattress can be lowered.

EXTRA SLEEPING CAPACITY

Whether you have houseguests regularly, your children have sleepovers, or you want to sleep near them when they are unwell, an underbed truckle – a slimline beds on wheels – is an invaluable buy. Simply pull it out when you need it.

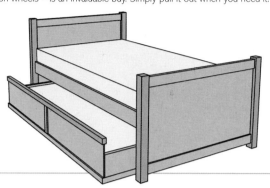

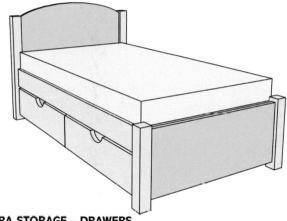

EXTRA STORAGE – DRAWERS

Drawers – whether built-in or separate – that occupy the space under a single bed are always useful. If the drawers are separate units, look for ones that roll out on wheels and have a lid, as dust tends to gather beneath a bed.

EXTRA STORAGE – WARDROBE

A raised bed with a wardrobe is the ideal buy if you need to store the maximum number of items within the minimum amount of floor space. Shop for a wardrobe with both hanging and concealed drawer/shelving options, as flexibility is key.

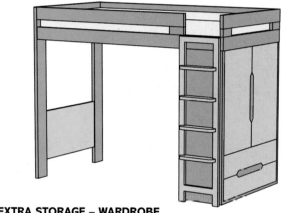

PLAY BED

If choosing a bed for a small child, you could opt for one with fun elements such as a slide or a wendy house area. If possible, choose one where the extra features can be stripped away when the child gets older.

BED WITH WORKSPACE

If your child needs a quiet place to study, a desk incorporated into the space under a raised bed will prove very useful. A model that also offers some storage, such as a chest of drawers, will ensure you make the best use of the space.

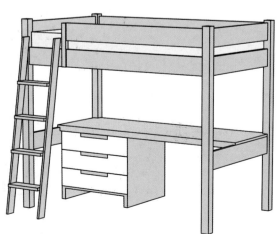

5 WAYS WITH
CHILD'S DISPLAY SPACE

Young children produce lots of paintings, models, and drawings that they – and you – will want to keep on show. However, the challenge is often in knowing how best to display them to create an attractive arrangement on your walls without it overtaking a room.

CORD AND PEGS

For a simple display that can quickly be taken down if you need the room to look smarter for visitors, fix lengths of cord across a wall and use clothes pegs to hang artwork and photographs.

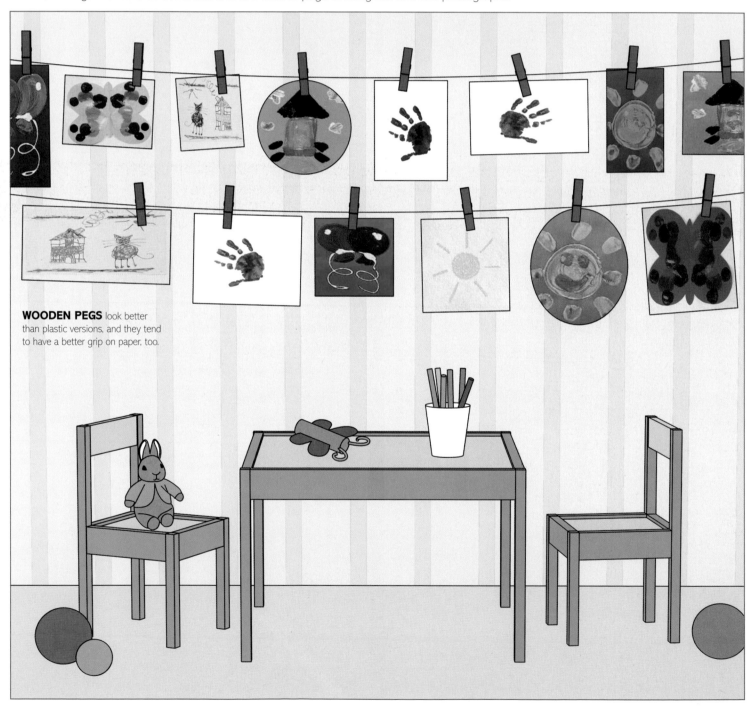

WOODEN PEGS look better than plastic versions, and they tend to have a better grip on paper, too.

BOX FRAMES

Painted box frames displaying models, collections, and awards can be hung on the wall or positioned on a shelf.

USE WALLPAPER within the frames if you want to create a more interesting background.

CORK BOARDS

Turn cork floor tiles into a pinboard or series of pinboards. Adhere the tiles to the wall in different arrangements and shapes.

LEAVE THE TILES natural or paint them to match or complement the wall colour.

BULLDOG CLIPS

Make a framework with slim wood battens and fix it to the wall with tacks. Attach bulldog clips to the horizontal battens with panel pins.

MAGNETIC WALL

Magnetic paint, applied as an undercoat before your chosen paint or wallpaper, can give you a whole wall on which to display artwork.

7 WAYS WITH
STORAGE

Children's bedrooms require storage for everything from clothes and equipment to toys and games. Unlike other rooms, the storage will need to be accessed easily – often at a low level, if your children are small – and be almost constantly on show, so it needs to be both functional and good-looking.

HANGING STORAGE BASKET

If you don't have free floor space, use baskets that hang from the wall or ceiling, and which are ideal for light items such as soft toys.

ENSURE THE BASKETS are fixed to the rafters within the ceiling so they won't fall down and damage the plasterwork or hurt a child if pulled or swung from.

WALL POCKETS

Colourful wall pockets are fun, practical, and decorative. Fix them low enough for a small child to be able to look inside the pockets.

UNDER-BED STORAGE

Make use of space under a bed with integral drawers or under-bed storage boxes, which are ideal for clothes, games, or toys.

SHELVING ON WHEELS

A storage unit on wheels gives you the flexibility to move it when space is needed for playing or other activities.

MAKE SURE there's a locking mechanism on the wheels.

SHELVING UNIT WITH BOXES

A shelving unit with a mixture of boxes or drawers and shelves is a good way to keep clutter out of sight and a room looking tidy.

BASKETS OR BOXES in a low-level shelving unit are ideal for concealing toys and encouraging a child to stay tidy.

STORAGE BENCH

A storage bench provides handy seating as well as somewhere to store away toys and games.

STORAGE BAGS

Large bags can be used permanently or temporarily for clothes, blankets, and toys, and are easy to store away when not in use.

HALLWAY

3 LAYOUT CONSIDERATIONS
FOR THE HALLWAY

A hallway is usually a long, thin area, with little room for manoeuvre, that has to accommodate a variety of bulky items while also making a good first impression. However, there are still ways in which you can improve the space immeasurably, both decoratively and functionally, and avoid ways of getting the layout wrong. Follow these layout tips to get it right first time.

CONSOLE TABLE

If your hallway is long and thin, you may only have one place for a console table – usually up against a left- or right-hand wall by the front door. If the hallway is too narrow for a table, hang a shelf at tabletop height on sturdy brackets in the same position, or perhaps over a radiator. If your hallway is wide, consider where the table might be best positioned from a decorative point of view. If you site it against a wall by the front door, position it centrally for balance; if it will stand opposite the front door, position it so it's the first thing you see as you come indoors.

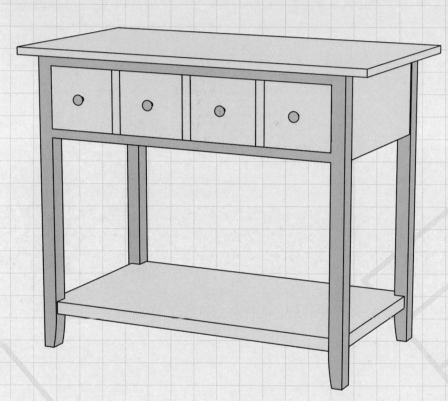

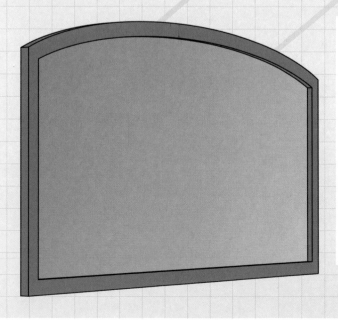

MIRROR

If you have room for a console table, hang a mirror centrally above it for a practical and decoratively attractive look. A wide mirror that matches the length of the console table will give a balanced look and help the hall to seem longer. If the room is too small for a table, place a long – even floor to ceiling – mirror adjacent to the front door (assuming the door has a glazed panel) to reflect natural light and make the hall seem wider. Or improve a small hall by hanging a large mirror opposite the front door.

COAT RACK OR STAND

A wall-hung coat rack is the best choice for a small hallway, as it takes up no floor space. Hang it on a wall with space either side so bulky coats won't be in the way. Think about how to conceal the rack and its contents – in a recessed space with a sliding panel or door in front, perhaps, or in an under-stairs cupboard – or buy a modern design in contemporary materials so that it looks as attractive as possible. A coat stand looks good in a hallway, but takes up floor space, so is best placed in a corner of a large hall.

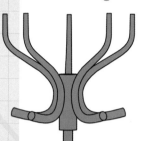

SHOE STORAGE

If you have a wall-hung coat rack, the natural place for shoe storage is beneath it (ideally not on show). Or store shoes in lidded baskets beneath the console table or in any deep drawers or shelves that the unit has. Narrow shoe storage units with hinged drawers that tip out (above) are also available, and you can use the top of the unit as a console table-like surface.

SEATING

If you have room near the front door, use the space for a bench or seat so that you can sit down to take off outdoor shoes. Or look for a bench with a lift-up lid so that it can provide more useful storage space for shoes and boots.

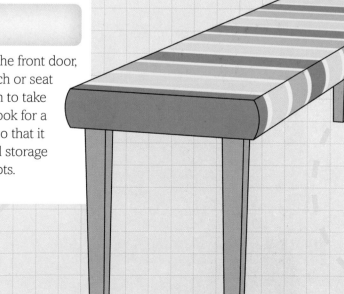

4 CHOOSE FLOORING

A hallway is the first impression you and your visitors have of your home, so the floor needs to look attractive. There's a huge range of good-looking yet hardy flooring available, but remember that this floor in particular is subject to lots of foot traffic, so it needs to be extremely hardwearing and easy to care for.

1 CHOOSE THE LOOK

While practicality is paramount, you will also want something that is stylish and consistent with the the rest of your home. Carpet is inviting, tiles look sleek or rustic, and wood floors can be both highly practical and attractive.

TILED

Tiled floors are the most practical choice for hallways, as they are easy to keep clean and generally easy to care for. Choose tiles in colours that hide dirt well. Lay the tiles diagonally to stretch the space visually if your hallway is small.

WOODEN

Wooden floors add warmth and character and, depending on which way you lay the planks, can make a short space feel longer or a narrow space look wider. Use parquet for pattern and interest if you have a plain scheme. Choose from a wide range of tones.

CARPET

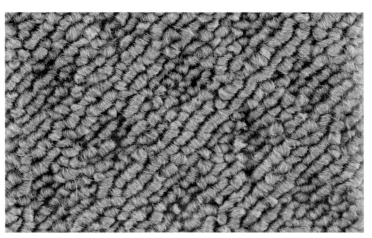

Bring colour and texture to your hallway with a carpet. Patterned designs are particularly good at hiding dirty marks and add interest to a plain room. The palest shades will show up dirt quickly, but don't be put off light tones, which will help a small space feel larger.

SEAMLESS

In open-plan ground floor hallways, poured concrete and poured resin floorings give a contemporary look. Think about the colour and finish when you consider this option – lighter gloss finishes will stretch the space visually, but may also show up marks and smudges.

2 CHOOSE THE MATERIAL

The material you choose for the floor needs to be resilient, easy to clean, and in a shade or finish that hides dirt. Tiles or wood are a practical option unless you are in the habit of taking off your shoes at the door, in which case a carpet will last well.

TILED

PORCELAIN
The smooth, non-porous surface of porcelain is easy to keep clean. It is available glazed (which may become slippery when wet) and unglazed in a range of prices.

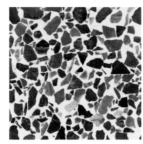
CERAMIC
Ceramic tiles are inexpensive and therefore a good choice if you have a large area to tile. They won't stain and don't need sealing, so are easy to look after.

TERRAZZO
These expensive, highly polished tiles of marble chips, cement, and colour pigment are hardwearing. They can be slippery if wet, so avoid them if you have children.

CONCRETE
Concrete tiles come in a range of colours and finishes, including polished, matt, or with exposed aggregates. These tiles are expensive yet hardwearing.

TERRACOTTA
This medium-priced porous tile is a good choice if you want a warm, inviting look for your hallway. Choose pre-sealed tiles or have your installer seal them.

TRAVERTINE
These expensive natural stone tiles come in various sizes and shades. They are also available with a sleek polished finish or a natural tumbled look.

LIMESTONE
High-cost limestone tiles are a good choice for brightening up dark hallways. Choose between highly polished gloss tiles or rougher matt finishes.

SLATE
The naturally uneven surface of dark slate tiles makes them less slippery than smooth tiles, and they won't show dirt. They are medium to high in price.

LAMINATE
These low- to medium-cost tiles offer a cheaper alternative to natural materials like slate and travertine, and you can fit them yourself to cut down on costs.

WOODEN

HARDWOOD
Medium to high in price this option is hardwearing and can be sanded to remove scratches and scuffs. To add more interest, consider using parquet flooring.

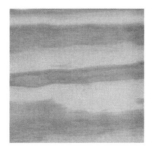
SOFTWOOD
If you like hardwood but don't have the budget for it, a low- to medium-priced softwood like pine is a good option. It may dent and mark, but it can be repaired.

ENGINEERED WOOD
This medium-priced floor looks like a solid wood floor, but can be fitted as a floating floor with an underlay, making it a good choice for uneven floors and flats.

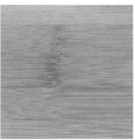
BAMBOO
Bamboo flooring is hardwearing, good-looking, and is medium to high in price. Choose a bamboo floor with an oil finish, which can be patch-repaired.

LAMINATE
If you're on a low- or medium-priced budget, laminate is a great choice. For the best effect, look for planks with realistic textured finishes and detailing or parquet.

CARPET

TWIST PILE

This low- to medium-priced hardwearing carpet has a coarse, rugged appearance. Patterns and heathers are better at hiding stains, so are good for hallways.

VELVET PILE

Medium to high in price, velvet pile carpet is hardwearing and feels comfortable underfoot. It has a dense low-cut pile and a smart, elegant look.

LOOP PILE

Loop pile carpet is made from yarn that forms loops on the surface of the carpet. Avoid if you have pets as their claws catch on the loops. It is medium priced.

SEAMLESS

CONCRETE

A modern option, polished concrete will give your hallway a contemporary, industrial look. Although expensive, it is extremely durable, and comes in a range of colours.

RESIN

Poured resin flooring comes in matt and gloss finishes and a range of colours. This expensive option suits open-plan spaces where the hall is part of the living area.

INSTALLING FLOOR LIGHTS

Recessed floor lighting can illuminate and add interest to your hallway, but it needs to be wired up before your flooring is installed.

- **The lights themselves will sit flush** with the floor, so they need to be recessed into the sub-floor. Get professional advice if your lights have to be recessed into a concrete sub-floor or you want to combine them with a carpet.

- **This type of lighting** creates a contemporary feel, so is best matched with a hard flooring such as tiles or wood.

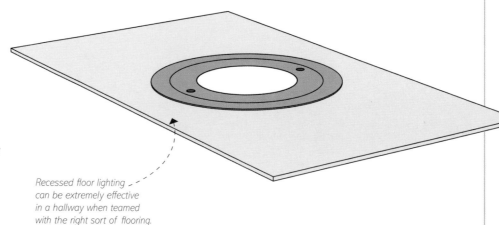

Recessed floor lighting can be extremely effective in a hallway when teamed with the right sort of flooring.

A LIVELY PATTERNED RUG can add colour and texture if you have opted for neutral hard flooring.

6 CHOOSE LIGHTING

A hallway is a tricky space to light because it tends to be a long, thin space, often with little natural daylight. The trick with lighting a hallway is to use it to make the space feel not just brighter but bigger. There are a number of ways to do this and a range of different lighting styles and types.

1 DECIDE ON A STYLE OF LIGHTING

If you are reworking your lighting plan from scratch, try to use a combination of accent and ambient lighting, however small your space, to allow you to create a range of lighting levels and atmospheres in what could otherwise be a characterless space.

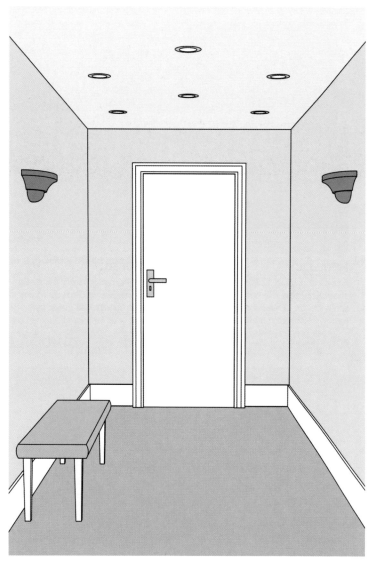

ACCENT

Accent lighting is all about creating an effect or an atmosphere. In a hallway, skirting board lights, or step lights on the stairs, can provide low-level accent lighting, while highlighting pictures on the walls is another good option. Clever use of accent lighting can make a hallway more interesting or exaggerate its proportions.

AMBIENT

The ambient lighting in your hallway should mimic natural daylight as closely as possible, so, unless yours is a very small space, it is best not to rely on a single pendant bulb that may be too weak to light the room effectively. Instead, consider recessed downlights or an arrangement of spotlights along the length of the ceiling, and find space for a table lamp to soften the mood when needed.

Consider your space first: a low ceiling won't suit a large pendant, but a grand hallway can accommodate a chandelier. Then think about the style of the lighting. A period home needn't have traditional lighting if contemporary options will work wonders.

CEILING LIGHTS

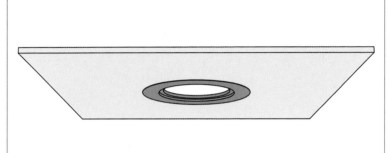

RECESSED DOWNLIGHTS

Recessed downlights are the perfect buy for a small, low-ceilinged hallway that needs to feel bigger and brighter, or a very long, thin hall, since the light they create tends to closely mimic daylight and is strong enough to throw light in every direction.

PENDANT LIGHT

If your hallway is small, a pendant light might suffice. Ensure that the shade hangs close to the ceiling so the tallest person in the house won't hit it if stretching up to put on a garment. Choose a shade, too, that's designed to throw light upwards and downwards – doing so will help to exaggerate space. If your hallway has a low ceiling, avoid pendants altogether.

STATEMENT LIGHTING

A statement light is ideally suited to a large, high-ceilinged hallway, and may need to be matched with other lighting styles, such as recessed downlights, to light the whole length of the hallway practically. Don't feel you have to stick to one piece if the hallway is large – a line of three or five smaller lights can be equally effective.

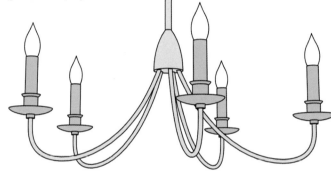

FIXED CEILING LIGHT

A fixed ceiling light should be picked for decorative effect. That means choosing a large chandelier or contemporary piece with a multitude of bright bulbs for a big, high-ceilinged hallway, or a line of attractive lamps for a long, narrow space that needs character.

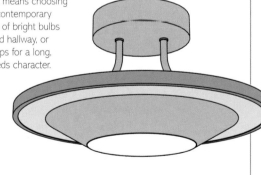

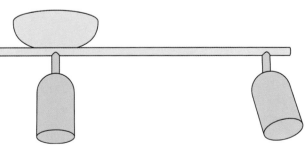

SPOTLIGHTS

A single lighting unit with directional spotlights will allow you to light the space practically and throw light onto elements of the room that you want to illuminate. This is an ideal choice if you are renovating a contemporary-style home.

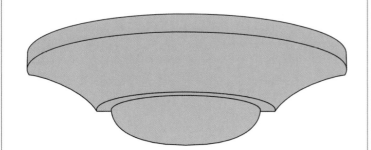

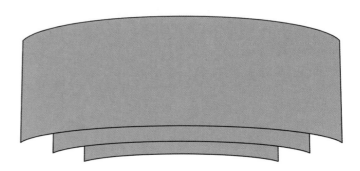

WALL UPLIGHTERS

If your hallway has a low ceiling, you should use every trick in the book to improve its proportions. The most effective way to do so is to use wall uplighters placed about two-thirds up the wall. These lamps will throw the light upwards to create a visual trick of raising the ceiling.

WALL LIGHTS

Using wall-mounted lamps is all about making the space look more interesting and playing with its proportions. A line of slim decorative pieces running the length of the hallway just above head height makes the hallway feel welcoming and, importantly, much longer.

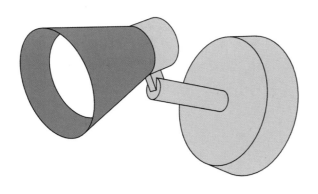

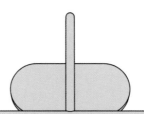

SINGLE SPOTLIGHTS

Single spotlights should be used to highlight an architectural detail, a picture, or a particularly attractive accessory such as a sculpture. The fittings themselves needn't be immediately visible, but the effect they create should be.

PICTURE LIGHTS

Picture lights won't light your hallway at all, but they will subtly highlight a favourite picture. They should ideally be used on medium to large pictures and, if you have a number of pictures, you should either light all of them, just the largest, or the picture hung in the focal point of the room – above the console table, for example.

FLOOR LIGHTS

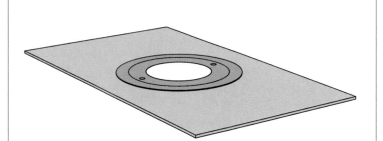

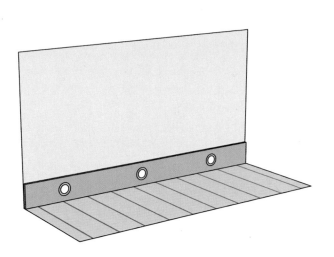

RECESSED FLOOR UPLIGHTERS

Recessed floor uplighters should be fitted along the length of a hallway, ideally on both sides. They are designed to sit close to the wall and subtly light it upwards; get a dimmer switch fitted so that you can vary the height the light travels, and bear in mind that it will highlight imperfections in the fabric of the wall.

SKIRTING BOARD LIGHTING

Typically set into the skirting boards that run up the length of one side of a flight of stairs, usually on every other step, skirting board lights can also be set into a flat floor every metre or so. Ensure that these lights are set low enough to skim the floor with light.

LAMPS

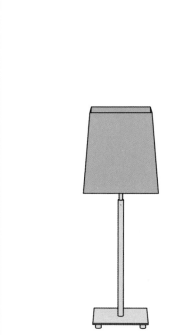

TABLE LAMPS

If you have a console table in your hallway, putting a lamp on it or, better still, a pair of matching lamps at either end, will make the room look more interesting decoratively and – once the task lighting is switched off – much more welcoming. If you only have room for a small corner shelf in your hallway, make space on it for a table lamp.

FLOOR LAMPS

A tall, floor-standing lamp, placed in a corner, is a good way to bring ambient lighting into a hallway that doesn't have room for a table. Ensure the shade isn't too bulky and won't be in the way as you walk past it, and that it's set at the right height – too low or too high and you'll be looking into the bulb as you walk past it.

FLOOR UPLIGHTERS

Floor uplighters are generally placed behind or adjacent to furniture to throw light upwards onto a wall. They create a similar effect to wall uplighters in terms of improving the hall's proportions, but their light tends to be less uniform and more about creating a dramatic effect.

5 WAYS WITH
MIRRORS

Putting a mirror in a hallway isn't just about having somewhere to check your appearance before you leave the house – or even about having a decorative piece to admire. Its main function is to improve the light and proportions of what might otherwise be a narrow, light-starved space.

LARGE MIRROR

A mirror hung over a console table just inside a glazed front door will reflect any light that comes through the door or a fan light window, if you have one.

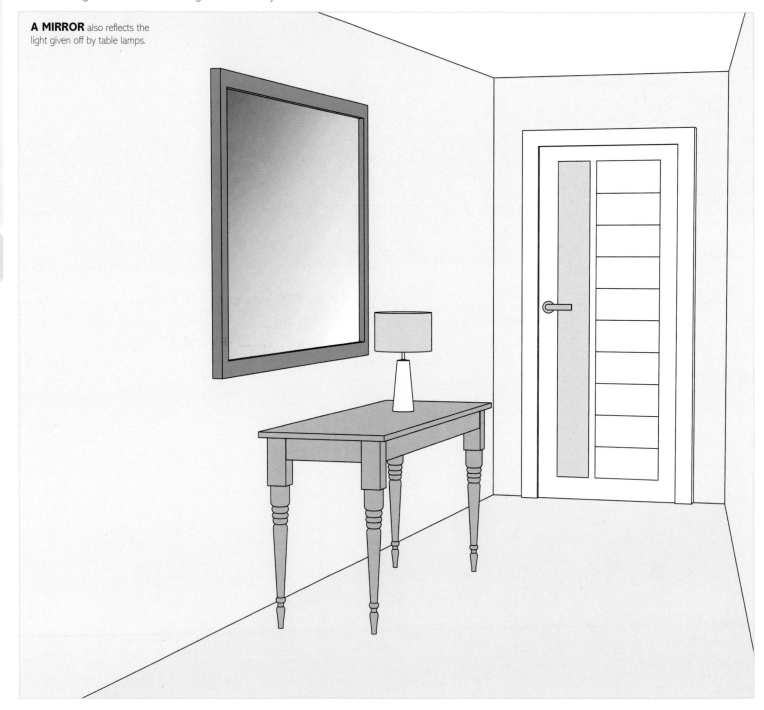

A MIRROR also reflects the light given off by table lamps.

FLOOR-TO-CEILING MIRROR

Small hallways will appear to expand when you hang a tall mirror. The taller the mirror is, the higher the ceiling will seem, too.

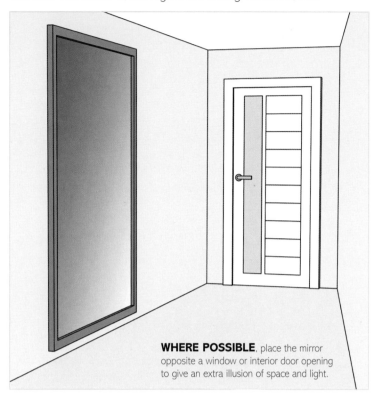

WHERE POSSIBLE, place the mirror opposite a window or interior door opening to give an extra illusion of space and light.

GROUPING OF VINTAGE MIRRORS

An assortment of vintage-style mirrors in varying shapes and sizes, and with different frames, will create a decorative and eclectic look.

TRY THIS look on a stairway wall, too.

END MIRROR

Hanging a floor-to-ceiling mirror at the far end of a short hallway will make the space seem longer.

MAKE THE MIRROR as wide as possible so it fills the wall space; this will help to widen the hall, too.

REGULAR GROUPING

Instead of hanging just one mirror over a console table, hang a grouping of smaller mirrors in a regular grid layout.

THIS WORKS with square, rectangular, and circular mirrors.

7 CHOOSE
HALLWAY STORAGE

As the first room you – and any visitors – will see when entering your home, your hallway should be kept as tidy as possible. Choosing the best storage solutions will help you achieve this aim. As hallways are generally narrow, busy areas, opt for streamlined pieces that can withstand everyday knocks and scuffs.

CHOOSE ITEMS

What you choose depends on your household's storage needs, so assess what you actually want to keep in the hallway: if you don't have space to store shoes in a bedroom wardrobe, for example, would a shoe rack in the hall be a satisfactory solution?

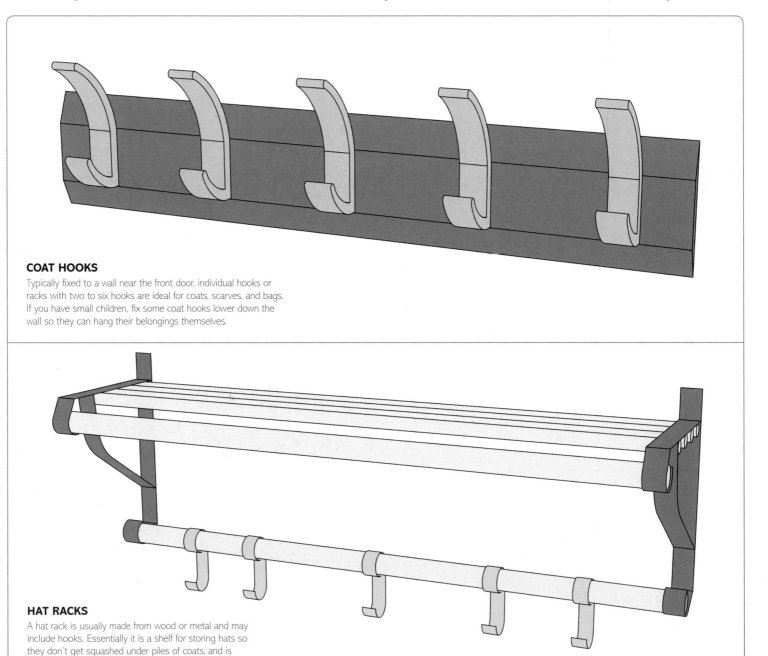

COAT HOOKS
Typically fixed to a wall near the front door, individual hooks or racks with two to six hooks are ideal for coats, scarves, and bags. If you have small children, fix some coat hooks lower down the wall so they can hang their belongings themselves.

HAT RACKS
A hat rack is usually made from wood or metal and may include hooks. Essentially it is a shelf for storing hats so they don't get squashed under piles of coats, and is normally hung just above eye level.

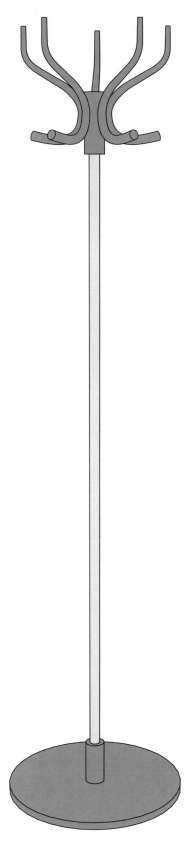

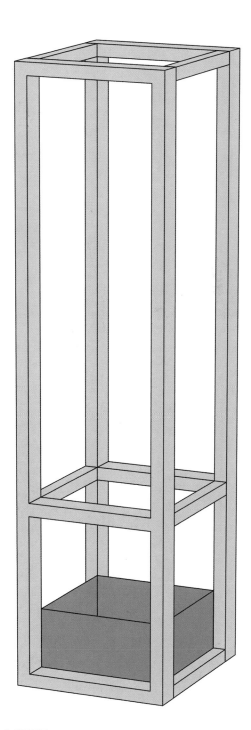

COAT STAND

Floor-standing coat stands are available in traditional and contemporary designs, with some also featuring storage space for umbrellas and hats. Try not to overload them with occasional-wear items, as they can take up quite a lot of space when full.

UMBRELLA STAND

If you regularly take an umbrella with you when you go out, a neat umbrella stand positioned near the door will help ensure you always have one in a convenient place, without taking up too much space.

7 WAYS TO
ADD CHARACTER TO A HALLWAY

While it is sensible to leave the hallway until after you have redecorated any other rooms, doing so means you risk running out of steam and creating a featureless space that doesn't work as hard as it should. Here are some tips on how to give your hallway a more stylish finish.

ADD A RUNNER

Add interest to a plain floor by adding a patterned or colourful runner. It will also add comfort underfoot in halls that have hard flooring.

A STRIPED RUNNER will give the appearance of a longer or wider space.

ADD STATEMENT LIGHTING

Make a statement with a striking ceiling light or, if you have low ceilings, an attractive table light.

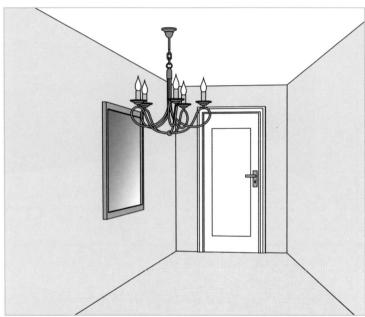

PICTURE GALLERY

Create a picture gallery using framed photos or art. This works successfully even in the narrowest of hallways.

HANGING FRAMES in one long line will draw the eye along the wall, making the hallway feel longer.

OPEN SHELVING

Wider hallways are the perfect place to add open shelving to store an overspill of books and display decorative objects.

IN SMALLER HALLWAYS consider hanging shallow shelves above and around door frames.

COLOURFUL FURNITURE

If you have space, use a sideboard or table painted in a bright colour, or a long footstool upholstered in a decorative fabric, to lift the room.

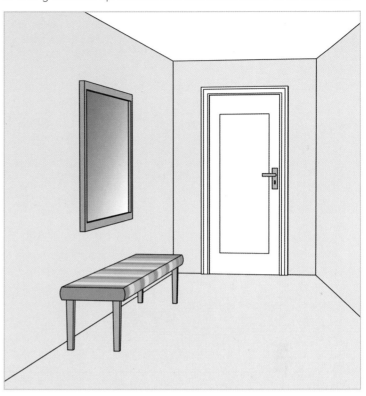

PAINT A WALL

One of the easiest ways to add character to a plain hallway is to create a feature wall using paint.

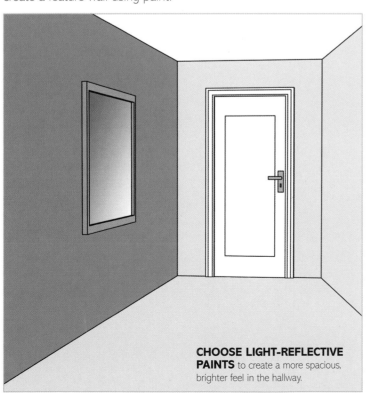

CHOOSE LIGHT-REFLECTIVE PAINTS to create a more spacious, brighter feel in the hallway.

STATEMENT WALLPAPER

Add personality to your hallway using a dramatic wallpaper with a large floral or geometric design.

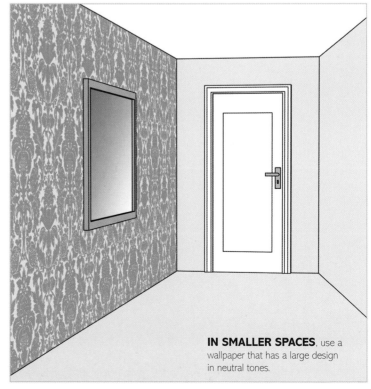

IN SMALLER SPACES, use a wallpaper that has a large design in neutral tones.

6 WAYS WITH
STAIRS

Although a staircase is an essential requirement if you live in a house or maisonette, you can turn it into an attractive feature or showpiece by adding character and individuality. Here are six durable, but good-looking, treatments for your stairs.

RUNNER

Lay a carpet runner, or use paint; apply a base colour to the whole staircase, then paint the central section in a contrasting shade.

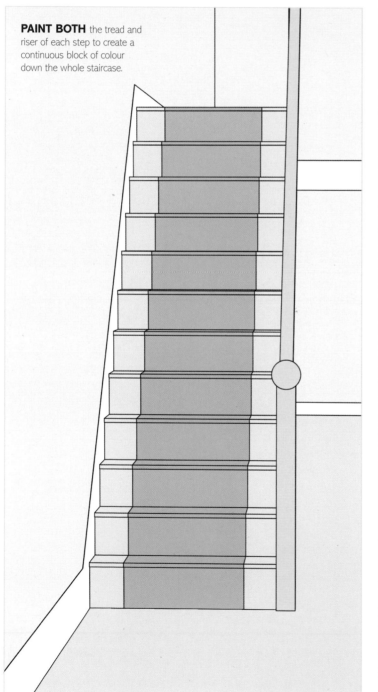

PAINT BOTH the tread and riser of each step to create a continuous block of colour down the whole staircase.

VARNISHED TOP, PAINTED RISER

For a classic look, varnish or stain the tread and paint the riser to match the rest of your woodwork.

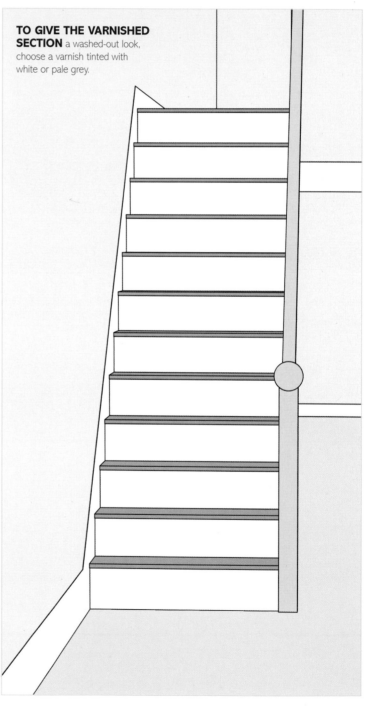

TO GIVE THE VARNISHED SECTION a washed-out look, choose a varnish tinted with white or pale grey.

CORK TREADS

Update tired treads by fixing corkboard floor tiles to each stair tread to provide a softer feel underfoot.

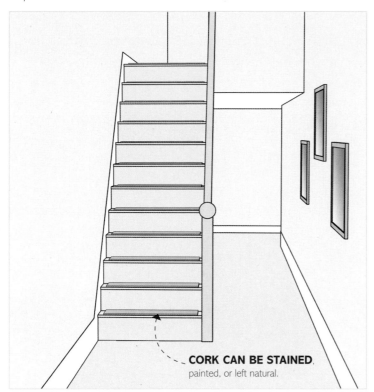

CORK CAN BE STAINED, painted, or left natural.

FULLY CARPETED

If your staircase is not made of an attractive wood that you would want to show off, fully carpeted stairs are a good option.

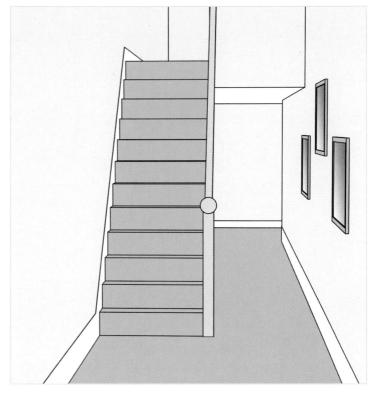

NUMBERED RISERS

Number each of your stair risers using either a painted stencil, transfer, or a number cut from paper.

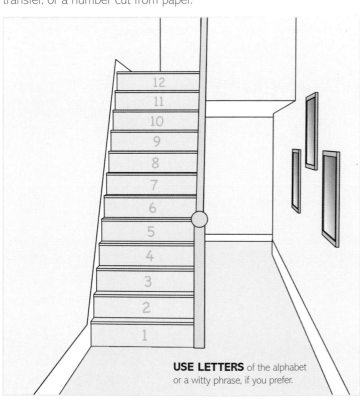

USE LETTERS of the alphabet or a witty phrase, if you prefer.

WALLPAPERED RISERS

Introduce pattern to your stairs by wallpapering the risers. Stick the paper down using wallpaper adhesive, glue, or double-sided tape.

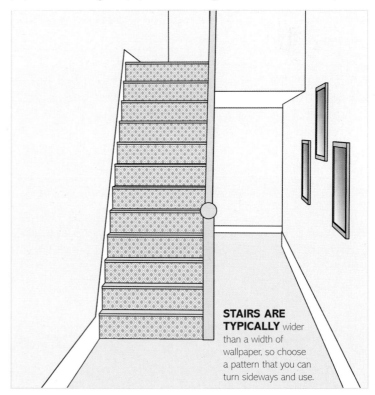

STAIRS ARE TYPICALLY wider than a width of wallpaper, so choose a pattern that you can turn sideways and use.

6 WAYS WITH
UNDER-STAIR SPACE

The area under the stairs is wasted in many homes but with proper thought and correct fitting-out it can become an invaluable space. Measure up the dimensions to see what you can realistically do with it, and consider whether custom-made furniture will help you to use the space more efficiently.

MEDIA UNIT

If your stairs are part of your living room, use the under-stair space to hide away your TV and other media equipment.

REMEMBER THAT YOU'LL NEED to install electric points if you choose this option.

UNDER-STAIR SEATING

Built-in seating can create a cosy nook for quiet reading, or to provide extra seating in your living room.

CONSIDER INCLUDING A WALL LIGHT or clip-on light to illuminate the space.

DRAWERS

Made to measure drawers use the space well and can be used to store shoes, scarves, gloves or equipment for outdoor games.

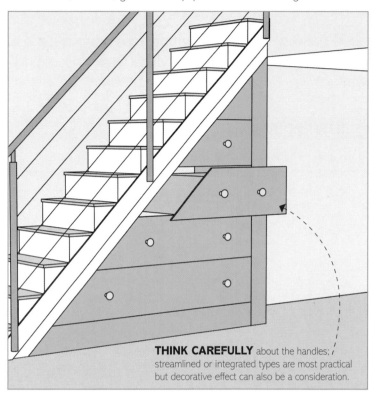

THINK CAREFULLY about the handles; streamlined or integrated types are most practical but decorative effect can also be a consideration.

PULL-OUT CUPBOARDS

Tall cupboards on runners are a good use of under-stair space. Shelving within will help keep them organized.

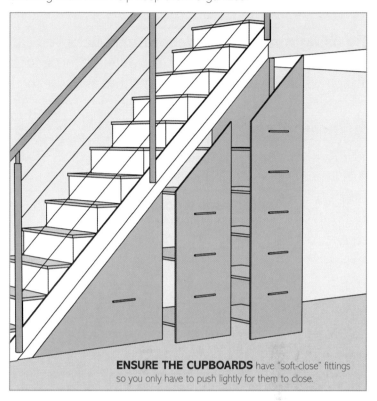

ENSURE THE CUPBOARDS have "soft-close" fittings so you only have to push lightly for them to close.

HANGING SPACE

Hang your coat rack under the stairs so that bulky outdoor clothes and bags won't encroach on the thoroughfare of the hallway.

YOU COULD ALSO add a shoe rack in the space underneath.

HOME OFFICE

If there's enough headroom, you can create a small home office area. Be sure to find furniture that will make good use of the space.

KEEP THE COLOUR SCHEME the same as the rest of the room so the workspace doesn't attract attention.

HOME OFFICE

1 WHAT TO DO WHEN REVAMPING YOUR HOME OFFICE

A home office will not be included in every home but if you are having one it will require careful planning to make sure it works not just decoratively but also functionally. Follow this schedule to get the appropriate tradespeople in and the work done at the right time.

1 DEVISE A BUDGET

If you're starting work from scratch, include plastering, wallpapering, and painting in your budget list. Include extra money for any wiring, equipment, and a good office chair, and allow yourself a contingency of at least 10 per cent.

2 PLAN THE LAYOUT

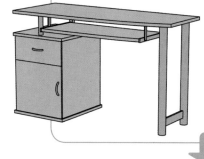

Draw a scale plan and include all doors and windows. Plot the position of the desk and, based on this, work out where to site the lighting and the phone/ internet and electrical points.

3 RETHINK THE HEATING

Consider whether you need to make changes to the heating system. You can easily become cold when sitting still at a desk and if the room was not an office to begin with, it may need better or more easily adjustable heating. Similarly, can you open the windows easily to cool the room?

4 BOOK TRADESPEOPLE

Contact an electrician, heating engineer, plasterer, and decorator to give you quotes. Ask a joiner or fitted furniture company for a quote for fitted storage, too. Ask them what their job entails so you get everyone in at the right time.

5 ORDER THE MATERIALS

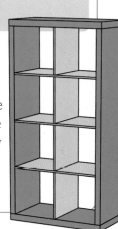

Once the quotes are in, order flooring, woodwork, doors, radiators, and windows, if being replaced. Furniture, wallpaper, paint, a carpet, and light fittings can be ordered once the main jobs are under way unless you have space to store them. If you are ordering new furniture, find out about lead times for delivery, as it may need to be ordered now.

6 GUT THE ROOM

Remove old wallpaper to see if the walls and ceiling need replastering or patching, rip out damaged woodwork and unrepairable mouldings, and pull up old flooring. Old electrics and redundant pipework should also be removed.

7 FIT NEW HEATING – FIRST FIX

Have the pipework for new radiators laid now, as it is a disruptive job and may stop other trades progressing.

8 INSTALL THE ELECTRICS – FIRST FIX

The electrician will lay cabling beneath the floor and into the walls and ceiling for the lighting system. The cabling and points for the phone/internet and additional equipment such as a printer should also be done now.

9 FIT NEW WINDOWS

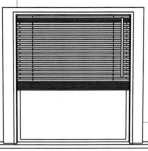

Tackle this task now before the room is replastered. If the windows are being renovated rather than replaced, prepare them for painting now.

10 PLASTER THE WALLS AND CEILING

If the walls and ceiling need plastering, employ a professional plasterer to do the work to get the best finish.

11 LAY THE FLOORING

While the plaster dries, lay hard flooring, such as a wooden floor, or a sub-floor for a carpet.

12 INSTALL FITTED FURNITURE

If you have chosen bespoke fitted office furniture, have the joiner install it before he fits the skirting and mouldings.

13 INSTALL THE WOODWORK

Once the fitted furniture is in place, the new woodwork – skirting boards, architraves, doors, door frames, and picture rails – can all be installed by the carpenter or joiner.

14 DECORATE

Fill fine cracks or dents in the walls. Prime and paint the ceiling, walls, and woodwork, and put up wallpaper last.

15 ORGANIZE THE SECOND FIX

The electrician can return to fix the light fittings and electric sockets, and the heating engineer to fit the radiator.

16 LAY THE CARPET

If you have chosen a carpet (or carpet tiles), now is the best time for it to be fitted.

17 ADD FINISHING TOUCHES

Any new furniture such as a desk, filing cabinets, and an office chair can be delivered now. Put up curtain poles or blinds, fix door furniture, connect up your equipment, and hang items like a noticeboard on the wall.

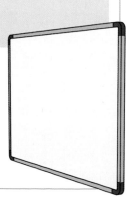

2 CREATE A MOOD BOARD
FOR YOUR HOME OFFICE

Whether your home office is large or small, it needs to feels calm and organized. Getting the colour palette, patterns, and furnishings right first time will enable you to create an area that's not only well put together and uses space effectively, but is inviting and comfortable to work in. Using a mood board will help you to create the most successful scheme for this often overlooked room.

1 FIND PICTURES OF HOME OFFICE ROOMS you like the look of by searching the internet and looking through magazines and books. Tear them out, print them off, or copy them and lay them all out on the floor. You might notice a theme begins to emerge, whether it's a liking for a type of wood or a furniture shape. This will be the starting point for your room scheme.

Edit your selection of home office pictures down to one or two favourites and stick them to your mood board.

2 PICK A KEY ITEM or a theme to help you find a direction for your scheme. Use it as inspiration for everything from colours and shapes to patterns and textures when searching for the other components of the room.

Your favourite item could be a retro filing cabinet, anglepoise lamp, or antique desk.

3 **PICK A BACKGROUND COLOUR** for the room. Whether you choose a light, soothing shade or a deep, welcoming tone depends on how much natural light the room receives, but both these options will be easy to live with. If you're covering most of the walls with shelving, storage units, and noticeboards, your background colour (whether paint or a wallpaper) will be less of a feature.

Paint a larger proportion of the mood board (or pin on a wallpaper swatch) in your background colour.

The intensity or subtlety of your main accent colour will also influence the atmosphere of your working space.

Second accent colours can help to add more depth and interest to your scheme.

A third accent colour might be a subtle variation of, or a complete contrast to, your main colour.

4 **CHOOSE TWO OR THREE ACCENT COLOURS**, which can be a subtle variation of your wall colour or a dramatic contrast to it. One will be your main accent shade; use the second fractionally less and the third minimally. Paint colour samples onto the board in the same proportions as they'll be used within the room to check that you have the right balance.

5 **ADD PATTERN & TEXTURE** with a rug, noticeboard, or fabric blind, for example; only small splashes are needed in an efficient environment like this. Keep the furnishings simple if you choose patterned wallpaper or, if the walls are plain, add wooden shutters or a desk with a grainy wood surface.

Stick some floor swatches to the mood board to help you decide which flooring will suit your scheme.

6 **CHOOSE NEW FURNITURE** Using the same tricks you used to narrow down your room's colour scheme, begin to look for furniture for your office. If the look of the room seems fairly plain so far, aim to add interest with a curvaceously shaped upholstered office chair, for example.

Displays of well-ordered colourful box files on shelves will add visual interest.

Stick any pictures of functional yet attractive furniture onto the board to build up your ideas.

7 **ADD FINISHING TOUCHES** Adding accessories and final touches, such as lighting, a chair cover, or picture frames, to a home office can turn it from purely functional to personal and individual, and help to pull your scheme together. This is the time to pick pieces in your third accent colour, whether they tone or contrast with your main colour scheme. These subtle touches will ensure the success of your scheme, so refer your choices back to the colour palette and style of your mood board first to ensure they will be right.

LAUNDRY ROOM

1 WHAT TO DO WHEN REVAMPING YOUR LAUNDRY ROOM

If you're lucky enough to have the space for a laundry room, you'll want it to be as useful a space as possible so plan the room carefully to get both the layout and work schedule right first time. Follow the timeline below to ensure that you include everything you need, when you need it.

1 PLAN YOUR LAYOUT

Draw a plan of the room to scale on graph paper and include all the items you require. It's worth keeping all plumbing to one side of the room to cut down on costs. Include a water supply for the sink and washing machine plus drainage, plumbing for a toilet and shower if required, electric sockets, task-focused lighting, an extractor fan, and space for a duct and exterior vent for the dryer if needed.

2 CONSIDER STORAGE AND DRYING OPTIONS

For storage, look for a combination of deep cupboard and drawer space; kitchen units are ideal. Plan in some worktop space to accommodate a laundry basket and folded laundry. Also consider whether you want wall- or ceiling-hung drying racks installed or floor-standing racks that can be folded flat when not in use. Think about where you'd like these to go.

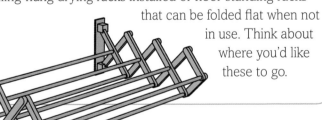

3 GET QUOTES FOR THE WORK

Line up quotes from at least three different plumbers, electricians, heating engineers, plasterers, and carpenters, and possibly tilers and decorators. Or ask one building company to take on the work and get in each trade itself.

4 ORDER YOUR MATERIALS

Ask your builder when flooring, sanitaryware, plumbing, electrical, and other supplies should be delivered. The washing machine and accessories can be ordered once work is under way.

5 GUT THE ROOM

Clear the room of everything that is no longer needed, such as old woodwork, sanitaryware, and flooring.

6 INSTALL ELECTRICS AND PLUMBING – FIRST FIX

The electrics for everything from underfloor heating to sockets, and the plumbing for washing appliances can start now. The electrician and plumber will need to return later to finish the installation of these (the second fix).

7 PLASTER AND MAKE GOOD

Once the pipework and wiring are in place, the walls and ceiling can be filled and replastered for decoration (some parts of the room may need some minor filling later). Prepare any walls that will be tiled so they are moisture resistant.

8 LAY THE FLOOR

If you are having electric underfloor heating, ensure that the sub-floor is level before installing it, then protect it with a hard floor suitable for a laundry room; tiles and concrete are practical choices. Seal the new floor if necessary and keep it well protected until other work is finished.

9 FIT WOODWORK

Once the plastered walls are dry, new skirting boards, door frames, and any other decorative mouldings can be put back into the room. If you are having built-in storage installed, this could be done at the same time.

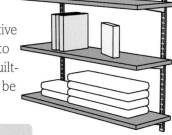

10 MAKE GOOD AND PAINT

Fill, prime, and paint over any fine cracks or damage to the walls by the woodwork being fitted. Start with the walls and ceiling, then the woodwork. Choose paint that has good water-resistance, as condensation will be an issue.

11 SECOND FIX – ELECTRICS AND PLUMBING

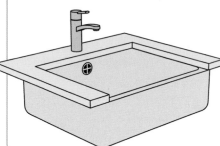

The plumber and electrician can return to plumb in the sink and connect the electric sockets and lighting.

12 TILE THE WALLS

Tiles withstand knocks and scrapes well, are easy to wipe clean, and are a good surface for rooms with moist conditions, so the more tiled surfaces, the better. Painted wood panelling around non-wet areas is another option.

13 INSTALL HANGING STORAGE

Fit wall- and ceiling-hung drying racks, hooks, pegs, and shelves. Vary the height of the hooks to accommodate clothes of differing lengths (fold-up floor-standing drying racks can be stored on wall hooks, too, when not in use).

14 ADD FINISHING TOUCHES

Include some fun details, such as pictures, old-fashioned laundry signs, peg bags, or decorative boxes to hold laundry products.

2 LAYOUT CONSIDERATIONS
FOR THE LAUNDRY ROOM

A laundry room will rarely be a very large space – more commonly it will be just about big enough. Planning the layout down to the last detail is therefore a must to ensure that you can fit in all the equipment you need, that everything is easily accessible, and that the room functions well. Follow these tips to find out how to plan your laundry room effectively.

WASHING MACHINE

Your washing machine, or washer dryer, and a sink will be the two most important elements in the room, so situate them first. They don't need to be next to each other, but it will cut your plumbing bills if the water supply and drainage for the two are nearby, preferably along the same wall. Check there is enough room to kneel in front of a front-loading washing machine and that opening the door to the room will not impede access to the drum.

TUMBLE DRYER

If you have enough floor space, a tumble dryer should sit next to the washing machine so you can transfer a load of washing easily. If there isn't enough room, put the tumble dryer on top of the washing machine (don't try it the other way round, as the washing machine will be too heavy). Most dryers don't need venting, but if your machine does, consider how best to work this into your layout so that it is placed on an outside wall.

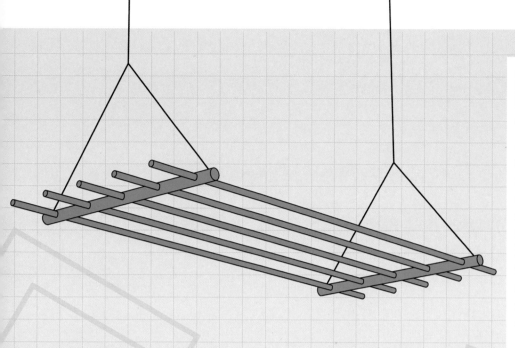

WASHING RACK

Wall- or ceiling-hung washing racks are useful, as they take up no floor space. Position them near a source of ventilation such as a window and above a sink or draining board so clothes can drip-dry. Also hang them high enough so that you can hang long items without them touching the floor or another surface. Otherwise, buy drying racks that will fold flat against the wall when not in use.

SINK

If you can place the sink near your washing machine, you will find it more practical: anything left to soak can be neatly transferred to rinse and spin in the machine without water dripping over the floor. Try to leave space either side, or to one side, of the sink for a draining board, and space below to hold washing powders and liquids.

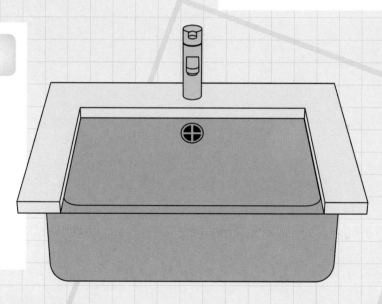

SHELVES OR CUPBOARDS

Any spare wall space within a laundry room can be filled with shelves or, for a neater look, wall-hung cupboards. If the room is doubling up as a downstairs cloakroom, fix shelves or a cupboard above the toilet and use the space above the sink to incorporate a cupboard with a mirrored front.

3 CHOOSE APPLIANCES

Your washing machine and tumble dryer are probably the most important purchases you will make when fitting out your laundry room. Think about where the appliances will be sited as well as your household's requirements, as this too may have a bearing on which models you opt for.

1 CHOOSE A COMBINATION OF APPLIANCES

When planning what appliances you need, consider the cost, the available space, and your lifestyle. With separate machines you will get through more laundry more quickly, but if space is at a premium, a single machine may be more practical.

WASHING MACHINE

The budget option: a one- or two-person household may be able to get by with just a washing machine. To do this comfortably, though, you will need space – indoors or outdoors – for line drying.

WASHER-DRYER

A combined washing machine and tumble dryer is a good option if you only have space for one appliance. Bear in mind, though, that these machines do not always dry clothes as well as a normal tumble dryer would.

SEPARATE WASHING MACHINE AND TUMBLE DRYER

If you have enough space for separate appliances, this is usually the best option, particularly for households of several people. The great benefit of this is that you can run both machines at the same time, thereby getting through more laundry. Arrange them side by side or stacked vertically (see panel opposite) depending on what works best in your space.

2 CHOOSE THE MODELS

With all laundry appliances, you should check that you are happy with the capacity, the cycles on offer, and the energy efficiency rating (they are rated A–G, with A being the most economical). Beyond that, consider the following.

WASHING MACHINES

FRONT LOADING

Preferred by many, front-loading washing machines can be built into a run of units under a worktop, which often represents the best use of space in a laundry room or kitchen. These machines also typically use less water than top loaders, so are more energy efficient. If you are stacking appliances, a front loader is, of course, essential.

TOP LOADING

Top-loading washing machines tend to be harder on clothes than front loaders, although you may find them more accessible if you have difficulties bending down to reach the drum. Top loaders tend to be cheaper than front-loading machines, so are a better buy if you are on a budget.

TUMBLE DRYERS

GAS OR ELECTRIC

Gas-powered tumble dryers are more energy efficient than electric models, and hence cheaper to run. However, they must be fitted by a gas professional. Electric machines are easier to install, although bear in mind that a vented machine must be sited against an outside wall (more expensive condensing models can sit anywhere in a well-ventilated room).

STACKING APPLIANCES

Stacking your washing machine and tumble dryer can offer a better use of space than positioning them both on the floor. Here's how to do it:

● Buy a suitable stacking kit or stacking frame. Try a "universal" kit or, for the best fit, see if the manufacturer of your appliances offers a more bespoke option.

● Always put the dryer on top of the washing machine, and ensure that the washing machine is on a sturdy, level base.

● Choose a washing machine that has a low vibration level when it's spinning to ensure the dryer isn't damaged.

● Check the manufacturer's instructions if you intend stacking a condensing tumble dryer, as this is not always recommended.

● Stacked appliances can easily be hidden within a tall cupboard built around them. Ensure the door, or doors, open in the same direction as those of the washer and dryer, and drill and cut ventilation holes in the door and the top of the unit to allow any residual heat to escape.

PLAN THE PERFECT
LAUNDRY ROOM

Your laundry room is, overall, a very practical space, and it's unlikely that many visitors will see it. However, that doesn't mean it can't look inviting while also being functional. Follow this guide to making your laundry room look as good as possible while accommodating all the equipment you need.

FIT SHELVING

It's helpful to have everything to hand in a laundry room, so don't underestimate the amount of shelving you should put up. Ideally, keep the shelves uniform – either running at the same height all the way around the room at just above head height or in a stack on a free wall – and within arm's length of the washing machine. Choose a theme for your laundry room (such as shabby chic, French laundry, or rustic country) and find shelves that will fit your look.

DISGUISE WITH BOXES AND BASKETS

You will find you have a whole array of things to put on your shelves, from washing powder to spare lightbulbs, pet supplies to candles. Don't feel they all have to be in their original packaging – the room will soon look like a supermarket storeroom if they are. Instead, buy a range of lidded boxes and baskets to hide things away. They'll still be accessible, but disguised by, for example, a country print fabric or a 1950s enamel tin.

INSTALL A STYLISH SINK

Don't be tempted to fit the cheapest DIY store sink you can find. Instead, look for a sink that will finish the room perfectly and can sit near the washing machine. Ideally, it needs to be roomy and flat-bottomed to hand-wash clothes, and there should be, if not a draining board, then a space for drip-drying clothes nearby. Look in antique markets and on the internet for old recycled ceramic sinks for a laid-back look, or hunt for old industrial stainless steel units.

STASH AWAY YOUR IRONING BOARD AND IRON

Fix a couple of hooks to a wall or the back of a door at head height to hang your ironing board from so it is off the floor and out of the way. The iron can sit on a shelf alongside your laundry powder. If you're opting for a contemporary look to the room, you can buy combined ironing board/iron holders that can be wall- or door-hung (assuming you have a solid door and it can take the weight).

HANG A DRYING RACK

If your laundry room is contemporary, there is a huge range of wall-hung or floor-standing metallic or plastic-finished hanging racks that will work perfectly well and will not look out of place. However, if you hunt around – in antique markets for example – you may find something more appropriate for a traditionally styled room, such as a Victorian ceiling-hung airer or a vintage-style linen rack in attractive solid wood.

FIND INTERESTING FLOORING

Whatever you choose for your floor, it must be as water-resistant as possible or it will be stained within no time. Since this is usually a small room, it makes sense to choose a light colour, and you can also stretch the space visually by setting any tiles diagonally. If you want to be adventurous and make the room look more fun, choose tiles, vinyl, or rubber in a bold pattern or bright colour.

CHOOSE A LAUNDRY BASKET

Even if you have a laundry basket elsewhere in your house – in your bedroom, family bathroom, or ensuite – it's handy to have an extra basket in the laundry room to transfer washing to. If floorspace is short, look for one with a lid that can sit on top of your washing machine, a quarter-circle- or triangular-shaped lidded basket that can sit in a corner, or bags that can be hung on a wall or the back of a door.

OUTSIDE SPACE

1 WHAT TO DO WHEN REVAMPING YOUR OUTSIDE SPACE

If you're considering redesigning your outdoor space – whether a patio, deck area, or small courtyard garden – it pays to plan well in advance. That way, you can get everything delivered at the right time, have labourers ready to spring into action, and get the whole job done efficiently.

1 MAKE A PLAN

Draw a rough plan to scale and include your needs – a sun deck, shed or storage unit, dining or barbecue area, or a garden structure or planting for privacy, for example.

2 CONSIDER YOUR BUDGET

Work out what you are able to spend, and what this will allow you to do, bearing in mind that the more structures and hard landscaping involved, the greater the cost. If you have to spread the cost over time, invest in landscaping first.

3 PLAN THE ELECTRICS AND WATER FEATURES

Check if you can afford decorative features such as lighting (controlled from within the house) and water features, which require electrical work, excavation, and plumbing. (Save money by buying solar-powered lighting and water features, though they are not as effective as electrically powered versions.)

4 ENGAGE A GARDEN DESIGNER

Just as if you were designing any room in the house, get the opinion of professionals. Some may offer a design service for free and others will charge, but the cost can be taken off their services, should you decide to engage them. A professional can be more cost-effective – though not cheaper – because he or she can project-manage, order materials at good rates, and offer clever design ideas.

5 GET QUOTES AND BOOK LABOURERS

Ask at least three people or companies (including builders, electricians, and plumbers) for quotes. Ideally, engage one landscaping company to do the clearing and hard landscaping for you (most will see the jobs right through), but if you have a very tight budget, getting people in separately may be cheaper. Do your homework now to save yourself money later.

6 ORDER MATERIALS

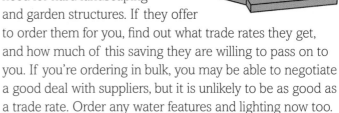

Ask your tradespeople to help you work out what materials you need for hard landscaping and garden structures. If they offer to order them for you, find out what trade rates they get, and how much of this saving they are willing to pass on to you. If you're ordering in bulk, you may be able to negotiate a good deal with suppliers, but it is unlikely to be as good as a trade rate. Order any water features and lighting now too.

7 CLEAR THE PLOT

Clear the space of anything that won't be needed, including old plants, weeds, storage units, paving, decking, and so on. Unless your outdoor space has direct access to the street, rubbish (and new materials) will be transported through your home. If you have ordered a skip that will sit on the street, apply to your local council for a licence first.

8 BEGIN HARD LANDSCAPING

The hard landscaping can now begin: levelling or shaping the plot, digging the foundations for walls, steps, structures, and the patio or deck, and excavating earth for any water features.

9 INSTALL ELECTRICS AND WATER FEATURES – FIRST FIX

As the hard landscaping begins, other tradespeople will need to lay pipework for the water features and electric cabling for the garden lighting, powering the water features, and power points. If you are having an outside tap fitted, get this done now.

10 ORDER PLANTS, TOPSOIL, AND FURNITURE

As the space takes shape, think about ordering the topsoil, plants, mulch, and garden furniture. The best time to plant out is autumn and spring, so delay planting if the work takes place in high summer or midwinter.

11 FINISH HARD LANDSCAPING AND ORGANIZE THE SECOND FIX

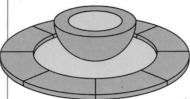

At this stage walls should be built and possibly rendered, steps and structures – whether pergolas or outdoor storage – constructed, and ponds or water features assembled. The plumber and electrician must return now to finish their work.

12 EXTERIOR PAINTING

Once any concrete or render is dry, and before you bring in bags of soil, paint or stain the outside walls, fences, trellis, pergolas, garden structures, or storage. Give them all at least two coats of stain or paint for effective protection.

13 FILL A WATER FEATURE

If you have a water feature, it can be filled now. Before populating it with fish or aquatic plants, follow the supplier's instructions to prepare the water properly.

14 PLANT OUT

Fill flower beds with soil and plants, either with mature specimens (if you have the budget for an instant, finished look) or seedlings that, with care, will soon shoot up to fill the beds. If you don't have flowerbeds, dot pots of plants that grow to different heights around the outdoor area to create the impression of a verdant space.

2 CREATE A MOOD BOARD
FOR YOUR OUTDOOR SPACE

Just as with rooms inside the house, creating a mood board for your garden, courtyard, or balcony will help you to decide whether all the elements you are considering will sit successfully together. Before you begin, it's worth also thinking about what type of atmosphere you want to create, especially if the space is to be used both as a relaxing and dining area.

1 FIND PICTURES OF OUTDOOR AREAS you like, or can use as inspiration, in magazines, websites, and books. If the room will have a dual purpose – as a dining and lounging area, perhaps – decide which element is more important to you. Then gather pictures of that type of outdoor room and work out how you can incorporate the other element within the space. Edit the pictures down to a manageable few and see if a colour scheme or decorative theme starts to emerge.

Stick a favourite image, or images, to the mood board as a starting point for your own outdoor scheme.

2 CONSIDER THE SUNLIGHT and where it falls on your space, as this will have a bearing on which colour palette you choose as a background, what type of plants you will buy and where you will site them, and where your outdoor furniture will sit.

Decide if you want a bright, neutral, or cool scheme according to how much sun or shade your space receives.

3 **PICK A BACKGROUND** for the room. Just like walls indoors, perimeter walls or fences provide a backdrop and dictate the look of other elements. Your choice won't just be paint shades for walls or stains for fences – you also need to consider the effect of the colours and textures of natural materials, whether brick, stone, or wood. Pin pictures of materials to the board or paint part of it in your chosen colour in proportion to how it will be used outdoors. This will also help you to choose other colours.

Your background should blend with both your furniture and planting scheme.

Stick swatches of accent colours onto the background to see if they work together.

4 **INTRODUCE ACCENT COLOURS,** which can be a subtle variation of your background colour or a contrast to it, or both. If you want a well-designed space, keep the colour palette to fewer than three colours other than green (although you can add a whole range of colours with flowers, if you wish). Use the first accent colour in greater proportion to the second, and the third minimally.

A contrasting accent colour will make your scheme look dynamic and stimulating.

Add images of furniture and other outdoor items to see if they will co-ordinate with your scheme.

Pick out one or more of your accent colours with particular plants and flowers.

5 **CHOOSE NEW FURNITURE** using the same methods as you did for your paint and plant colours. Work out if your choices offer what you need practically, but also if they will enhance the space decoratively. Sketch the layout of the space to be certain that everything will fit.

6 **ADD PATTERN** in the form of a design on your garden chair covers or cushions. This should be sufficient for an outdoor space, as flowers and plants can provide added pattern and colour. Stick pictures or fabric samples to your mood board to ensure that you're working along the right lines.

Look for a fabric design and plant pots that match your colour palette.

Pictures of various accessories in similar colours and tones on your mood board will help you get the mix right.

7 **ADD FINISHING TOUCHES** such as outdoor candles, crockery, lighting, and garden pots. You can choose individual pieces rather than a matching set of crockery, for example, to give your outdoor room a more individual look, but they should all tone in terms of colour, material, or texture if the room is to work successfully.

3 LAYOUT CONSIDERATIONS
FOR OUTSIDE SPACE

If you have an undeveloped outdoor space, you really have a blank canvas on which to impose a layout. However, there are several things to consider that will affect your plans, such as how to gain privacy if you are overlooked, where the sun falls and when, and even how well you can hide some components of this area. Follow these layout tips to create the most successful space possible.

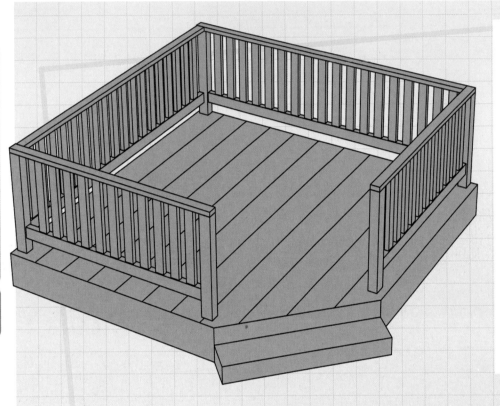

PATIO OR DECKED AREA

Think about how much of your patio or deck you want in the sun, in dappled shade, or in full shade. If you want to combine space for sunbathing, dining, and a kids' play area, you might want to position part of it in full sun for lounging and part in dappled shade for dining and playing. If you'll only be using this space for dining, it makes sense to site it right outside the back door. Ideally, this area should be screened from your neighbours' view: you may have existing features, such as a wall or trees, that you can take advantage of, or create a screen using trellis, pergolas, or planting.

DINING AREA

Where you position your dining furniture depends on where your patio or decking area is, where you have dappled shade (if your garden is south-facing, you may have to create shade with a pergola, planting, or a large parasol), and how close to the house you want to dine. When calculating what size of table to buy, allow an extra metre (3ft) all round it for the seats to be comfortably pulled in and out.

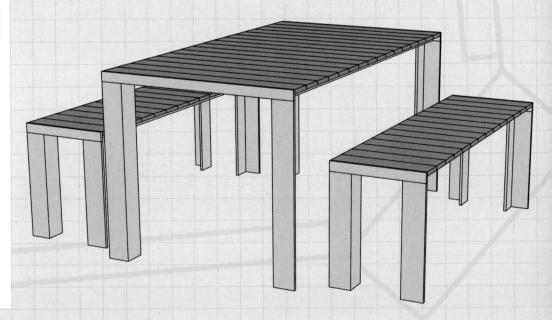

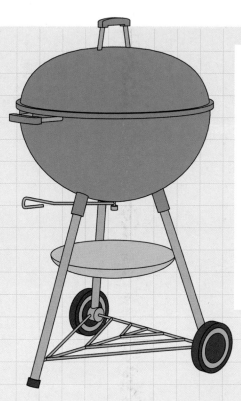

COOKING AREA

The most convenient place for an outdoor cooking area is near the house. If you are planning a fully functioning outdoor kitchen, it will also be easier to install the electrics and/or gas if the house is nearby. Choose a shady spot for your cooking area, or create one using a pergola or clever planting – but be careful not to create a fire hazard.

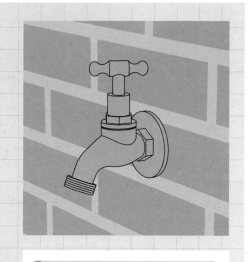

WATER SUPPLY

Fix a tap to the back wall of the house next to a boundary wall (not centrally, where it will take up space), with a stashable hose attached to the wall next to it. If you have children, it pays to also have a hot tap fitted so you can fill a paddling pool easily. If you want an outdoor shower, site it in a sunny spot where the shower area will dry out quickly.

STORAGE

Tuck a shed or storage unit out of sight at the end or the side of the garden, or hide it with clever planting such as climbers or tall, bushy plants. If your space is very small, a bench with a lift-up lid and storage beneath is a good option. Any small units can sit against a wall of the house so they aren't visible from indoors.

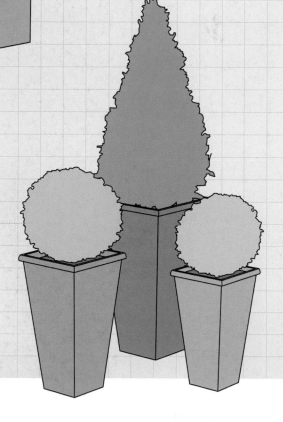

PLANTING

Plants can be used as screening for privacy, to hide ugly views or features, for shade, or simply as decoration. Plant tall trees around your boundaries if you need to screen your outdoor space, or train climbers over a pergola or a trellis to hide a seating area. Hide an ugly view with tall, bushy planting or climbers trained over trellis.

4 CHOOSE OUTDOOR FLOORING

Shop for outdoor flooring in the same way that you would when deciding what to lay on your floors indoors. Think about the style and finished look of the outside space, its size, how you'll be using it, whether you want a low-maintenance surface, and, of course, what your budget can accommodate.

1 CHOOSE THE TYPE

Paving, decking, and gravel are the three main types of hard outdoor flooring. Selecting the right one is as important as selecting the right plants, so consider how it will go with your overall scheme.

PAVING

Paving sizes range from small stones to large slabs laid in various patterns for different effects (opt for a sawn edge for a contemporary look). Prepare the ground with sharp sand or a cement foundation and lay out the blocks as you want them before fixing them in place.

DECKING

This is a versatile surface that can be used to create a patio leading out from the house, a separate raised area, or for levelling off a sloping garden. Fit the decking on a frame so it is clear of the ground and air can circulate underneath, and ensure there is good drainage.

AGGREGATE

Gravel, or aggregate, is the cheapest hard surface, so it's a practical option for large areas. Check the ground is well compacted, cover it with a weed-suppressing membrane, and scatter the gravel over it to a depth of at least 2.5cm (1in). Weed the area regularly.

CHECKLIST

● **Ensure that the flooring** you choose – whether tiles or decking – is non-slip when wet.

● **Rainwater needs to runs off** a patio or deck, so ensure that there is adequate fall and drainage.

● **Decide whether you want** your outdoor flooring to match that of the connecting room indoors. Doing so will unite the two spaces and make both seem larger.

● **Is the flooring you've chosen** suitable for your family? If you have children you may be better off with a softer floor such as wood, for example.

2 CHOOSE THE MATERIAL

Each type of outdoor flooring is available in various materials, sizes, and colours. Look at all the available choices – taking samples home, if possible, to see what they look like in situ first – before making up your mind.

PAVING

SLATE

Ideal for contemporary patios, this blue-black stone can run from indoors outside via a wall of glass doors. Its low-to-medium cost makes it good value for money.

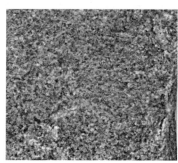

GRANITE

Hard and extremely durable, granite comes in a variety of greys, reds, and greens. Run it from inside onto the patio for a seamless transition. Its cost is medium to high.

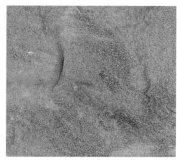

LIMESTONE

Available in various shades, limestone is smooth, low-maintenance, and hardwearing, and suits minimalist modern patios. Prices range from cheap to expensive.

SANDSTONE

Sandstone has a subtle texture, varies in colour, and is very hardwearing, which makes its low-to-medium cost good value for money. It may need sealing once laid.

FLAGSTONE

Comprised of flat stones with a non-slip surface that provide rustic charm, flagstones develop an attractive weathered look. The medium-cost tiles are irregular in shape.

CONCRETE

Hardwearing concrete can be coloured, textured, or patterned. Choose slabs or blocks depending on how you want your patio to look.

TRAVERTINE

The advantage of medium-to-high cost travertine is that it doesn't heat up, which makes it ideal for sunny patios as it always stays cool underfoot. It's also slip-resistant.

BRICK

Brick paving is made of clay or concrete that is then dyed, which is cheaper but less durable than clay. This medium-cost surface is available in different shapes.

DECKING

HARDWOOD

Durable hardwood decking is medium to high in price. Oil it occasionally to prevent it drying out. It can become slippery when wet, so opt for a textured finish.

SOFTWOOD

Easier to work with than hardwood, though not as long-lasting, softwood requires regular painting or staining. Its prices range from low to medium.

MAN-MADE

Weather-resistant UPVC lacks the aesthetic appeal of timber, but is nearly maintenance-free. Medium-cost composite decking is low-maintenance and looks like solid wood.

DECK TILES

Wooden tiles, which are low to medium in cost, can be laid over an existing patio to create a deck without the need for a frame. They are slip-resistant and easy to lay.

AGGREGATE

SLATE CHIPPINGS

These low-cost flattish stones in varying sizes are easier to walk on, and wheel a barrow over, than gravel. They also deepen in colour and intensity when wet.

LIMESTONE CHIPPINGS

Pale grey or buff limestone chippings are bagged according to the size of stone, so check which size suits your space. Their low cost makes them good value for money.

FLINT CHIPPINGS

This low-cost, hardwearing, angular gravel is available in tones of grey, white, or gold. Its warm, mellow appearance makes it a popular choice for outdoor surfaces.

BEACH COBBLES

These large, smooth, medium-cost pebbles give a relaxed, seaside feel. They are tricky to walk on so use sparingly in borders, or in place of randomly selected paving stones.

PEA SHINGLE

Composed of crushed stones through a sieve, low-cost pea shingle is available as a rounded or slightly jagged shape. The bags may be mixed or uniform in colour.

RUBBER CHIPPINGS

Made from recycled tyres, low-cost rubber is economical because it goes much further than other aggregates. It's also a child-friendly alternative to sharp stones.

LAWNS

There are dedicated gardening books and resources that provide much more advice on lawns than this book is able to do, but lawns are of course a major consideration when it comes to planning your outdoor flooring.

● **Is your outdoor space** suitable for a lawn? Grass does best in a well-drained site that has some sunlight – too much shade will make the lawn patchy. Find out which grass type will best suit your garden's exposure to sunlight (establish, too, which type will be best for your planned usage).

● **Thinking about how** you will use your lawn will help you decide the most suitable shape for it. If it is to be a practical play area, a simple square, oval, or circular lawn will be best. If you want to enhance your garden's design, consider a more dynamic shape, with curves carved out to create interesting edges for borders.

● **You can create** a lawn by laying down turf or sowing seed. Either way is simple enough to do, with seed being the cheaper option and turf being quicker. Whichever approach you choose, be prepared to give it lots of water in the early days.

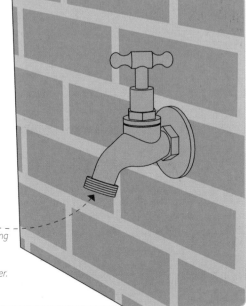

An outside tap is invaluable for watering a lawn, especially a newly laid one that needs plenty of water.

WOODEN OUTDOOR FLOORING gives a warmer feel than stone or concrete but needs careful weather-proofing.

6 WAYS WITH
PATIO AND DECK SHAPES

Add extra interest to your outdoor space by including a patio or deck in a dynamic shape, or enhance a regular rectangle or square patio with clever seating and planting arrangements. Choose a design that fits the dimensions of your space and complements the style of your planting scheme.

DIAMOND

If you have space, create an interesting patio design using two squares interlinked to form a diamond design, with planting displayed around it. This works well in a courtyard garden.

A BORDER in a different colour will give the patio shape more definition.

STRAIGHT EDGE

A straight-edge patio or decked area will usually run the full width of your house and can be any depth, depending on the space you have available in your garden.

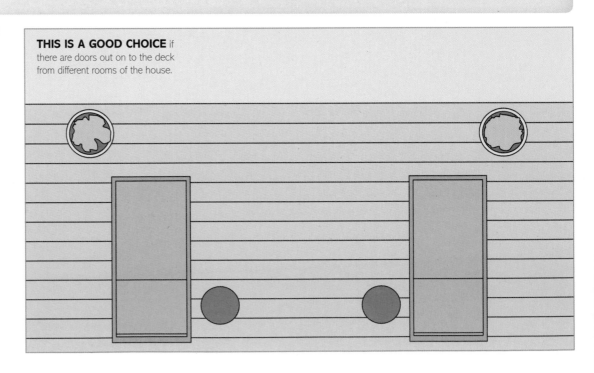

THIS IS A GOOD CHOICE if there are doors out on to the deck from different rooms of the house.

45° CORNERS

Add interest to a square or rectangular area of decking with 45° corners at the ends. Planting in the corners will give privacy.

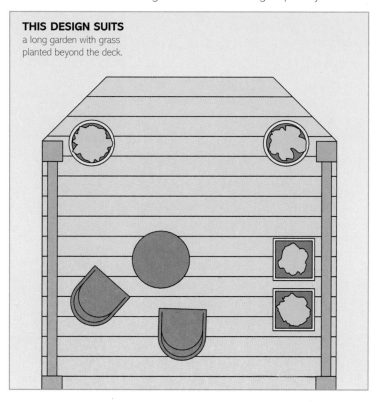

THIS DESIGN SUITS a long garden with grass planted beyond the deck.

CURVED

Curved edges can give a less formal look to your garden and the soft edges will blend in with the planting beyond.

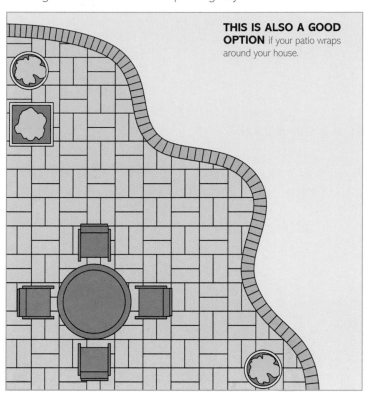

THIS IS ALSO A GOOD OPTION if your patio wraps around your house.

ROUND

A round patio creates a focal point in the centre of a garden and softens any hard edges. Highlight the shape by planting around it.

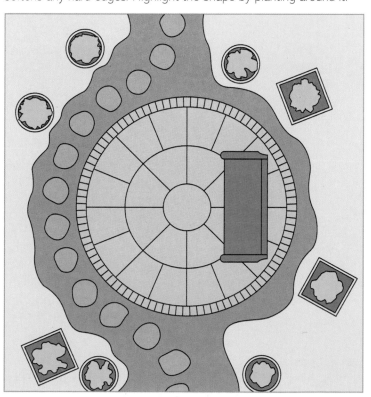

SQUARE

In small gardens, square patios and decked areas work well. Break up their formal look with planting among the paving or with large pots.

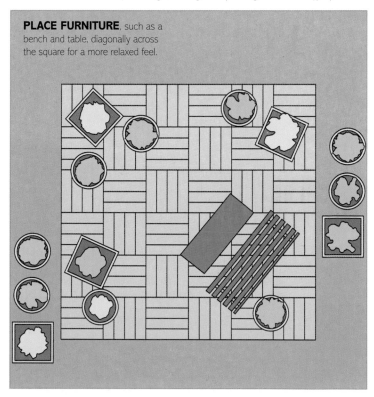

PLACE FURNITURE, such as a bench and table, diagonally across the square for a more relaxed feel.

6 WAYS WITH
SLAB PATTERNS

Laying a patio isn't as basic as it may seem – there are a great many different designs you can create by using certain slab shapes in particular arrangements. Achieve a modern, traditional, ordered, or relaxed look to suit your outside space. Here are a few ideas to consider.

HERRINGBONE

Laying bricks or concrete blocks in a herringbone pattern will create a smart, neat look that works for wide expanses and pathways alike.

IF YOU LIVE in an old property, use reclaimed bricks for a more authentic look.

DUTCH

This design is created by laying two different sizes of square slab in a repeating pattern.

USE ALL THE SAME colour or two different colours – one for the large squares, another for the small squares.

CRAZY PAVING

Irregular sizes and shapes of stone or concrete paving can be used to create a random pattern.

ALTHOUGH CRAZY PAVING is often a cheaper option to buy, it's more complicated to install than other paving options.

RANDOM

Obtain slabs of four or five different sizes and shapes, ensuring they will tessellate, and arrange them into a random pattern.

THIS DESIGN will require careful planning to ensure that the slabs all fit.

SLABS AND COBBLES

Create your own design using a mixture of slabs and cobbles. Use the cobbles to form borders to the slabs.

LIKE OTHER DETAILED PATTERNS, this design will make your patio look "busy", so keep the pots and planting simple.

COBBLES OR SETTS

The rustic look of cobbles or setts will give a relaxed, country feel, but you can make them feel more formal using geometric patterns.

IF YOU ARE PLANNING an intricate pattern, draw it out to scale on graph paper first.

MAKE
A SAIL SHADE

Create a lightweight triangular shade to give you a retreat from the sun on warm summer days. The shade can be secured to trees, fence posts, or whatever else you have in your outdoor space, as long as the fixtures are sturdy enough to take the extra stress. Avoid using in high winds.

WHAT YOU NEED

- Fabric
- Needle and thread, or sewing machine
- Scissors
- D rings
- Cord

1 MEASURE THE FABRIC

MEASURE UP THE AREA where you want the shade to go and sketch out a scale drawing, including the points you want to attach the corners to. Use this drawing to determine the size of your shade. It is very likely that you will need to attach two pieces of fabric to make the necessary width, so make a plan for where the seam should go and where the fabric will need to be cut.

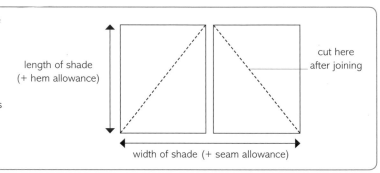

length of shade (+ hem allowance)

cut here after joining

width of shade (+ seam allowance)

2 JOIN THE FABRIC

1 **PLACE THE TWO PIECES** of fabric together, right side to right side, and sew a 2cm (¾in) seam to create the central join.

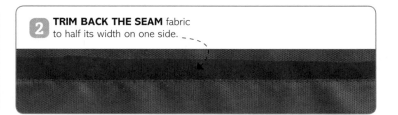

2 **TRIM BACK THE SEAM** fabric to half its width on one side.

3 **OPEN OUT FLAT** and fold the wider side of the seam fabric around the narrower side.

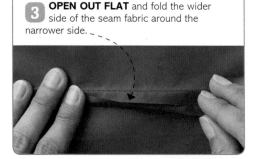

4 **FOLD DOWN FLAT** against the fabric so that the raw edge is tucked away.

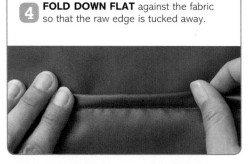

5 **SEW AGAIN** to secure, creating a flat seam. Now you can make the diagonal cuts to create your triangle.

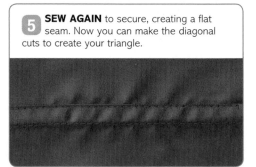

3 HEM THE SIDES

1 **ON EACH OF THE THREE SIDES**, create a double hem by folding once, then folding again to conceal the raw edge, and sewing.

2 **AT THE CORNERS** where the folded hems meet, a tail will be created. This can be left loose for now.

1 PASS THE TAIL through a D ring at each of the corners. Fold the fabric over the straight edge of the ring and stitch to hold in place.

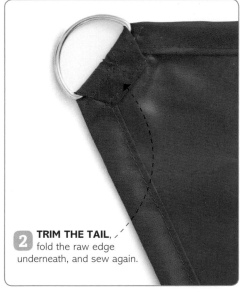

2 TRIM THE TAIL, fold the raw edge underneath, and sew again.

3 ATTACH THE CORD to each of the D rings. Your shade can now be tied in place.

5 CHOOSE OUTDOOR LIGHTING

As in the house, good use of lighting in your outdoor room will help enhance the space, highlight attractive features, and provide the necessary illumination for whatever activities are to take place there. Opt for a combination of different lighting types – maybe three or four types if it is a large space.

CHOOSE YOUR LIGHT FITTINGS

Consider how you use your outside space – and how you would like to use it – and try to identify lighting that will meet your practical needs, as well as suiting the proportions of the area.

WALL-MOUNTED LIGHTS

WALL LIGHTS

Wall lights are best used singly above, or in pairs at either side of, a door. They are most useful if they also have a security function. As with all outdoor electric lighting, ensure the switch is positioned inside, by the door.

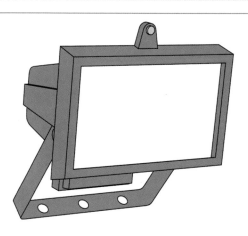

FLOODLIGHTS

If you have a large outdoor space and regularly use it at night, for entertaining, sports activities, or as a play area, a floodlight will provide the most generous illumination. Remember though, if you live at close quarters with your neighbours, to be careful how a light like this is aimed.

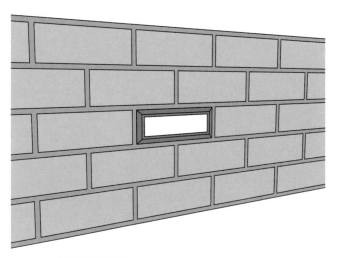

BRICK LIGHTS

If you want to create subtle lighting around a patio area, set brick lights into the wall of the house or boundary. They can be positioned at various heights, with each variation creating a different effect: the lower the lights, the softer the overall lighting will be.

CEILING LIGHTS

HANGING LIGHTS

A hanging light is often placed above a front or back door, often within a porch. If you have an outside dining area or outdoor kitchen shaded by a pergola, plan out a scheme to site a hanging light above the dining table. Hanging lights are available in a wide range of designs, including hanging downlights, traditional-style lanterns, and opulent chandeliers.

FLOOR LIGHTS

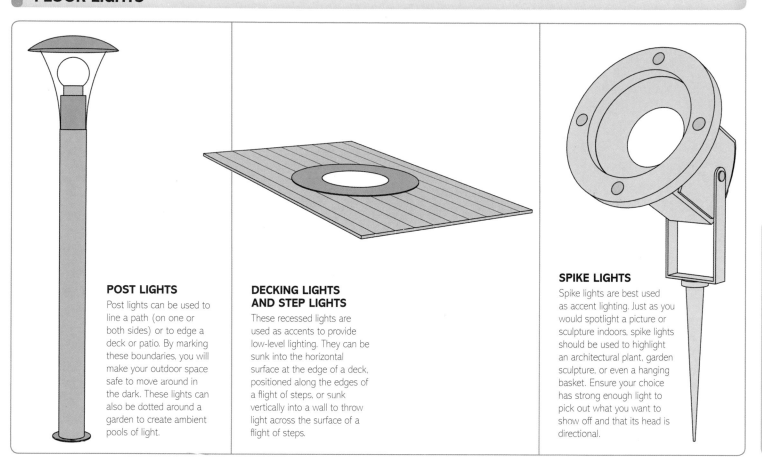

POST LIGHTS

Post lights can be used to line a path (on one or both sides) or to edge a deck or patio. By marking these boundaries, you will make your outdoor space safe to move around in the dark. These lights can also be dotted around a garden to create ambient pools of light.

DECKING LIGHTS AND STEP LIGHTS

These recessed lights are used as accents to provide low-level lighting. They can be sunk into the horizontal surface at the edge of a deck, positioned along the edges of a flight of steps, or sunk vertically into a wall to throw light across the surface of a flight of steps.

SPIKE LIGHTS

Spike lights are best used as accent lighting. Just as you would spotlight a picture or sculpture indoors, spike lights should be used to highlight an architectural plant, garden sculpture, or even a hanging basket. Ensure your choice has strong enough light to pick out what you want to show off and that its head is directional.

DECORATIVE LIGHTING

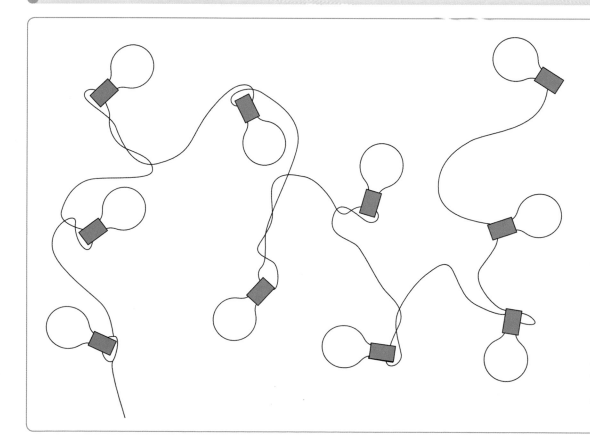

STRING LIGHTING

String lighting provides little ambient light, but will make a patio, deck, or balcony look pretty if strung around its edge. This form of lighting can also be twisted around the uprights of pergolas or hung from their upper beams, and twined around the trunks and branches of trees and plants to make a garden look magical.

7 WAYS WITH PLANT POTS

Potting plants in pots needn't just be about creating a bright, pretty display of your favourite flowers. It can also be about defining the style of your garden, delineating a certain area, or screening an ugly view. Carefully choose pots in styles that complement both the plants and the design of your outdoor space.

BORDER

Use pots to create a low border around the edge of your lawn, patio, or path. They can also create a safety barrier at the edge of a raised deck.

RECTANGULAR TROUGHS work well, but you can use any pot shape you like.

WINDOW LEDGE

Instead of window boxes, use several pots of flowers or herbs to brighten up a window ledge, provide privacy, or screen an ugly view.

USE PAINTED POTS that will add colour if the flowers aren't in bloom.

DIFFERENT HEIGHTS

For a relaxed look, create an interesting grouping of different-sized pots. Mix the shapes and colours of the pots, too.

GROUP THE POTS and plants in odd numbers for best effect.

EITHER SIDE OF A DOORWAY

Position identical pots at either side of a front or back door to frame it. This look works very well with large pots and architectural plants.

FOR THE BEST EFFECT, the planting in both pots should match.

ON STEPS

If you have garden steps, place one pot at the edge of each step. Mix the pot shapes for variety, or use the same style for uniformity.

IF YOU HAVE WIDE STEPS, consider sitting groups of several pots on each step.

WALL MOUNTED

Add visual interest to a plain wall or fence by vertically mounting a series of pots that diminish in size the higher up they are.

DISGUISE A FENCE or wall by planting a combination of trailing plants.

ÉTAGÈRE

Add interest and height to a corner of your garden using an étagère, which allows you to display many pots at different heights.

SEMICIRCULAR and circular étagères allow you to plant against flat walls and around trees.

6 CHOOSE OUTDOOR FURNITURE

The outdoor furniture you choose will depend on a number of factors, such as the type of material you like, how contemporary or traditional your space is, and its size. Small spaces need compact pieces, while a bigger garden may lend itself to large pieces. Check, too, how easy it will be to store, move, and clean.

1 CHOOSE A DINING SET

Start by thinking about the dining area. What size and shape of table will be best for your space? Tables are often sold in a set with matching seating, but you could also buy separate pieces that complement each other more subtly.

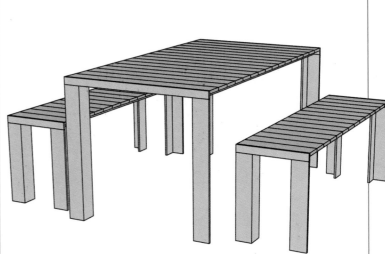

TABLE AND CHAIRS

Separate tables and chairs are available in a wide range of sizes, from neat café-style tables that seat two people up to large rectangular, circular, and oval tables that can seat many people. You can buy these pieces in sets or individually, which means you can choose chairs that suit your space and comfort requirements.

TABLE WITH BENCHES

A table with benches is a good choice if you often need to seat lots of people, (although bear in mind that benches are not suitable for children under three), to eat at the same time. Benches are not always comfortable to sit on for long periods, so if possible, complement them with at least a couple of chairs.

PICNIC TABLE

Picnic tables have fixed benches, so you don't have to buy separate seating. However, climbing over the benches to sit on them can be awkward. They are a good choice for families or small gardens. You can buy rectangular and round versions.

2 CHOOSE ADDITIONAL FURNITURE

When choosing additional furniture, think about what you want to do in your outside space. Do you want a chair on which to sit and read or drink a cup of tea, or are you looking for something you can stretch out on and sunbathe?

CHAIR

If you intend to leave garden chairs outside all year round, choose a material that is durable and resistant. If you want to store them away, it makes sense to buy folding or stackable chairs. Consider buying separate seat cushions to make the chairs more comfortable.

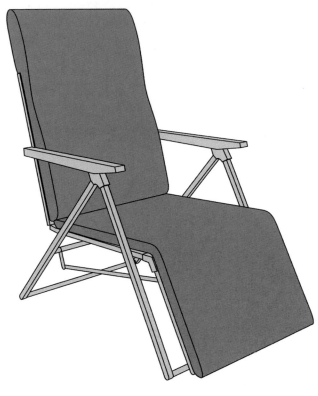

RECLINER

Recliner chairs adjust from an upright to near-horizontal position, and are ideal if you have little space to store both dining and lounging chairs, since you can use them for both dining and reclining. They are available in a range of materials and with or without filled cushions.

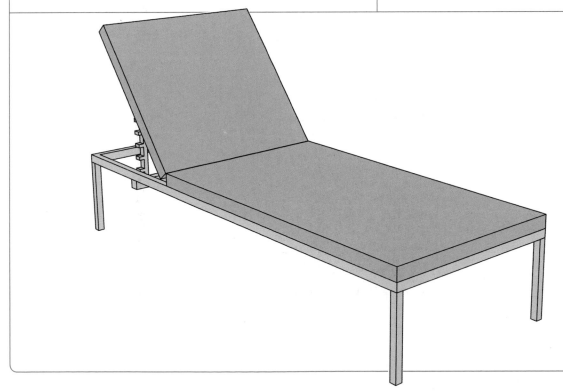

LOUNGER

If you like to sunbathe, a sun lounger – typically made from wood, plastic, or metal – is the most comfortable option. It features an adjustable back, which can be raised for reading or laid flat for stretching out. Some, usually fixed models, can be left outside all year round, while others can be folded away for easier storing.

BENCH

Available in a wide range of sizes and styles, and in a choice of wood or metal, garden benches can either be used as extra seating for dining or placed in a quiet corner for you to enjoy your outdoor space. Find a permanent spot for a bench, as it won't provide the same flexibility as individual outdoor chairs.

SOFA

Garden sofas are usually made from a woven plastic or a treated rattan. Not all garden sofa materials can be left outside in all weathers, so check before you buy if you don't have somewhere to store it in winter. They are often sold with seat pads for added comfort.

SWING

Garden swings typically have a fixed frame with a hanging swing seat (normally to seat two or three) and a canopy that offers protection from the sun. This furniture takes up a fair amount of space, so is more suited to large gardens.

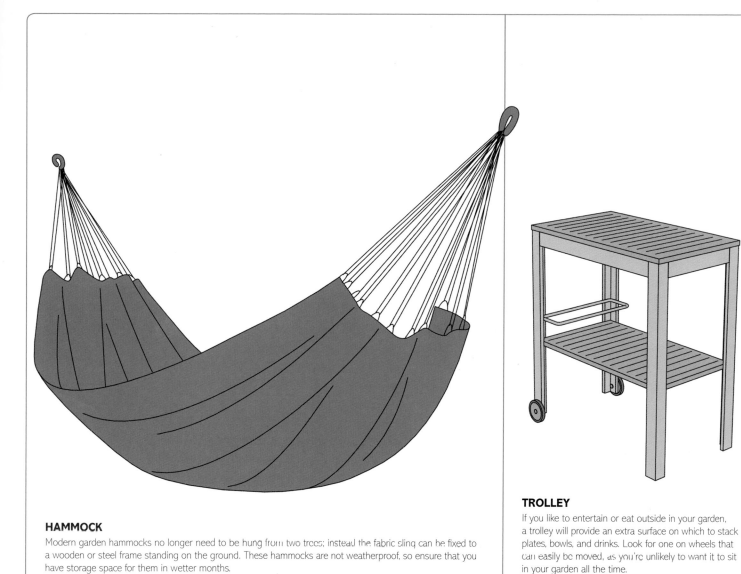

HAMMOCK

Modern garden hammocks no longer need to be hung from two trees; instead the fabric sling can be fixed to a wooden or steel frame standing on the ground. These hammocks are not weatherproof, so ensure that you have storage space for them in wetter months.

TROLLEY

If you like to entertain or eat outside in your garden, a trolley will provide an extra surface on which to stack plates, bowls, and drinks. Look for one on wheels that can easily be moved, as you're unlikely to want it to sit in your garden all the time.

3 CHOOSE THE MATERIAL

When choosing garden furniture, consider whether the material it is made from will suit your outdoor scheme, how durable it is, and whether it will need annual maintenance.

   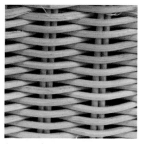 

WROUGHT IRON

Medium to high in cost, furniture made of heavy wrought iron is often traditional-looking and ornate. It can be uncomfortable, so consider seat pads.

PLASTIC

Available in a range of prices, plastic furniture comes in many different colours and designs, and is easy to clean. It is extremely lightweight.

CAST ALUMINIUM

Cast aluminium is lightweight, so can be moved around easily. It is typically low to medium in cost and can be left outside all year round.

RATTAN/WICKER

Medium to high in cost, natural wicker and rattan furniture gives a relaxed look. Choose a synthetic version if you will be leaving it uncovered in wet conditions.

WOOD

Wooden furniture, available in a range of prices, is durable and hardwearing, but often heavy. Most woods need to be treated or stained every 6–12 months.

MAKE
CUSHIONS FOR GARDEN CHAIRS

Add an extra touch of comfort to your outdoor seating area with these chair cushions, which can be made to fit any shape and size of garden chair. Covering both the seat and chair back, they have ties to secure the seat pad in position and elastic that loops over the chair back to keep the back pad upright.

WHAT YOU NEED

- 2 flat foam pads (about 2.5cm/1in thick)
- Scissors
- Coloured fabric – use curtain-weight cotton material
- Pins
- Thick elastic
- Sewing machine, or needle and threads

1 MEASURE AND CUT

1 **MEASURE THE DIMENSIONS** of your chair, recording the height of the chair back, the depth of the seat, and the width of the seat and back. Cut the foam pads to size.

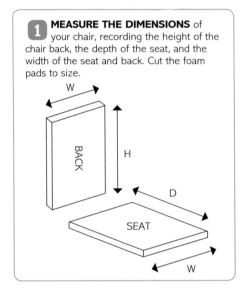

2 **FOR EACH CHAIR COVER**, cut out two large fabric panels, plus two smaller pieces for the ties, as follows.

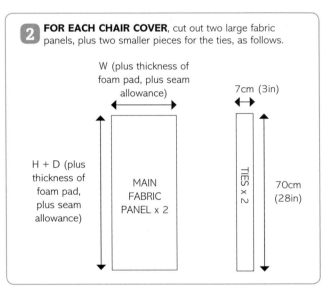

W (plus thickness of foam pad, plus seam allowance)

H + D (plus thickness of foam pad, plus seam allowance)

MAIN FABRIC PANEL x 2

7cm (3in)

TIES x 2

70cm (28in)

2 MAKE THE CUSHION COVER

1 **PLACE THE TWO** large pieces of fabric face to face, and pin all the way round the edges.

2 **PIN THE ELASTIC** across the width of the cushion cover, about a quarter of the way down from the top of the fabric.

3 **SEW AROUND** three sides of the fabric, leaving one short end open.

4 **TURN THE FABRIC** inside out through the open end so it is the right way round. Check the elastic is securely fixed.

3 INSERT THE SEAT PAD

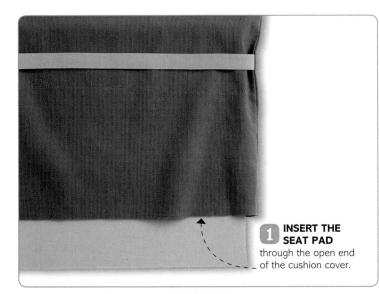

1 **INSERT THE SEAT PAD** through the open end of the cushion cover.

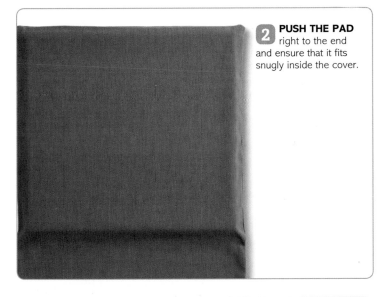

2 **PUSH THE PAD** right to the end and ensure that it fits snugly inside the cover.

4 MAKE THE TIES

1 **FOLD OVER THE SHORT ENDS** of each tie, then the long ends, and then fold the tie in half lengthways.

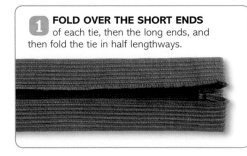

2 **PIN THE FOLDS** to secure them in place.

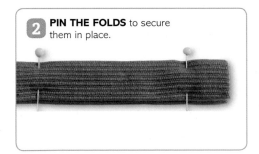

3 **SEW** neatly around the edges.

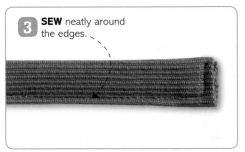

5 SECURE THE TIES

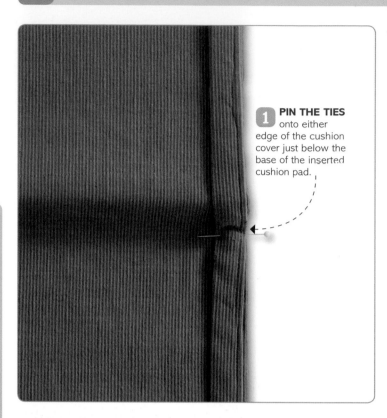

1 PIN THE TIES onto either edge of the cushion cover just below the base of the inserted cushion pad.

2 SEW ACROSS THE BASE of the pad and through the centre of each tie to secure them in place and create a "hinge" in the seat cover.

6 INSERT THE BACK PAD

1 SLIDE THE BACK PAD into the remaining section of the cushion cover through the open end.

2 FOLD AND PIN the open end of the cover so the seam will rest against the chair back.

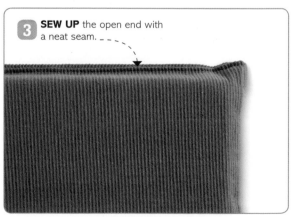

3 SEW UP the open end with a neat seam.

8 WAYS WITH
TINY OUTDOOR SPACES

Having a small garden doesn't necessarily mean that you will be severely limited in what you can do with it; there are plenty of ways to be creative with a restricted space. The key is to build a versatile area with hidden storage, built-in seating, and clever features.

BUILT-IN SEATING

If you can't find furniture that fits the proportions of your garden or makes best use of its space, consider having made-to-measure furniture built.

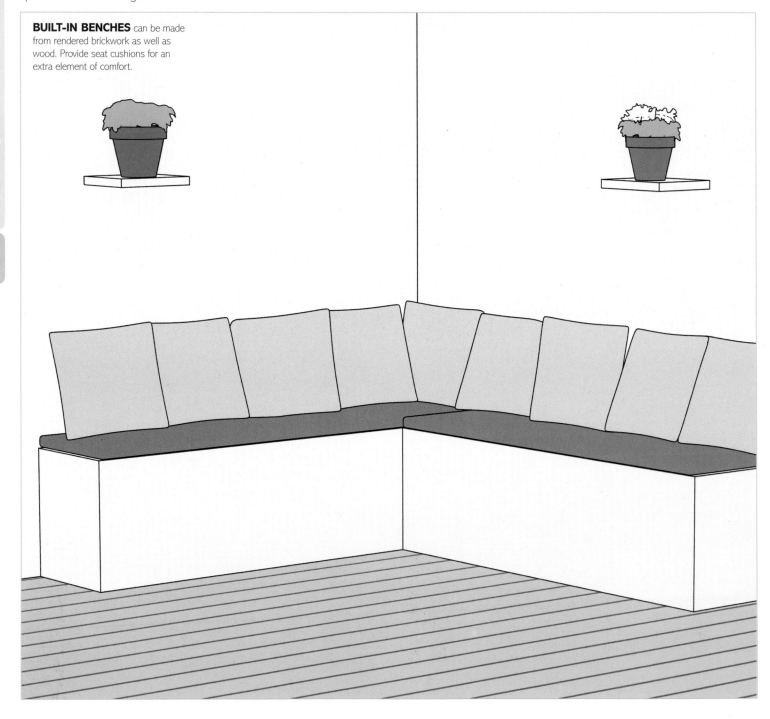

BUILT-IN BENCHES can be made from rendered brickwork as well as wood. Provide seat cushions for an extra element of comfort.

WALL ART

Add interest to a plain wall with a decorative wall hanging or some shelves that can be used to display small pots or garden sculptures.

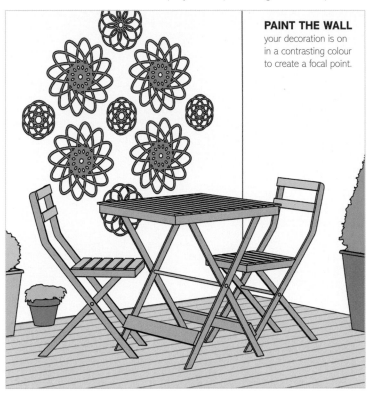

PAINT THE WALL your decoration is on in a contrasting colour to create a focal point.

ADD A LIVING WALL

Plant a living wall using purpose-designed modules or panels that contain soil for plants like herbs, grasses, and ferns to grow.

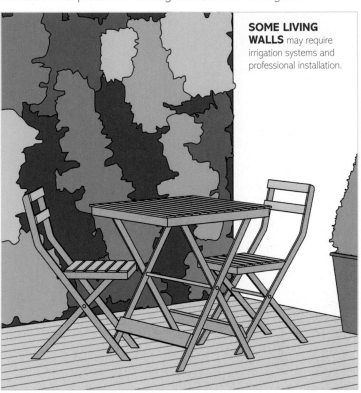

SOME LIVING WALLS may require irrigation systems and professional installation.

HANG FOLDING CHAIRS

Where space is tight, look for tables and chairs that can be folded flat and hung out of the way on the wall.

ENSURE THE FURNITURE is weather resistant, or have covers made to protect it.

ADD A MIRROR

Using mirrors in a garden will help reflect light, making the space feel larger. Look for a weatherproof acrylic mirror.

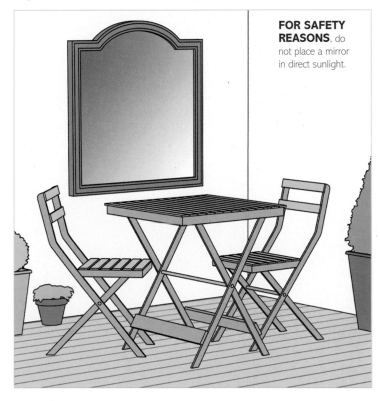

FOR SAFETY REASONS, do not place a mirror in direct sunlight.

CREATE A MEZZANINE

A small mezzanine will provide an extra level that you can use for planting or even a seating area. The space underneath will also offer some shade.

CHECK WHETHER you need planning permission before starting any work.

ADD DECORATIVE LIGHTING

Create a party mood using decorative lighting. Highlight seating and dining areas using hanging lights, string lights, or lanterns.

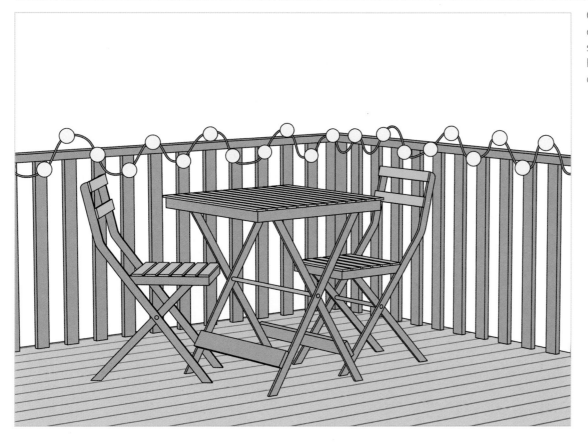

DUAL-PURPOSE FURNITURE

Make the most of your space by choosing furniture that serves more than one function – such as a bench that has a lift-up lid with space beneath for storing away cushions.

ALTERNATIVELY, look for furniture that can be used indoors and out.

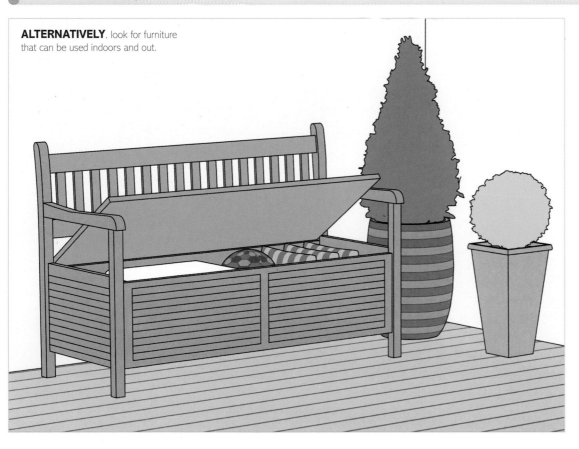

PLAN THE PERFECT
OUTDOOR KITCHEN

If you love entertaining and eating outdoors, you may prefer to have an outdoor kitchen installed so you can cook and serve more than just basic barbecued food. You need to employ many of the same rules as you would for designing an indoor kitchen, and what you include depends on how much space you have.

POSITION THE COOKING AREA

Unless you are an aspiring cook or live in a suitable climate, you will probably only want the most basic of cooking equipment. This is likely to include a grill, perhaps a gas hob, and possibly a stove. The cooking you do in an outdoor kitchen will be far more sociable than indoors, so bear this in mind – can you position the cooking area safely so that it faces out on to the rest of your garden or patio, where guests will be sitting waiting for their food?

ALLOW FOR ADEQUATE WORKTOPS

You need to allow adequate worktop space at either side of your cooking area – at least 60cm (24in), and more if possible. Don't plan for your cooking area to be at one end of a run of worktops – incorporating enough space for food preparation and serving at either side is a must.

CHOOSE A LIDDED BIN

Having a bin in your outdoor kitchen is essential, because it will allow you to clear plates quickly, which means that you won't be overrun with insects. Either ensure your bin is incorporated within a self-closing cabinet within a run of units or choose one that is free-standing, but sealed with a lid.

ALLOCATE STORAGE SPACE

Lots of efficient storage isn't as important outdoors as it is indoors, but since you're unlikely to have much worktop space outdoors, it is good to have somewhere to store cooking utensils, serving dishes, and plates, even if these will all be cleared away into the house once you've finished eating. Open shelving is easy to access, while units with well-sealed doors are also practical.

FIND ROOM FOR A SINK

If you have the room to add a sink to your outdoor kitchen, you will find it invaluable. Without one, you will have to make room for a large bottle of water for cooking and a storage area for dirty cooking utensils and pans to be stashed away. Ensure that the sink is within easy reach of both the cooking area and bin.

GIVE YOURSELF SPACE

Build in enough room – at least 1.25m (4ft) – as a thoroughfare for your cooking area, and ensure that people who aren't cooking don't have to use it as a route to and from the house. You may also want to protect yourself (from sun or rain) with a non-flammable roof; make sure it is constructed so that the ventilation is as efficient as possible.

MAKE ROOM FOR SEATING

Make sure there is room for tables and chairs (or benches, which take up less space) nearby. You can also incorporate bar stools into your kitchen design, for guests to perch on while you cook. Allow at least 60cm (24in) width per stool so each person has enough elbow room.

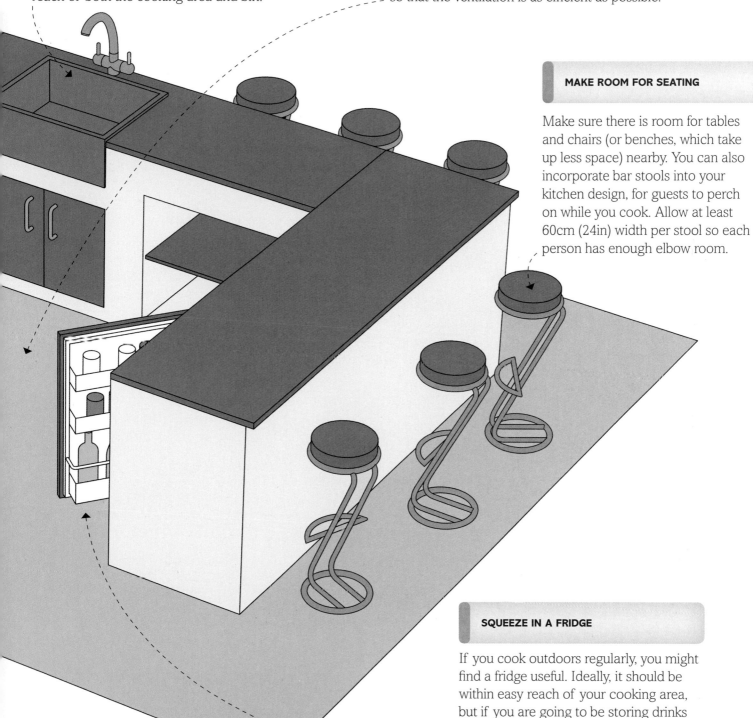

SQUEEZE IN A FRIDGE

If you cook outdoors regularly, you might find a fridge useful. Ideally, it should be within easy reach of your cooking area, but if you are going to be storing drinks in it for other people to access while you cook, place it nearest the patio area at the end of a run of units.

USEFUL RESOURCES

This is a selection of UK and Australian organizations and companies that cater for the home designer and decorator. Some are huge multinationals, others are magazines or smaller design studios, but all are good sources of information or products.

General Info

The House Directory
www.thehousedirectory.com
A directory of over 3500 companies, covering every possible aspect of home design and decoration.

KBSA
www.kbsa.org.uk
"Kitchen Bathroom Bedroom Specialists Association" – association of over 300 accredited kitchen, bathroom, bedroom and home office suppliers. Website has articles, FAQs and image galleries.

Planning a Room

House to Home
www.housetohome.co.uk
General guide, featuring "how to" articles and ideas for interiors.

Home & Design
www.homeanddesign.com
Architecture and interior design magazine.

homelife
www.homelife.com.au
Guide featuring articles on room planning and interior decoration, as well as blogs and a selection of web forums.

Elledecor
www.elledecor.com
Style magazine, with ideas, information and products to help you design and decorate.

houzz
www.houzz.com
A home design photo database. Includes thousands of images from top designers.

Freshome
www.freshome.com
Weblog devoted to latest developments in interior design, with hundreds of pictures and articles.

hd directory
www.homedesigndirectory.com.au
Home design resource website, with featured designers and products, and helpful articles.

Home Improvement Pages
www.homeimprovementpages.com.au
Australian design and decoration web directory with company listings and articles.

General Suppliers

IKEA
www.ikea.com
Global home products retailer.

John Lewis
www.johnlewis.com
Department store group.

Homebase
www.homebase.co.uk
Home improvement chain.

B&Q
www.diy.com
DIY and home improvement supplier.

Wickes
www.wickes.co.uk
DIY Specialist and building material stockist.

Argos
www.argos.co.uk
General goods supplier, selling home products ranging from bedding and furniture to lighting.

Fired Earth
www.firedearth.com
Dealer in floor and wall tiles, paint, bathrooms, kitchen furniture and wood flooring. Also offers a design and installation service.

Wall Coverings

Wallpaper Direct
www.wallpaperdirect.co.uk
Online wallpaper supplier. Offers free samples.

Wallpaper Central
www.wallpapercentral.co.uk
Online business selling wallpaper from the leading design companies.

Cole & Son
www.cole-and-son.com
Seller of hand-printed wallpapers.

Arthouse
www.arthouse.com
Designs and sells wallpaper, wall art and tiles.

Graham & Brown
www.grahambrown.com
Supplier of a wide range of designer wallpaper designs and paint.

Rasch
www.rasch.de
Internationally renowned wallpaper design company.

Dulux
www.dulux.co.uk
International paint supplier.

Crown Paint
www.crownpaint.co.uk
Major UK paint producer.

Wall Panelling Ltd
www.panelmaster.co.uk
Lancashire-based wall panelling suppliers and consultants with over 25 years of experience.

The Wainscotting Company
www.thewainscotingcompany.co.uk
Contractor specialising in tailored wood interiors, wood panelling and cabinetry.

Tiles

Walls and Floors
www.wallsandfloors.co.uk
A leading tile stockist, supplying cermic, porcelain and stone tiles in hundreds of styles.

Topps Tiles
www.toppstiles.co.uk
Britain's biggest tile specialist, with over 300 stores throughout the UK.

Tile Choice
www.tilechoice.co.uk
Midlands-based tile company.

Tile Giant
www.tilegiant.co.uk
Owned by Travis Perkins, this expanding tile business has over 100 stores.

Amber Tiles
www.ambertiles.co.au
Australian wall and flooring company.

Flooring

Flooring Supplies
www.flooringsupplies.co.uk
UK's largest online flooring company.

UK Flooring Direct
www.ukflooringdirect.co.uk
Specialist in wood and bamboo floors.

Carpet Right
www.carpetright.co.uk
One of the UK's largest suppliers of flooring materials with over 700 stores.

WovenGround
www.wovenground.com
London-based rug dealer.

Puur
www.puur.uk.com/
Seamless resin and concrete floors.

Meadee Flooring
www.meadeeflooring.co.uk
Supplier of rubber, vinyl and specialist floor coverings.

Kitchens & Bathrooms

Magnet
www.magnet.co.uk
A leading UK kitchen specialist.

Betta Living
www.bettaliving.co.uk
Kitchen designers and fitters.

Sinks.co.uk
www.sinks.co.uk
Online sink retailer. Also sells bathroom products.

Sinks-taps
www.sinks-taps.com
Online sink specialist, with a very wide range of tap styles.

Axiom
www.axiomworktops.com
Producer of a several styles of worktops including solid surface, solid wood and gloss.

Bushboard
www.bushboard.com
Major UK worktop producer.

Caesarstone
www.caesarstone.com
Leading quartz composite worktop company.

Concreations
www.concreations.co.uk
Produces polished concrete work surfaces.

Corian
www.corian.co.uk
Dupont's international solid surface worktop and sink business.

Kitchen Connection
www.kitchenconnection.com.au
Australian kitchen design specialist, supplying wide range of kitchens and accessories.

Kitcheners
www.kitcheners.com.au
Australian kitchen design company.

Living Rooms

DFS
www.dfs.co.uk
Major sofa and furniture supplier.

Sofa.com
www.sofa.com
London-based sofa business, with an extensive selection of fabrics.

Furniture Choice
www.furniturechoice.co.uk
Online furniture company.

Sofas&Stuff
www.sofasandstuff.com
Sofa supplier with showrooms in Yorkshire and the home counties. Most of its sofas are hand-built in workshops outside Nottingham.

Bathrooms.com
www.bathrooms.com
Online bathroom supplier.

bath store
www.bathstore.com
UK-wide chain of bathroom stores.

bathroom heaven
www.bathroomheaven.com
Company offering a wide range of modern and traditional bathroom products and accessories.

Bedrooms

Hammonds
www.hammonds-uk.com
Leading fitted bedroom company.

Sharps
www.sharps.co.uk
Bedroom and home office specialist.

Building Materials

Jewson
www.jewson.co.uk
Material suppliers with branches all over the UK, supplying products ranging from doors and windows to flooring and paint. Also has a kitchen and bathroom design service.

Travis Perkins
www.travisperkins.co.uk
Building material chain. Products include kitchens and bathrooms, decorating materials, landscaping, joinery and plumbing.

CALCULATING FABRIC QUANTITIES
FOR MAKING CURTAINS

To make curtains such as the ones demonstrated on pages 178–181 and 246–249, you will need to know from the outset how much fabric you need. To establish this, follow the steps below. Making these calculations can be tricky if you are inexperienced and we recommend that you do your workings-out twice or more until you are confident the figures are correct.

MEASURE THE LENGTH OF THE TRACK OR POLE
You will need to know this later when you establish what width the curtains should be. If you are fitting a new pole, aim to use one that extends 15–30cm (6–12in) beyond the window or recess, excluding any decorative ends.

ESTABLISH THE USABLE WIDTH OF FABRIC
With plain fabric, the usable width is simply the width minus any seam allowances. It is likely to be less for patterned fabric, where it will be dictated by the repeat of the pattern.

ESTABLISH THE FINAL LENGTH OF YOUR CURTAINS
You typically work out the final length of your curtains by measuring from the top of the track or pole to the point where you want the curtain to finish, whether this is just below the sill or just above the floor (if you want curtains that are long enough to pool on the floor, measure to the floor and then add on an extra 20–30cm/8–12in). You will need to bear in mind different headings, however. For instance, with tab tops, the curtain proper starts lower down, so take your measurements from the bottom of the pole rather than the top.

CALCULATE THE CUT LENGTH OF THE CURTAINS
The cut length of the curtains is the length you will need to cut the fabric to in order to achieve the requisite length of final curtain. To make the curtains in this book, using plain fabric, calculate the cut length by adding 25cm (10in) to the intended final length, for hem allowance and top edge allowance. Again, if using patterned fabric, you will need to take the repeat of the pattern into account

ESTABLISH THE MINIMUM WIDTH OF THE CURTAINS
Curtains should always have a certain "fullness" – essentially, this is about there being enough fabric to hang in attractive loose folds. The fullness is dictated by the headings, and as a result, different styles of curtain need to be made to different widths, even if the window is the same size. For tab top curtains (pages 178–181) to hang nicely, the width of each should be half to three-quarters the length of the pole. For the pencil pleat curtains (pages 246–249) to hang nicely, the width of each should be roughly equivalent to the entire length of the track or pole.

CALCULATE HOW MANY WIDTHS OF FABRIC YOU WILL NEED
To do this, divide your figure for the intended final width of the curtain by the usable width of fabric. This will almost certainly not result in a whole number – round up, not down, to establish how many widths of fabric will be required to make a curtain of the necessary width.

CALCULATE THE TOTAL QUANTITY OF FABRIC REQUIRED
You now know both the length the fabric needs to be cut to (the cut length of the curtains) and how many widths of fabric are required for each curtain. Multiplying these two figures together will give you the quantity of fabric needed for the main front panel of each curtain.

DON'T FORGET THE EXTRAS
You are nearly ready to order your fabric, but first you need to take any extra pieces into account. Tab top curtains, for example, have a back panel at the top, which also needs to be accounted for, plus the tabs themselves. You can calculate the extra fabric needed for the back panel by repeating the above steps, assuming a length of 25cm (10in). To calculate how much additional fabric is needed for the tabs, first work out the size of one tab – 20cm (8in) wide; length dependent on the thickness of the pole. You then need to work out the number of tabs: they will be positioned at 20–30cm (8–12in) intervals so divide the final width of the curtain by 20, 25, or 30. The resulting figure, rounded up to the nearest whole number, represents the number of tabs. Work out how many tabs you will get from a width of fabric, and calculate the fabric you need accordingly.

REMEMBER THAT for tab top curtains like these, you will need to order additional fabric with which to make the tabs.

PROJECT
TEMPLATES

If you have been inspired to try the projects in the "child's bedroom" section of this book – the appliqué cushion on pages 264–267 or the wall stencil on pages 254–255 – and are keen to use the same designs, use the templates on these pages. To increase or decrease the size, either photocopy the page using the "enlarge" function or scan and resize. Alternatively, try the projects with designs of your own.

TRACE AROUND THIS IMAGE, or an enlarged version of it, onto a piece of bondaweb and you are ready to start your appliqué cushion.

PLACE A SHEET OF ACETATE over this page, or a photocopied enlargement of it, and trace around the shape using a marker pen. You can then cut the shape out to create your template.

INDEX

R

radiators 126, 127, 175, 196, 197, 245, 270, 302, 303
recessed downlights 55, 113, 171, 241, 283, 311
recessed floor uplighters 113, 285
recliners, outdoor 368
refreshing a bathroom 120–1
refreshing a kitchen 72–3, 78–81
refrigerators
  choosing 41
  outdoor kitchen 381
  positioning 24, 26–7
resin flooring 48, 50, 101, 132, 134, 276, 278
revamping tiles 73
revamping a wardrobe 232–5
roller blinds 58, 116, 121, 122, 173, 174, 243, 244, 313, 314
  making 118–19
Roman blinds 58, 116, 173, 174, 175, 243, 244, 313, 314
  making 60–3
rubber chippings 356
rubber flooring 48, 101, 252, 336, 343
rugs 16, 199, 251
  care 189
  choosing 188–9
  living room 129, 190–1
  for zoning 50, 190
runners 292
  carpet 188, 191, 273, 295, 298
  for hallways 188, 273, 294, 295, 298
  painted 294, 298
  as rugs 188, 191
  for stairs 273, 294, 295

S

safety, bathroom electrical 91, 113, 114
sail shades, making 362–3
sanding wooden floors 136
sanitaryware 84, 90–9
  choosing 86
  installing 85, 270, 271
  positioning 88–9
scheduling the work
  bathroom 84–5
  bedroom 196–7
  hallway 270–1
  home office 302–3
  kitchen 20–1
  laundry room 330–1
  living room 126–7
  outdoor space 348–9
screens 326
  outdoor 352, 353
seamless flooring 48, 50, 100, 101, 132, 134, 252, 276, 278, 336
seat pads
  for garden chairs 372–5
  for kitchen chairs 68–71
seating
  hallway 275, 296
  outdoor 368–70, 376, 381
  see also benches; chairs; sofa beds; sofas
self-levelling compound 202
setts 361
shade 352
shade sails, making 362–3
sheet flooring 48, 50, 100, 101, 252, 336
shelves 121, 297, 315
  box shelves 163, 185
  displaying on 16, 147, 184, 185
  around doors 163, 293
  fitting 164–9
  floating shelves 120, 162, 166–9, 184, 185

shelving 331, 337
  bedroom 230
  hallway 293
  laundry room 333, 342
  living room 162–3
shelving units 185, 263
shoe cabinets 275, 290
shoe racks 288, 290
shoe storage 231, 275, 288, 290
shower baths 91, 92
shower cubicles 85, 89, 92, 93, 94, 122
shower curtains 92, 94, 121, 122
shower rooms 111
shower screens 88, 92, 93, 94, 122
showers
  choosing 86, 92–5
  installing 85
  outdoor 353
  overbath 88, 92, 94
  positioning 89
shutters
  bathroom 115, 117
  bedroom 243, 245
  home office 305, 312, 314
  kitchen 57, 59
  living room 173, 175
side tables 159
sideboards 23, 161, 293
sinks
  bathroom 86, 88, 96–7, 110
  Corian® 21, 39
  kitchen 21, 25, 38–9, 40
  laundry room 330, 331, 332, 333, 342
  outdoor kitchen 381
skips 349
skirting board lighting 285
slab patterns 360–1
small outdoor spaces 376–9
sofa beds 153, 327
sofas 128, 129
  choosing 17, 150–3

ACKNOWLEDGMENTS

Author's acknowledgments

Clare Steel would like to thank Gary for his support and patience, and Lucy Searle for her constant guidance and advice.

Publishers' acknowledgments

Dorling Kindersley would like to thank Zoe Browne and Alison Smith for creating the craft-based projects, Jane Coulter for creating the index, Barry Cox and Kit Jolliffe for set building, Sara Emslie for interiors styling, and Samuel Grant for the DIY projects.

Thanks also to the following suppliers, who assisted by donating samples to be photographed:

Bamboo Flooring Company – bamboo flooring
www.bambooflooringcompany.com

Bushboard – laminate worktops
www.bushboard.com

Churchfield sofa bed company – sofa fabrics
www.sofabed.co.uk

Concreations – concrete worktops
www.concreations.co.uk

Decorative Aggregates – rubber and stone chippings
www.decorativeaggregates.com

Flooringsupplies.co.uk – wooden flooring, engineered wood flooring, laminate flooring, carpets
www.flooringsupplies.co.uk

Fritztile – terrazzo tiles
www.fritztile.com

Furniture Choice – sofa fabrics
www.furniturechoice.co.uk

Glassact – glass worktops
www.glassactuk.com

Granitesolutionsdirect– granite and quartz composite worktops
www.granitesolutionsdirect.co.uk

London Stone – Yorkstone paving
www.londonstone.com

Meadee Flooring – rubber, vinyl and lino flooring
www.meadeeflooring.co.uk

Puur – Seamless concrete and resin floors
www.puur.uk.com

Q Stoneworks – granite and lavastone worktops
www.qstoneworks.co.uk

Sofa.com – sofa fabrics
www.sofa.com

Sofas&stuff – sofa fabrics
www.sofasandstuff.com

The Sofa Company – sofa fabrics
www.sofa-company.co.uk

Tong Ling Bamboo Flooring – bamboo flooring
www.tlflooring.co.uk

Walls and Floors – tiles
www.wallsandfloors.co.uk

Wallpaper direct – wallpaper
www.wallpaperdirect.co.uk

Wilsons Flooring – Saxony carpets
www.wilsonsflooringdirect.co.uk

Wilton Carpets – velvet pile carpets
www.wiltoncarpets.com

Picture Credits

Dorling Kindersley would like to thank the following for their kind permission to reproduce their photographs:

(Key: a-above; b-below/bottom; c-centre; f-far; l-left; r-right; t-top)

Alamy Images: Ivan Barta 51; *The Garden Collection*: Nicola Stocken Tomkins 357; *Getty Images*: Neo Vision 14tr; *IPC+ Syndication*: Hallie Burton / Livingetc 16bl, Ideal Home 135; *Photoshot*: Red Cover / Ed Reeve 16cb, 16crb, Red Cover / Ken Hayden 279, Red Cover / Mary-Jane Maybury 16br; *www.jordicanosa.com*: 205

All other images © Dorling Kindersley
For further information see: www.dkimages.com

About the Author

Clare Steel has worked across a broad selection of national interiors magazines in the UK, from *Ideal Home* to *House Beautiful*, and regularly contributes to property and design websites, such as channel4.com/4Homes. She has spent the majority of her career conceiving, designing and creating rooms and cameos for photo shoots. She has also transformed countless magazine readers' homes with room and house makeovers, and regularly contributes written features to magazines and websites on everything from choosing colour schemes to picking out flooring.